Haydn Paul was born in 19
wife and three children. H
of a Nepalese girl for the 'V

He has been an astrologe
astrology interpretations tl
esoteric spiritual training w............... School,
and through the Servants of the Light and has been involved
in the human potential movement since 1973.

He is the author of *Phoenix Rising*, *Revolutionary Spirit* and
Visionary Dreamer (the Outer Planets Trilogy), which explore
the astrology of Pluto, Uranus and Neptune respectively, and
of *Queen of the Night*, a forthcoming book on the astrology of
the Moon.

YOUR STARCHILD

An Astrology Guide for
Every Parent

HAYDN PAUL

MANDALA
UNWIN PAPERBACKS
London Boston Sydney Wellington

First published in paperback by Unwin Paperbacks,
an imprint of Unwin Hyman Limited, in 1990

Haydn Paul 1990

UNWIN HYMAN LIMITED
15–17 Broadwick Street
London W1V 1FP

Allen and Unwin Australia Pty Ltd
8 Napier Street, North Sydney, NSW 2060, Australia

Allen and Unwin New Zealand Pty Ltd in association with
the Port Nicholson Press
Compusales Building, 75 Ghuznee Street, Wellington,
New Zealand

British Library Cataloguing in Publication Data

Paul, Haydn
    Your StarChild: An Astrology Guide for Every Parent.
1. Children. Personality. Astrological aspects
1. Title
133.5'8155418
ISBN 0 04440649 5

Typeset in Palatino 10 on 11½ point by
Computape (Pickering) Ltd, Pickering, North Yorkshire
Printed in Great Britain by
Cox & Wyman Ltd, Reading

Your StarChild is dedicated to these important people:

All parents and children everywhere
To my father, Dennis, and my late mother, Irene
To my wife, Carol
To my children, Kai, Sarah and Lauren
And to all who seek to build a bright future for the world
May your star burn ever brighter, illuminating the way.

CONTENTS

CONTENTS

INTRODUCTION

'Man, Know Thyself' – The Eternal Quest

Are there any perfect parents starting to read this book? If so, why bother, because you obviously believe that you know it all anyway. But for the rest of us, who admit and acknowledge our lack of perfection, this book can help to build a better relationship with our children through a deeper understanding of the nature of the child that we have been privileged to bring into this world.

Like the myth of the perfect parent, the truth is that the perfect child does not exist either. Whilst most adults find it easy to start the process of creating new life, many are less well prepared for the consequence: the birth of a child. Being a parent is often a challenging and difficult task, even when it is drawing out unconditional love and joy from us for our children. Raising a child is a daily tension for many, even in our technologically advanced Western society, and children have a knack of evoking a wide variety of powerful emotions in mothers and fathers, emotions that can often be negative and potentially violent too, as well as the positive ones of love and caring. Babies cry, sometimes incessantly through the night, children misbehave and have 'temper tantrums', adolescents clash with their parent's views and assert their own individuality and freedom; all of these create stresses in the parent and in the family relationship over the years. Anger and frustration at genuine attempts to raise the child are common. Many mothers who are practically housebound with young children bear the brunt of parenting; spending hours with a demanding child is often difficult, tiring and limiting for the mother. A father coming home after work is often not in the right mood to have to cope with an unruly

1

child, whose excitable ebullience is in direct conflict with his need to unwind and relax. Many fathers see little of their children except at weekends.

Acknowledging that being a parent is not an easy responsibility, and one which really lasts a lifetime, is a first step towards looking for an alternative way to understand your children and perhaps to transform that relationship into one which can be easier and more positive for all concerned. *Your StarChild* is designed to deepen mutual understanding of your son or daughter, and is an attempt at illuminating both child and parental personality patterns so that individual development of talents and potentiality can successfully occur throughout childhood.

The source of this illumination is Astrology, one of the oldest techniques of understanding life that exists in our knowledge. It is the art and science of planetary influences upon the psychological and physiological aspects of the human being. A newborn child is not just an empty shell waiting to be filled by human social conditioning and socialization, Astrology therefore proposes that the time, place and date of birth is important in indicating the intrinsic personality patterns of that child. Generally this is associated with the sign of the zone in the heavenly zodiac where the Sun was positioned at the time of birth. This is known as the Sun sign, and is the facet of Astrology widely known by the general public, indicating to them which one of the twelve archetypal signs they are. Children tend to reflect their Sun sign and Ascendant quite clearly, as do adults, although as time passes the influences of the other planetary factors play a more powerful and differentiating role, which can only be considered by calculating a full natal chart and analysis.

Holding a newborn baby is an emotional moment. There is joy and relief that the tension has passed and all is well, but it is also a time which gives rise to all sorts of questions; what will the child be like, what sort of life will the child have, what talents will be unfolded over time? All parents wonder these things, as they peer in delight at the small hands, feet and features of their creation. Astrology can offer some indications to answer these questions, in the descriptions of probable personality characteristics that the child will begin to display. As many parents fail to understand their own inner personality patterns and motivations, it is unlikely that they will develop great insight into those of their children either; the results can be misunderstandings and eventual conflicts, or attempts to force the child to fit parental expectations in ways that are totally unsuitable for the well-being of the child.

Obviously genetic heritage will play a powerful role in the forming of the child, as will environmental influences, but it is through the lens of Astrology that insight can be gained into those patterns of personality hidden deep in the psyche. This is the real value of contemporary humanistic Astrology which explores those psychological levels of the individual. If a parent can understand his or her own psychology better, and the psychological type of the child (as perceived by Astrology), then through greater understanding, a more harmonious and creative relationship can be built. The aim is to help children to release their full potential, to exploit natural gifts and talents (whatever they are) and not to destroy or inhibit them through ignorance and a lack of sensitivity.

Similarly, the same is required of every teacher, whose challenge is even greater in that they deal with the education of many children, whose nature and background they know little about. It could be very valuable for a teacher to have a basic knowledge of the signs of children they teach, because this can provide insight into how to deal individually with the children, and would show how they best absorb information and learning. Also, professionals who deal with children, such as social workers, child psychologists, probation officers and youth community workers, could at least have a basic insight into each child's nature through astrological typology, which could be most beneficial in developing a therapeutic relationship.

We live in a time when many families have been disrupted through divorce and separation, and this leads to many children living with a step-parent. This is often a difficult situation with underlying stresses and tensions, with the traumas of marital breakdowns, where relative strangers can suddenly be living together. An astrological look at the personality patterns which are involved can be beneficial in building 'bridges' through greater insight and understanding. A step-parent could study the *StarChild* sign of the children, and gain some immediate sense of the type of personality that they have now taken responsibility for. They could then consider their own parental sign in respect of their probable tendencies in dealing with such a child. Seeing such tendencies can be the key to changing them if they are not suitable for that child. For instance, a parent could determine their own Sun and Ascendant signs; then, when dealing with the child, they could observe that if they are expressing the qualities of the Sun sign, that the relationship with the child is not so good, but if they are expressing the qualities of their Ascendant, then the child's response is much better and less friction occurs. So that could be the key to a better relationship. These are the astrological concepts of affinities and disaffinities, and are associated with the elemental types which are discussed later in the book.

The intention of *Your StarChild* is to be a guide to every parent in understanding their children better, helping latent potential to unfold, and enabling a more loving, supportive and caring relationship to be built, which is positive and creative for all concerned.

Before entering the astrological analysis of children's signs, it may be beneficial to consider the phases of physiological and mental development in children, which can offer a structure against which your child's development can be set.

Each child is unique, and has his or her own individual pattern which will be demonstrated over the years. Acknowledging the individuality of each child is important, and leads to understanding and respect. Some babies tend to sleep a lot, whilst others require less sleep, or regular naps; some seem to be always awake. A child's 'nature' is reflected by the astrological types, and is also inherited from parents, as is general physical appearance, intelligence, and often, skills. The immediate environment is also important in influencing the development of the child and in the release of natural potential. Factors such as parents, home, diet and teachers are all influential, as well as factors like love and caring for the child's physical, emotional and mental needs. All of these either support the full expression of each child or inhibit and destroy that potential.

Children develop 'from the top downwards' with the activation of mind–brain control directing the body's limbs and coordination. Standard average times for such physiological milestones are as follows: six weeks, smiling at Mother; six months, a steadier back and head needing less support; six to twelve months, hand skills start to develop, simple holding and grasping; seven to nine months, able to sit without parental support; twelve months, able to stand upright, walk a little with support, crawl easily; thirteen to fifteen months, walking without support, although still tends to fall over; by eighteen months, the average toddler can walk unaided; by five years old, body coordination and all basic skills should have been learnt and the child should be proficient in these and relatively independent.

Yet it should be understood that all such timings are average, and that children develop skills at the right time for themselves. A child is not necessarily advanced if he or she learns a skill more quickly than other children, and neither is the child backward if that skill takes longer to learn. Children vary – some do not start walking until nearly two, yet the same child could have a vocabulary of over fifty words six months earlier.

Learning skills also have their average 'timetable'. In those first six years of life, the average child succeeds in learning more than she ever will again in her life. Many parents fail to recognize the sheer volume of learning that children absorb and apply in those early years, probably because it is forms of information that parents take for granted, yet fail to appreciate just how alien they are to a child. A child's mind and senses are much more alert than in adult life, when most adults shut off many of life's experiences due to familiarity.

In childhood learning, most information is not easily retained in the memory, and is mainly absorbed through repetition and practice. It is only when the child is giving his full attention that information is retained. Between birth and six months, hand–eye coordination develops and learning develops through the visual senses; between six and nine months, manipulative hand skills start and learning occurs through touch and exploring physical objects; by twelve months, the child is mobile, through crawling or by supported standing, and learning comes through environmental exploration. Over those first two years development occurs by the child learning through his or her physical senses and body activity in exploratory play. After the age of two, more imaginative play commences, and from that age until school-going age, the cognitive or thinking skills become alive and active; concepts and creative play emerge. Body coordination is greatly improved, and the ability to repeat words and understand symbolic and representative human words and language evolves. Speech is word symbols associated with physical objects, feelings, sensations and ideas and is in fact extremely complex. Between the ages of two and two and a half, the average child can say fifty words. The child becomes increasingly self-controlled and is slowly able to function as an independent being. Toilet training can commence around the age of two, as the child can communicate through words or signs the need for the potty, and at this time some degree of body control is to be expected. The child can then recognize – through daily repetition – those body feelings and sensations that involve waste release, and can notify the parent of his or her need.

Later important stages in child development are puberty and adolescence. Puberty is the phase when the child's body begins to change and develop into a young adult's body. The average age is over twelve for girls, and over fourteen for boys, although each child has his or her own body clock and hormonal mechanism that is right for them and these average times can be earlier or later in individual cases. Adolescence is a phase of growth in the emotions and mind of the teenage child, and starts later than puberty, as the adult patterns of the child's nature begin to form and take their place. These teenage physiological and psychological changes are extremely powerful and confusing for many children, and often leads to renewed family friction and unsettled relationships because of moody and erratically behaved children and their attitudes to parents.

Suitable toys for specific childhood phases of development and unfoldment are: three months old, bright colourful shiny rings, rattles, mobiles above the crib for baby to watch moving in the air, toys to help develop eye coordination which can be reached for and grasped; six months to a year: noisy rattles, rings and bells, wooden or plastic bricks, toys to bang and make noises on, teething rings, toys for hand skills; one year to two years: cuddly toys, favourite fluffy animals, baby walking aids, bath toys, building blocks, balls to kick and hold; between two and three, simple crayons, pastels and colouring books and paper can be introduced for 'artistic scribbling'; between three and four, picture books with simple stories and full page drawings can fascinate, and artistic expansion to include paints and blackboards and chalk can be made; creativity with Plasticine or Playdoh is enjoyed, as well as garden play in sand with water, buckets and spades, toy animals are popular, or adventure characters, toy cars and spaceships, as are miniature household items, like cups, plates, utensils; dolls are loved, and dressing or undressing is reflective of their own abilities; riding toy bicycles, rocking horses, etc. helps their mobility and coordination; between four and five, cutting and pasting and creating collages help hand skills and creativity, simple jigsaws tax their visual skills (and often their patience too!), and outdoor play is more popular with balls, climbing frames, swings and slides. Early

educative training can be made if the child is naturally receptive, and story/picture books, old rhymes and songs, and basic
alphabet and number work can be introduced.

SUN SIGNS AND THE ASCENDANT

The emphasis in this book has been placed upon the Sun sign
and the Ascendant, plus their corresponding Elemental affinities. This is to make it reasonably accessible for the general
reader, as understanding and interpreting a properly constructed natal chart or horoscope is a more complex matter,
and can only be achieved when using the specific personal
information of time, date and place of birth. Yet within the
scope of basic astrology and using the Sun sign and
Ascendant, much can be revealed of the child's nature and
also of the probable characteristics of each parent, and thus
the 'triangular relationship' of the basic family unit.

The 'Sun sign', which is the most public face of astrology
through newspaper and magazine columns, is the Sun's
position in the sky and, depending upon the time and date of
birth, the Sun will be located in one of the twelve signs of the
Zodiac. It is only a part of the full natal horoscope, which also
includes the positions of the planets in our solar system, and
these positions are superimposed upon a system of 'houses' to
form the natal chart of that individual personality and
potential. Each of these houses also represents a specific
sphere of life experience that will be important for that
individual, especially those where planets are positioned. The
chart of Princess Beatrice, (see p. 12), daughter of the Duke
and Duchess of York, is a full natal chart, although her early
environment may be slightly different from your children!

The Sun sign symbolizes the essential core self of the child,
and deeply influences the personality that will unfold over her
lifetime. It indicates those inner motivations and natural
potential that are present in the child, and those tendencies
that will both vitalize and inspire the child onward towards
the dreams of later achievement in adult life. This involves

personal styles of expression, strengths and weaknesses, creativity and abilities, and natural affinities to friends and parents; even the astrological bias of teachers will influence their relationships to children in the classroom. The Sun sign is the centre or heart of that personality, and reveals those essential values, qualities and individual characteristics. In adult life, most people strongly express the Sun sign characteristics or a combination of that and the Ascendant.

The other astrological aspects in a full chart reveal more individual variations and specific personal factors, and tend to come into effect as the child grows older and towards adulthood. For instance, from birth to two years old, the Moon is activated; from two to four, the Sun and Mars; from four to six, Venus awakes; and from six to ten, Mercury, Jupiter and Saturn begin to perform their role as the mind awakens. Planetary aspects – which are certain relationships between planets in the horoscope – tend to be more influential within the later teenage years and through the adult life. So focusing on the Sun sign and Ascendant is usually sufficient to gain a clear perspective on the more simple life of the child.

It is these differences in each person's chart that distinguishes each as an unique individual, and not just simply one of twelve personality types within a system of astrological analysis. Variations in time, date and place of birth makes for the differences in the astrological map of the personality, even though most Taureans or Aries have much in common with others of the same sign. Each has his or her own destiny and potential to fulfil. Essentially the twelve Zodiac signs reflect the twelve types of personality that emanate from the 'collective unconscious', and embody group characteristics within individual uniqueness. The 'collective unconscious' is a term coined by the psycholgist Carl Jung to describe the personality and consciousness roots which lie deep within the nature of all human beings, and is called 'collective' because it is something that we all share and participate in at a very deep level of the psyche, and which is the pattern of our common human nature or species.

The Ascendant is the sign of the Zodiac which is rising on the eastern horizon at the time and place of birth; this position is also used for the setting up of the house division in the chart. The Ascendant corresponds to the 'persona' or social mask that everyone develops, and many fall into the error of identifying too stongly with this partial self. This mask is the created interface between our real nature (Sun sign) and the world, often concealing our true character from view. It is a form of psychological adjustment to the world, and shows our immediate response to our environment and people. This is the social personality, the impression that we make on others, our 'image'. It is like a psychological door through which we express and direct our real inner motivations to affect others and the world. In most people the dominant qualities and personality characteristics are those of the Sun sign, and the Ascendant qualities are secondary, being either complementary or conflicting with those Sun sign impulses. Such conflicts between opposing energy tendencies can account for many personal inner difficulties.

When evaluating your child's astrological characteristics, the Sun sign is probably the most important, so check which is the relevant sign for the child's birth date, and read that. Other tendencies of the child can be accounted for by determining the Ascendant, so refer to the tables in the appendix to establish the Ascendant, as well as noting the corresponding element type from Part 3.

In each of the twelve signs of the Zodiac, there is an alternation of the sex of the 'featured child', so that in Aries for example, the child is considered to be a boy or girl expressing those astrological characteristics. The twelve signs are divided into six 'positive' and six 'negative'. The 'positive' signs are Aries, Gemini, Leo, Libra, Sagittarius, Aquarius; the 'negative' signs are Taurus, Cancer, Virgo, Scorpio, Capricorn and Pisces. The Fire and Air elements are the positive signs, whilst Earth and Water are the negative. What this means is that the negative signs do not have detrimental implications, but refer more to tendencies of more personal introversion and social sensitivity, being less socially outgoing or impulsively spontaneous. They are more self-reflective. The positive signs are more socially extrovert, needing a more public style of self-expression, tending to be impulsive and spontaneous in action, rather then being as self-absorbed or preoccupied.

In the pre-school child sections, there is an indication regarding the type of birth that the child born to each sign often has; it may be worth mentioning that the type of birth related to each sign could be either the child's Sun sign or Ascendant, so that for example a Leo birth Sun sign with a Scorpio Ascendant could have the more traumatic birth that can be associated with Scorpio.

The short sections on ideal and suitable careers are included to suggest several directions that your child could be temperamentally suited to follow, using those natural talents, gifts and interests. In a perfect world, we would all be employed to perform work that we enjoyed; meanwhile, back in the real world, this is unfortunately not often the case, and many have to earn a living performing tasks and duties that fail to fulfil their inner needs. However, it is obviously preferable to encourage our children towards achieving suitable and satisfying employment, and these astrological career affinities are included as direction pointers.

Without using the proper astrological ephemeris (astrological data table showing predicted daily positions of planets) for the planetary position, it is impossible to be 100 per cent accurate with either the Sun sign or Ascendant. If the child's birthday falls on either the first or last day of any of the Sun sign periods, then you cannot be totally sure that the child is, for example, a Scorpio; this is because on those days the Sun may be either passing out of Libra into Scorpio, or out of Scorpio into Sagittarius. Also, a similar problem can arise with the attempt to provide the Ascendant position, where during a day the Ascendant passes through each sign, and can spend variable amounts of hours and minutes in each sign. During some hours, the Ascendant moves clearly between two signs, and these are indicated on the tables; if so, an approximate guide is to consider the first sign to indicate the first half hour, and the second to cover the second half of the hour.

Having made these qualifications, the majority of readers should be able, at least, to clearly determine the Sun sign of their child, and many will be able to establish an accurate Ascendant too. For those who wish to have a properly calculated natal chart and analysis for themselves or children, please contact the StarLore address at the back of this book.

THE CHART OF PRINCESS BEATRICE

Princess Beatrice has a Leo Sun and an Aquarius Ascendant, with the element of Fire prominent in her chart – Sun, Mercury, Mars, Saturn, Uranus are all placed in Fire signs and the MidHeaven in Sagittarius.

As a child of the Royal Family, she will experience a privileged upbringing, shielded from many life experiences and economic concerns that affect most families, and her social status will open many doors for her in later life. In addition, it is likely that a powerful influence on her will be that of a nanny, who will be responsible for her early rearing and training, due to the commitments of her parents, the Duke and Duchess of York. The astrological type of the family nanny will also have a conditioning impact on Beatrice.

A Leo–Aquarius combination with an emphasized Fire element will result in a wilful individualist, who is impulsive, a little self-centred and a person determined to choose her own way. For someone born into a high-profile family, she should be able to adjust to the inevitable media pressures that will occur; she will 'enjoy' the attention focused on her, amplifying that personal sense of a unique individuality. However, she will not appreciate comment on her later adult actions and choices, especially when she has made her decision to move in specific directions.

Beatrice conformed to the dramatic entrance of the Leo child, being born on the auspicious 8 August 1988, at 8 p.m. with the accompanying media circus at the birth of a new member of the British Royal Family. Leo is an apt sign for an imperial birth, and Beatrice is likely to display such characteristics as she grows older, having a natural tendency towards issuing commands, and expecting to be obeyed, even as a young child. Performing a regal role will be ideal for her! And she will act it out in a most impressive manner; certainly she will provide many column inches in the tabloid press in later years. That impulsive and independent spirit will be very prominent in her temperament, and she may often fail to look before she leaps into action; royal advisers will inevitably need to be consulted, and their public relations department had better prepare for the time when Beatrice enters the social whirl during her later teenage years.

She'll be a loving child, and her family will be of great importance to her to provide stability and security. Hopefully, the commitments of the Duke and Duchess will not prevent them spending sufficient time with Beatrice, or she may begin to feel insecure, and feeling loved by her parents is essential to her. The substitute surrogate parental figure of her nanny will need to ensure that a careful balance is attained between childhood nurturing and disciplining, to avoid any repression of the warm-hearted Leo temperament. The section on the Leo and Aquarius child and the Fire element will greatly amplify an understanding of her essential characteristics.

Taking a look at Beatrice's parents, the Duke and Duchess of York, Andrew and Sarah, can also highlight some interesting factors. Andrew is a Pisces Sun and Leo Ascendant, and tends to reflect several images of a 'romantic hero'. In recent years, his image had been enhanced by his involvement in the Royal Navy as a helicopter pilot, fighting in the South Atlantic during the Falklands conflict. His persona (Leo Ascendant) has portrayed him as a more macho action man, and this emphasized masculine activity has helped to define his identity through the media lens. His involvement with the actress Koo Stark also helped this process. Yet beneath the more public Leo mask of confidence and assertion, he is still the Piscan romantic dreamer, emotionally empathic, and often moulding his character through association, interaction and absorption of those with whom he is closely involved – as at Gordonstoun, during his schooling, where a spartan self-reliant regime of personal independence is the aim, or through his Royal Navy officer colleagues. His more sensitive Piscean nature shines through in his interest in photography, where images replete with mood and dramatic atmosphere are frozen in time for later contemplation. He is attracted by the glamour and creativity of film and theatre, and has a personal desire to be respected for his own photographic artistry, rather than because of his social status. In many ways, there are two distinct Andrews; the public and private individuals, reflected by his Ascendant and Sun; the royal figure and the husband and father.

As Pisces, Andrew will have immense love for Beatrice, and she will be extremely meaningful and important to him, more than he would often acknowledge. If he allows her to, she will soften his heart and his action image. He will often find it difficult to resist her entreaties, and will tend to let her have her own way, unless he is reminded of those royal obligations and duties with which they are expected to conform. These are the imprisoning gates around their free social standing. As she grows older, both Andrew and Sarah will try to encourage any natural talents that Beatrice has, helping her to unfold her creative potential, both as a means of childhood development and schooling, but also for a possible future career if necessary.

The Duchess of York, Sarah, is a Libra Sun and Scorpio Ascendant, and is a more intelligent and self-determined character than people may believe. Several factors which would have attracted the Piscean Andrew are depth of character, inner strength, independence and self-will. Sarah will help Beatrice to mature, and will relate to her as an unfolding adult rather than a child, although when wills clash there will be little doubt who is in charge. Beatrice will have more failures in trying to manipulate Sarah by using her appealing childish ways than she will with Andrew. Sarah should have a

14

natural affinity with Beatrice, and will help her to realize the importance of considered choices in life, perhaps trying to restrain Beatrice's impulsive tendencies through encouraging careful forethought. The cultural and creative aspect of Beatrice will also be enhanced by Sarah and Andrew, and the quality of the home environment and lifestyle will reflect an artistic sensitivity. A Libran parent can be a good match for a Fire child, and further information concerning the likely tendencies of Pisces and Libra parents can be found later in the book, in Part 2.

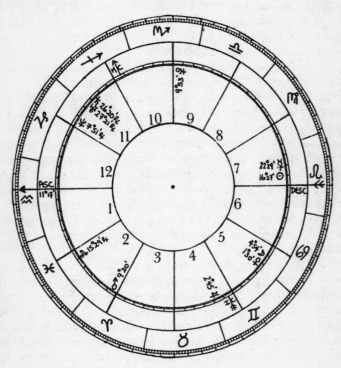

NATAL CHART

STARLORE ASTROLOGY INTERPRETATIONS

FOR: PRINCESS BEATRICE OF YORK

EQUAL HOUSES	PLANETARY ASPECTS

EQUAL HOUSES

BIRTH TIME: 8.18PM (B.S.T. Adjusted: G.M.T. 7.18PM)

BIRTH DATE: 8.8.1988

BIRTH PLACE: LONDON

LATITUDE: 51°30'N   LONGITUDE: 0°5'W

RULING PLANET: ☉   RULERS HOUSE 7

ELEMENTS   FIRE   : 5 + MC. ☉ ♀ ♂ ♄ ♅ ♐

EARTH : 1 ♆

AIR   : 1 + ASC. ♃ ⚷ ♒

WATER : 3 ☽ ♀ ☿

CARDINAL : 4 ☽ ♀ ♂ ♆

FIXED : 3 ☉ ♀ ♇

MUTABLE : 3 ♃ ♄ ♅

PLANETARY ASPECTS

	☉	☽	☿	♀	♂	♃	♄	♅	♆	♇	ASC
☉			☌⁶		△⁷			☌⁸	☌³	□⁷	☌⁵
☽				☌³	□⁴		△⁴	△⁵		△⁵	
☿							☌⁵	☌⁴	☌⁶		
♀					□⁸		☌⁶		□¹	□¹	
♂											✳²
♃								☌¹		✳²	
♄											
♅											
♆											□¹
♇											
ASC											

PART ONE

Children's Zodiac Signs from Aries to Pisces

ARIES
(MARCH 21 to APRIL 19)

Planetary Ruler: Mars

Element type	Fire
Type	Positive/Masculine
Triplicity	Cardinal
Symbol	♈
Image	The Ram
Part of Body	Head
Theme of Self	I Am
Key Qualities	Active, energetic, initiator
House Affinity	1st House

Famous Aries Personalities: Vincent Van Gogh, Thomas Jefferson, Nikita Krushchev, Marlon Brando, Bette Davis, Peter Ustinov, Jeffrey Archer, Dudley Moore, Tracy Chapman, Severiano Ballesteros, Herbert Von Karajan, Michael Heseltine.

THE PRE-SCHOOL ARIES CHILD

All prospective mothers know the approximate date of their future child's delivery and, if it is due during the period of the Sun in Aries, then the mother has probably experienced several of the basic Aries characteristics before the birth. Aries is active, restless, legs kicking, arms and elbows poking out, a bundle of movement, as though someone is thrashing around searching for the way out. That small body is already filled to bursting with physical vitality, just waiting for the opportunity to be where the action is: birth itself may come with an energetic rush to be free, and may happen quickly. The Aries

19

child may announce his presence in the world with a raucous cry.

During that first year, the child will be quite demanding, letting the parents know whenever he feels that his needs are not being met by loud noises, kicking of the legs and pumping of the arms, a minor whirl of motion in the crib. You will not be able to ignore him; he'll demand your attention fast, and will lack patience in waiting for his needs to be satisfied.

Because of that fundamental vitality coursing through his body, Aries will soon be looking for greater physical activity. He will not be content to remain a passive baby for longer that is necessary; as soon as coordination begins, he'll be trying to move around on his own. He will use a lot of energy in his attempts to reach that toy over there, and will feel frustrated if he is unable to attain his purpose. It is likely that he will begin to walk earlier than the average age, and will be extremely thrilled when he can manage to stand up with the support of the furniture. This can often happen by the age of ten months, and once he has achieved that, his early attempts at taking the first steps will soon follow. He perseveres; with plenty of energy he'll try and try, because if he can succeed, he intuits that a whole new world of independence and freedom will open for him. Once he's tasted freedom, you'll find that he does not really settle into play-pens or enclosed cribs. He'll rattle the 'bars of his cages', be noisy in the hope that you'll give in to his demands. He may be erratic with his sleep patterns; usually he'll only go to sleep when exhaustion strikes, and then he's likely to sleep deeply whilst his energy re-charges . . . and then he'll spring back to life, ready for action! The question is, who becomes exhausted first? You or baby Aries?

The essential Aries characteristics emerge more clearly between ages one to two, stimulated by increasing independence as the child grows more mobile and capable of exploring a limited environment of home and garden. You have already recognized that he has a will of his own, now his opposition and 'No . . . ' becomes a more regular response. He wants to do whatever he has decided. He is determined, and he'll set himself against the parental will. If frustrated, he will get very upset, probably rolling violently around the floor being very noisy; after all, that energy has got to go somewhere. He'll settle again once he's released his frustrations. What will suit him at this age are toys that he can be active with, toys to bang, toys that make noises, bricks, balls, anything that involves using physical energy and body coordination. Life may not be especially restful or quiet around Aries children.

By the age of two to three, young Aries is growing up, and speech ability has greatly improved. Aries will respond to the encouragement to talk only if he receives enjoyment and pleasure from 'disciplining his mouth'; he loves making noises, but speech may sometimes be a concentrated effort that diverts too much from playing and running around. When he talks the emphasis will be on 'I want . . . ', 'No . . . ', 'Do this . . . '; he can be very assertive, sure of his own needs and demands. How you will repond to his insistence is the issue; sometimes it will amuse, sometimes it will enrage. You may need all of your persuasive powers at times; otherwise, when he's made his mind up, and it differs with your intentions, armed conflict may occur!

Aries does not always respond well to tight routines, as spontaneity and freedom seem more preferable, and domestic routines can fail to fit in with his little plans of perhaps running around in the garden, or using the furniture as a trampoline. Aries finds that the imposed order of routine can clash with his will; one way for a parent to handle the Aries child can be through involving him more in the routine activity, by giving him apparent choices, such as 'Which of these jumpers are you wearing today?' or 'I think you look very grown up in that shirt, don't you?' Choice and involvement can make him a participant in routine daily activity, rather than a passive (and sometimes antagonistic) recipient of the parental intention.

Aries loves adventuring and physical exploration; climbing, hiding, delving into dark plant-filled areas of the garden can

21

involve him for hours. He can be a little foolhardy though, and through sheer physical exuberance often hurts himself. Aggression could develop, where in playing with children of a similar age group he becomes over-excited and acts too physically for them, resulting in tears and tellings off . . . The Aries self-image at this time is associated with physical vitality, and he can be very proud of his physical capabilities and coordination.

Between three and four years, this physicality begins to transform into another Aries characteristic; the competitive spirit, that urge to be recognized as a leader, or more superior than others. Competition begins to take on a role as a motivating impulse in the young Aries. Some express this quite openly, some may do it in a more secretive manner, depending on how much confidence they possess. The secret competitors will be inwardly striving to develop their embryonic abilities, so that whilst they may not achieve the number one spot yet, the day will come. . . . In several ways, this impulse can work to the parent's advantage in that the canny parent can use it to encourage the child to do things more quickly, learn things, behave better, especially if there are other small children in the family or peer-age friends around. Aries does not like to be shown up as being incapable of doing anything and, in the recognition of minor failures, can then decide that it will not happen again, and buckle down to learn properly.

Around the age of four, young Aries can be at his most aggressive and demanding. He thinks that he is ready to take on the world, life revolves around action and play, the more rough and tumble the better, although he certainly does not enjoy being hurt. Sometimes his 'body battery' gives in under the strain; he can suddenly tire, as though his body had deflated like a punctured tyre. At times this can be reflected in illness, where he just 'seizes up' for a couple of days, as if his body wisdom decides that he needs to have a forced stop to rest.

Relationships with parents can be a little touchy before the age of five. That potential aggressive assertiveness can lead to conflict and, if they begin to lose that self-control, can be difficult to deal with. Firm action may be required, although being aggressive back is not really the answer, because in life aggression tends to breed an aggressive reaction. One approach of reducing such situations could be a revitalized effort to involve their choices in situations (carefully created so that they choose from acceptable choices of your own). If they believe that they are getting their own way, then what can they object to?

That vitality can make her irritating at times; a rush of activity around a weakening parent is not the best thing to improved frayed tempers. Sometimes she may tend to work other children up, energizing them so everyone starts to become out of control, especially if she has younger brothers or sisters. Her spark lights other sparks, and before long you are struggling to put the flames out. After all, Aries is a Fire sign. You will just have to put up with the noise; try to occupy her with active participating toys, turn her loose in the garden, give her challenges that force her to develop to achieve, try some early education to involve mental effort which will redirect some of that body vitality.

By the time he's allowed into school, around the age of five, he will be more ready to change; and you will be ready for a rest (unless you have other smaller Aries children, in which case you'll soon be ready for a rest home). He'll still be active, and is graduating to climbing higher trees, but that vitality is being spread around his nature more evenly. Independence does involve choices and decisions, and with more freedom, he has to use his mind more, and that begins to absorb his excess energy. Aggression is expressed more through speech, and you may observe that he tends to be cheeky with you; he may need reminding of his place, which certainly isn't always number one! You may decide to offer 'bribes' for good behaviour; whilst this is not necessarily advisable, in practical terms it can help the parent cope with child-raising demands. Aries is likely to respond well to praise and encouragement, to make him feel important and capable can be even more valuable than sweets or toys to his development. Stimulate his imagination through suitable stories, this linked with his television watching of adventure cartoons will give him a fund of ideas that his budding imagination can build on, creating all sorts of exotic adventures in such mysterious locations as the garden. He'll love making up such stories and adventures himself, and then performing them with playmates, with him as leader of course. Leave him be; it'll soak up all that energy, and he'll be ready for bed all the sooner.

THE ARIES CHILD PERSONALITY

As you watch Aries growing up, you'll become aware of her direct approach to life, an eagerness to experience and explore the strange world in which she finds herself. She is keen to attempt any new challenge, tending to rush enthusiastically and impulsively into action, often before she has really thought out what she is doing. This deep need for fun and excitement can lead her into some situations of possible danger, so you certainly need to keep a watchful eye on her actions.

Whilst he is soon physically coordinated, those sudden spurts of energy can make his arms and legs a little jerky, which can lead to clumsiness around the home and accidents. In that impulsive eagerness to be up and active, he often forgets what is in his immediate environment. So be prepared for household breakages, spilt drinks, marks on the furniture, and have plenty of plasters, bandages and soothing words, because it is likely that Aries will need them!

They'll need plenty of sleep to replenish their drained body energy, yet you may find that they are resistant to going to bed because there are still things to do. Generally, the health and physical constitution of Aries is good, with sufficient vitality to recover from those normal childhood illnesses. Resilient is the word for Aries, always capable of springing back into action.

Aries can be very self-centred and demanding, determined

to have his own way. Because of his often simple assertive approach of ' I want . . . ', coupled with a persistent spirit, he can be difficult to resist. Once his mind has been firmly fixed on a desire, then he totally focuses on attaining it. Yet there can be a peculiar charm about his self-centred demands and desires, which are presented in an expectant innocent manner, as if the thought of rejection was unthinkable. (This trait continues into the adult Aries. . .) Because Aries wants, he believes that Aries should naturally get, and can be surprised when those desires are not always met. The failure of that disarming simplicity, and the shock of a 'No' response, can throw him into a temper and noisy anger. Any frustration of his attempts to achieve something will also build up in him, until he suddenly explodes in a fit of temper to release his repressed anger at his failure; yet this is more healthy then holding this blocked energy within for prolonged periods of time, and once the tension is released, his basic good humour reasserts itself quickly.

Aries reacts strongly to the imposition of the parent's will, yet always attempts to assert her own will on others. She will pass through stages of open defiance, challenging her will against the supremacy of the parent or teacher; she can be disputatious at times, looking for confrontation as a test for her own power, physically or verbally. Direct power clashes – which Aries tends to create – are not the best approaches to deal with her sometimes confrontational and adversarial tendencies. The best approach when dealing with an Aries who is causing school or family problems is to use tact and diplomacy, to try and find out from her why she is being so aggressive or contrary. Encouraging her – without immediate condemnation – to look at how she is behaving, to see the effect it has on others, and to appeal to that often hidden emotional side of Aries, can often work in allowing her to become more aware of her own actions, and then willingly choosing to alter her own behaviour.

Otherwise the power of Aries can feed off other power energy and, even if it loses the battle, will be more trained and sharpened for the next encounter. Eventually, Aries has faith in that he will win, and become number one. You can observe Aries taking control of a group of playmates over time, once he has established his dominance. He'll be the prime initiator, leading, providing ideas, and giving energy to the group; leader of the gang. The Aries forcefulness can have a negative effect on other children, at least from a parental or teacher's standpoint, as they are encouraged to follow the leader and perhaps to act in ways that normally they would not, under the influence of the Aries abundance of energy.

Aries has a straightforward outgoing energy, but the inner character has a tendency to be contradictory. As has been mentioned, there is a hidden emotional side to Aries, a generous and soft heart, which is part of the Aries who has a secret inferiority complex, who is not totally convinced of her capabilities or that she is lovable. This side gets overshadowed by the energetic Aries, who exudes confidence and makes assertive demands. This more sensitive personality reflects the Fire element in its more imaginative, idealistic dimension, and Aries has a strongly optimistic enthusiastic attitude to life, plus simple, naive ideals. There is a 'gentle soul and a pushy personality' in Aries, an odd combination of outer extrovert and inner introvert that often sit uncomfortably together. One side becomes repressed, rarely displayed, and often this is the sensitive soul, although there are adult Aries who seem more like Pisces in character, who have repressed that dominant assertive Aries characteristic.

The more gentle Aries can become an idealistic dreamer, who suffers considerable pain if her dreams collapse, or when her enthusiasms are met by an uninterested response. But she normally manages to maintain her optimistic view of life, even if it means hiding her dreams away out of sight.

One of the main accusations against Aries is a roughriding insensitivity. Often this is accurate, because there is a lack of awareness of others, through an excessive self-preoccupation; but this can be modified and balanced by a parent becoming aware of the more gentle dimension of their child, the one that easily demonstrates real affection and love, and by reassuring the child that it is OK and safe to allow expression. Certainly an adult Aries would benefit from a personal acceptance of that aspect, and an adolescent could find that it made the passage to adulthood more easy, once that emotional and idealistic self was acknowledged.

Aries has to learn social responsibility, cooperation and not competition; he'll compete anyway, and he needs to become more sensitive and aware of others coexisting in the world. His clever mind will grasp a common-sense explanation of the values of cooperation and living in harmony with people, and his heart will understand why it is wrong to make unnecessary suffering for people. An Aries who develops in a balanced manner could offer much to society. He could unfold that latent sensitivity, develop his idealistic dreams for a safer world and a higher quality of living for everyone, and determinedly apply his powerful energy to making that dream move a step closer to reality. It is perhaps a wiser way to guide the growing Aries, than to allow that more self-centred spirit to be number one. The sensitive Aries recognizes that he is 'number one amongst a world of number ones . . . '

Suggest a suitable ideal for Aries to work towards; if it is apt, he will apply himself. He develops better when praised for his efforts and achievements, and will try to attain those levels that are expected of him. Try not to set an impossible standard for him to attain but always one that is within his reach, but which also challenges him to stretch and improve, releasing his potential.

It is likely that Aries will rush into adolescence, and that puberty will take place earlier than with most. He will probably mature more quickly in his personality, showing distinct signs of impending adulthood throught a responsible attitude. He is eager to explore adult life, with perhaps a little naivety, and may be overenthusiastic and impulsive in his decisions and actions. That assertive, competitive tendency is probably prominent, and those self-centred demands may become irritating. But his innocent charm and romantic nature can persuade many to satisfy his desires. He'll rarely show you that inner vulnerability; it's too hidden behind the confidence and optimistic outlook. He's sure that he will succeed in adult life, that the world is just waiting for him to burst onto the scene!

THE ARIES CHILD AND EDUCATION

Young Aries are often very bright and clever, appearing to be relatively advanced for their age in their manner and style of expression. As they progress through school, their vitality moves towards awakening their mental capabilities, and a better balance with physical activity is achieved.

One of the main Aries characteristics is the enthusiasm with which she commences new projects or subjects; the problem can lie in her ability to complete a project, or maintain interest in the subject. Aries is a great initiator of ideas, but lacks the staying power; ideas and novelty turn her on, but after a while, if something new attracts her attention, she'll move all her energy towards that and ignore what she has already started. Sometimes she lacks all interest in results, and her most enjoyable preoccupation is in the launching of something new; sowing the springtime seeds.

Whilst younger children have a commen tendency to lose interest quickly and have a short attention span, the developing school-age Aries child may have to learn to finish one project at a time before diverting attention to the next apparently more interesting one. Both teachers and parents may need to guide the child in the disciplines of completion, otherwise he may grow up with a tendency to leave things uncompleted; leaving school work unfinished, leaving his bedroom half tidy, leaving jobs and relationships, running away from commitments and responsibilities, starting business schemes but never lasting long enough to make them work, or maybe becoming that frustrating type of handyman who rushes around the house starting jobs, disrupting rooms and never finishing them. In raising children, parents can bequeath problems for future sons- or daughters-in-law. . . . Aries needs to be shown the sense of satisfaction and achievement that can be experienced in the successful completion of a project, and that all ideas fail if they are only partially finished. Considering the Aries characteristic of wanting success and acknowledgement as an achiever, such praise and encouragement should be effective in redirecting this tendency.

Being challenged tends to evoke a corresponding response from Aries. They are determined to show that they can do it; or at least have a good try. Challenging them can be a good parental or teaching strategy, but it is best reserved for those times when you think that they have the potential but are being lazy. Over-use of such a tactic will eventually diminish its effectiveness and, remember, you'll need all those cunning tricks to play at opportune times whilst they are growing.

Aries prefers to initiate actions, and would rather be free to explore and discover things for herself. Her attitude is one of experimentation, and usually she will learn from making mistakes and this is part of her nature. Excessive interference and supervision tends to irritate her, so it is best to show her what to do, and then withdraw, watching her progress from a distance. Resist that temptation to jump in if she is doing something wrong, and wait awhile to see if she thinks through her mistake or problem, and alters her approach accordingly. If she doesn't perhaps ask if she's getting on OK, and let the request for help come from her. Interference may just cause her to lose interest through frustration at not being allowed to discover the way for herself.

Aries will want to be creative in some way, it's a natural impulse for him, and there may be signs of talent at an early age. Much of this can spring from an active imagination, sometimes overactive, which can weave fantastical tales around ordinary situations if the Aries has become a verbally explicit youngster. Tales of fantasy and heroic knights and adventurers can engross his attention as he identifies with the daring deeds and noble chivalry. Aries does prefer to personally set his creativity in motion, through self-motivation and choice, rather than have it imposed upon him. Any signs of natural gifts and talents should be encouraged, helping the child to develop them in his own way without too much direction from the parent. It is best to take the cue from the child, such as 'What do you want to do?' or 'How do you want to do it?' rather than imposing your own wishes directly on to him. To cooperate and collaborate is the key; acting in an obviously superior way to the Aries child is likely to stimulate a negative reaction over time. Also, as Aries tends to be competitive in attitude anyway, it is wiser not to attempt to encourage him by implying a competitive dimension to the situation. Whilst in the short term it may be effective in making him actively participate, repetitive arousal of that spirit can make him an almost obsessive competitor in adult life, a tendency that does not make for good relationships with others as Aries is always looking for an opportunity to demonstrate superiority.

Aries can be impatient; give him a toy that is too old for him, and after several failed attempts at mastering it he's likely to ignore it or may try to break it. He would hate being beaten by a toy!

School life should help to balance young Aries more, modifying those tendencies of independence into ones of group cooperation and participation, where she will discover that it can be rewarding fun to work with others in a small group, all exploring new ideas and knowledge about the world. She has a lot of nervous energy though, and a teacher may find her to be a restless, agitating child in the class, who sometimes struggles to keep any semblance of concentration on the topic that is being taught. That energy needs focused channels to be released along, and the wise teacher should try to ensure that Aries is kept busy, perhaps with lessons that slightly stretch her but are within her capabilities. Otherwise Aries could become more troublesome and disruptive in the classroom.

Unless young Aries is especially dominated by that impulse to succeed and to be top of the class, he often fails to really settle into school life. Aries children are quite capable of success, and can enjoy basic schooling and education, reading and writing, but it is the nature of the school environment that will never deeply appeal to them. They want to live freely and spontaneously, and the discipline and routine of school is often rejected. This, plus that style of self-assertion, can lead them towards clashes with teachers or authority figures, whether at school or later in employment situations. The routines of a job are not appreciated either and, like the Aries reactions to teachers, an employer who orders Aries is likely to receive a less than enthusiastic response. The Ram is often too self-assured to welcome such attitudes of coercion, and values the freedom not to bow the knee in obedience. Yet a relationship which tends to ask Aries to do something will usually have a more positive response, as Aries still feels that he has a freedom in choosing his response. Authoritarian parents, teachers and employers will provoke an antagonistic reaction. Having said that, Aries will still need some form of structured discipline to which he has to conform, or else problems will occur in adult life as he could refuse to conform to adult responsibilities.

As teachers can soon discover, Aries children have imagination, which tends to embellish and exaggerate events, especially those where they are at the centre of things. Careful guidance may be needed to modify this tendency, so that they begin to perceive and express real events in a common perspective, and start to restrict their more extravagant flights of fancy to those times which are appropriate. But never try to force them to suppress their imaginations; they could develop into imaginative writers or artists and you know how successful they can be in today's consumer world.

Aries is rarely the dedicated student; the discipline and perseverance puts him off, unless he has fixed his mind on achieving some clearly defined goal, then he'll contradict that opening statement. The question is, does he want to be the King Ram of the herd? If so, it'll be very hard for someone to stop him; if his focus wavers, and his intention is not firm, then he'll be more loose and relaxed. Whenever he chooses, he is capable of learning quickly and effectively. It depends on his application, although few Aries welcome homework and at times it may be a battle to persuade him to do it; sometimes suggesting to him that 'It is all right, if you can't do it then just ask the teacher for help' may galvanize him into activity designed to show you that he can do it perfectly correctly if he so chooses. But it's a subtle strategy, and if you over-use it, he'll become aware and refuse to fall for it in the future.

Aries will respond better to supportive positive encouragement, rather than any parental or teacher humiliations and implications of inadequacy. It is best to build up a child's confidence by praising whatever they can do and achieve, rather than by highlighting their failings and lack of talent in certain aspects. Each child has its own abilities and latent potential, and these may not always be obvious or suited to being expressed through mainstream schooling. Parents, teachers and society attitudes are all to blame for the early repression of many children's talents, through lack of insight, lack of supportive training, and an emphasis on children having to conform to societal expectations and prescribed lifestyles.

Aries tends to do well if she studies in a school environment that is personally encouraging, where the teacher has a more personal relationship with the child, and offers a clear acknowledgement of the value of Aries' work. If this doesn't happen, then the child can become demanding of the teacher's attention, as a form of asserting her presence in the room: 'Hey, look at me!' Juvenile perhaps, but a common need amongst children, and one that Aries is prepared to assert.

Often Aries needs some teaching concerning relationships with other children; some can cause trouble just by unconsciously being too physical, and a few can become bullies as an expression of that need to be number one. Most of this is just a lack of awareness and sensitivity, and is not something to worry unduly about, providing that he responds to a clear explanation of the suffering that he is causing for other children and changes his ways. Young Aries is not innately unkind, but in his over-abundance of energy can forget his sensitivity in relating to others. Such parental or teaching guidance would need to involve teaching Aries to think more, and to consider the possible consequences on others that his actions may create. Using his mind to project results of his choice is a talent that Aries may need to develop, and one that can help to improve adult life. Spontaneous decisions do not always lead to the right choices to follow. Encouraging him in sport and physical recreation can positively use any excess physical energy, and he may become quite skilled in certain sports, and appropriate professional training may help him in channelling any sporting ability towards higher achievements.

If Aries does not settle at school, and under-performs, then they still have the capability of success at a later age. Some children never seem to wake up until they enter the adult world, and in that shock they realize that they need to shake themselves in order to achieve anything. Further education could be required for them to catch up, and to create potential opportunities. But Aries can never be 'written off'; if they want to they can achieve, when they decide the time is right.

ARIES CAREERS

Most Aries prefer the sort of employment that offers them some personal space, and where there is sufficient freedom to express themselves. A job involving repetitive work will not be suitable for them, as they are liable to lose interest rapidly in an unchallenging occupation. What they prefer is a career which offers the potential of a full involvement of their energies, something that can maintain their natural enthusiasm.

As Aries does not take kindly to the imposition of orders, the ideal employment is one where he has some independence from superiors, so that friction does not begin to develop as Aries attempts to assert himself, or tries to act as a superior too. Either being independent or a manager are the suitable positions from the Aries standpoint. Yet he can thrive on career competition, vigorously entering the cut and thrust of certain professions' 'rat races', intent on rising to the top.

Aries likes to initiate projects, to bring inspiration to a new idea so that it is successfully launched, and can be the right person to act as an enthusiastic pioneer and ideas person with the devising of new schemes, businesses, etc. Aries people love this role, as it enables them to fire off a lot of possible ideas, 'brainstorming' through their feasibility, and sowing the foundational seeds for the birth of the project. Setting wheels in motion is the Aries talent, but once the basic patterns of the new project are established, they'll lose interest in the equally important finer details that are also necessary to ensure success. It is the dream or ideal that turns Aries on, who is in a rush to move onto the next scheme, even before the first one has been completed. There can be an interest in working with those more crusading projects which have social repercussions; these attract the Aries who is drawn to idealistic social visions.

They will enjoy working in an environment that embodies intrinsic change; the media could attract, and be suitable. Television, radio, journalism and newspapers could fascinate Aries, where several of their talents and personal needs could be satisfied. A more active lifestyle such as being an athlete, applying that competitive edge to gain greater success, or being a world traveller and explorer could also appeal.

Military life may seem to suit the late teenage Aries, although whether the discipline of obedience would is dubious; being an officer or a leader of men would be a natural role though. The idealistic Aries may wish to move towards political involvement, locally or nationally, where he can move into the spotlight and express his own solutions to current social problems. His vitality and enthusiasm could make him an active people's representative, although his tact and diplomacy could sometimes be lacking.

Medicine is another sphere, where Arian skills can be

demonstrated, and a certain degree of independence found, such as being a surgeon, doctor or dentist. Some Aries enter the world of the craftsmen, applying their talents in a creative manner, to make attractive, practical or aesthetically pleasing pieces, although here the challenge is for them to realize their dreams fully and complete the work. The challenges of mechanical engineering could attract the Aries temperament, especially through the initial ingenuity and skill required to design and construct machines capable of performing new tasks and which add to technological progress.

TAURUS
(APRIL 20 to MAY 20)

Planetary Ruler: Venus

Element type	Earth
Type	Negative/Feminine
Triplicity	Fixed
Symbol	♉
Image	The Bull
Part of Body	Throat, neck
Theme of Self	I Have
Key Qualities	Practical, determined, materialistic
House Affinity	2nd House

Famous Taurus Personalities: Queen Elizabeth II, Adolf Hitler, Oliver Cromwell, Sigmund Freud, Orson Welles, Gary Cooper, Bing Crosby, Barbra Streisand, Pope John Paul II, Cher, Lloyd Honeyghan, Michael Palin, Shirley Maclaine, David Shepherd.

THE PRE-SCHOOL TAURUS CHILD

For the mother who is destined to have a Taurus child, there is likely to be less activity in the womb than with the active Aries. As Taurus is a sensual type, the experience of protective warmth and sustenance found in the womb will be a very pleasurable state to remain in and, until the actual time of birth, Taurus will not be acting as if it is imperative to leave. This tendency can display itself in the nature of the birth, where, in a normal birth situation, Taurus is often cautious in arriving in this world, preferring to wait in that hidden familiar home, and being wary about emerging into the

36

unknown light. Once that time for action occurs, the birth should happen naturally and easily; but you may have to wait a little while for Taurus to be ready.

Once those early wrinkles are smoothed out, Taurus is usually an attractive baby with a fairly agreeable disposition. You'll have to make sure that you keep baby content, through regular feeds and plenty of love, affection and cuddles, because all this enforces that sense of protection, security and stability that Taurus needs. They'll let you know when those needs are not being satisfied; like the bellowing of the Bull, the noise will make you pay attention to them!

Over the first year, Taurus may seem to be passive, and perhaps a little slow in developing, Yet she is a happy child, alertly taking in the world through all of her senses, sight, hearing, touch, smells, and in her own way is gradually familiarising herself with life. She's one of those babies that goes stiff when upset, as if she daren't allow all that pent-up anger and energy to come out, and when she's older you'll see her sometimes pawing at the ground, like a bull working itself up to charge. That retention of energy and emotion will occur in varying contexts through the Taurean life. Sleep is important to Taurean well-being and humour, and she'll enjoy all sorts of physical and sensual pleasures; usually, bathtime is great fun for her. Even at an early age, regular lifestyle patterns of feeding, bathing and sleeping are of value to her, helping to enhance that feeling of stability for the developing personality.

It is unlikely that Taureans will be early walkers or talkers, and they will still have that cautious approach towards each stage of development. Sitting in a safe playpen can suit them, and give Mother a rest too. Taureans move at their own pace, and hate being rushed by anyone; the fact that they can be irritatingly slow does not seem to bother them. Encourage the child to experiment with walking and talking, but don't expect immediate progress; Taurus will take her time, wait until she is ready, and then with a broad grin amaze everyone. Once she breaks through the barriers of her own caution, progress can come quickly. As a physical support, she may be one of those children who have to carry a favourite teddy bear or toy wherever they go. When she realizes how much physical enjoyment there is in using her limbs and the freedom that she has through her own mobility, her physical coordination and capability will rapidly increase, as will her talking, and those parental concerns about any slow development will soon be forgotten.

Taurus will be an affectionate child, and will demand a lot of physical contact and clear demonstrations of love, or sensual stroking and bonding. She will tune into enjoyable physical sensations, and can appear to enter a light trance-like state when such pleasure is available. Her appreciation and enjoyment of the natural world and its impact on her senses will come more alive now, once she can play in the garden or experience open spaces. Food can become another source of tactile pleasure, and she may annoy by playing with food rather than eating it; spreading it all around is the game! If this happens, let her enjoy it, and protect the carpet and furniture by putting a plastic sheet around her chair, so that any mess can land on that. The phase will pass, and she'll soon make sure that she's eating enough, because that too is enjoyable for a Taurus.

By the age of two, signs of the Taurus fixity of will and stubborn determination begin to shine through. Taurus can become very demanding, and persists in those demands even when a parent is equally determined to deny them. He can be obstinate, unreasonably stubborn, and very hard to persuade. This can be displayed in a developing fussiness concerning food, and anger at not being given his favourite choices. He will sit there, mouth firmly closed, a belligerent, determined look on his face. 'That food is not crossing my lips . . . '; he'll even toss the whole plate onto the floor to avoid eating. When Taurus says 'No', it seems as if it's fixed in tablets of stone that he's swallowed. The 'terrible twos', it's been called, full of resistance and temper tantrums, and Taurus is like a fixed immovable object, clashing with the irresistible force of the parent. Something has to give, and it's often the temper of the parent, but even in defeat, Taurus will still voice a noisy opposition. And in any case, it's only a battle that has been lost and not the war, he thinks . . .

Whilst it is a common symptom at the age of two or three, Taurus children can have difficulty with toilet training and bowel movements. It relates to that tendency to rigidity and stiffness when retaining anger or emotions when desires are not met, plus that fixity of will. The term is 'anal retentive', and unhealthy constipation and refusal to release bowel movements can be a young Taurean trait. Often at the transition to proper toilet training, children who used to go regularly suddenly become irregular, as if fear of accidents unbalances natural movements. Taurus, who tends to dislike change, is one sign that has an uneasy response to this change in their lives. Part of this is related to unease with emotional power, and can occur in later life, reflecting the 'fear' of Earth (physical body, Taurus) at the eroding power of Water (feelings/emotions). If this develops, you may need to take medical advice to confirm that there is nothing physiologically wrong. Often, the simple answer is that Taurus has decided that he does not like bowel movements, and by sheer force of will, he is not going to have any! Usually as they grow older, and other interests and life demands divert their attention, this problem resolves itself by the age of three to three and a half.

The Taurus child can be a little shy with other children, but once she settles into a more familiar, regular relationship with them – such as at a playschool – she becomes more sociable. She'll prefer playing with either one or two children at a time, rather than with a larger group and, once she feels more relaxed and secure with friends, can begin to show a somewhat bossy side to her nature.

She's generally an active child, loving to play in water, sand and mud. Let her dig in an unused part of the garden and she can spend hours happily exploring the earth. She can be quite self-contained if need be, playing on her own, lost in her own imaginative world. Taurus often has an artistic talent, especially a gift of the hands, and she will enjoy the tactile pleasures of Plasticine, paints, chalk, coloured pencils, so give her plenty of paper, or sticky glue and scissors, and you can be assured of some peace and quiet!

Taurus domesticity can emerge, where he'll offer to help, and may choose to help by tidying around. Sometimes when children are being 'helpful', they are really more of a hindrance; but the wise parent should grimly bear it, hoping that such tendency will continue until they are old enough to be a really reliable help in the house, but unfortunately it seems to have completely disappeared by adolescence.

A favourite Taurus response is 'In a minute . . . ' When time is short, and you are rushing around trying to get ready, Taurus sits there, placid and calm, doing nothing . . . She's adept at this; and if you hurry her, watch out for passive resistance, she'll even slow down more . . . Taurus has an odd relationship with time, 'Plenty of time . . . ', and they'll do nothing until they are late or have to rush unreasonably.

By the age of four, Taurus is quite proficient in the practical, physical demands of life, and takes considerable pride in these abilities. His concentration has improved, and he will put a lot of effort and time into doing those things that he especially enjoys, and effort and will into avoiding anything he doesn't like. Playing is very important to him, and it is an apt time to encourage him in some pre-school training. He can be quite receptive, and is likely to enjoy those 'lessons' that involve drawing, colouring, painting or early writing and reading from this age onwards. He will make progress if he perseveres, but allow him to dictate the pace of development; try not to force him.

Whilst she is more independent, she still requires that sense to be reinforced, and you should take time to ensure that you do still give that physical comforting and clearly show your appreciation for her efforts in growing up. Possessiveness of toys can become highlighted, especially with friends or younger members of the family. Taurus will be choosy about her friends and playmates; generally she will have a few close friends with whom she feels safe, and can be shy with children and people that she isn't familiar with.

When the time to start school arrives, Taurean children will be ready for the next step, even though they are really domesticated home lovers. The change into school routines and education rhythms may seem frightening to them at first, although the enjoyment of focused play and primary teaching should quickly enable them to adjust and relax more. Their first teachers should be ready to make allowances for that tendency to be slow in doing things, whether it is eating, dressing or doing what they have just been told. It is a part of their nature, even though it can be annoying, and the Bull is very capable of resistance. They'll move at their own speed, or not at all.

THE TAURUS CHILD PERSONALITY

Taurus is an attractive child, and can be genuinely loving, although can veer at times towards emotional sentimentality, especially in older boys who may have difficulties with their emotions, as during adolescence. Physically displayed loving affection is vitally necessary to them, and the more cuddles, hugs and kisses there are, the better for the younger child. Qualities that will be expressed by the adult Taurus are in open evidence in the young, such as supportive love, sympathetic understanding, loyalty and devotion; even though the child may be young, the awareness of the value of emotional support is present.

Taurus is an Earth sign, and has the characteristics of reliability, support, endurance, perseverance and predictability; yet hiding deep within them is an emotional vulnerability and sensitivity that reflect the other 'feminine groupings' of the Water signs. The polar opposite sign to Taurus is Scorpio, and water is the main element capable of eroding the discipline and control that the earthy Taurus often displays.

Much of the vitality of Taurus comes from these inner feelings, and this can fade if she is not receiving sufficient love and attention that 'waters the inner dry arid land'. A Taurus child can become quite stolid, lacking vitality if those feelings become inhibited. Words alone seem inadequate in providing that vitalizing spark, but physical loving contact recharges those batteries, and brings joy back into their world. You'll notice that a sullen, moody child can often be drawn out of their mood through physical attention and caring.

The Earth and Water tendency can be an odd mixture. Like a swinging pendulum, their temperaments move between the two complementary opposites, and can fail to find that point of balance. Often young Taurus gives the appearance of being mature and confident for their age, and often this is true, but this appearance is not as real as it may seem, because hiding within is a personality that has feelings of insecurity and a lack of self-confidence. The Earth is aware of the eroding power of Water, and of its tidal ebbs and flows, and doesn't know how to deal with such sensations. Taurus often attempts to cope with this by emotional control, damming those inner waters; boys and men are most prone to this tendency, because such sensitivity is not easily expressed in the more masculine-dominated world. Girls and women find it much easier to direct and channel this in their lives, as mothers and home-makers offer natural ways in which sensitivity and a loving nature can be shared with others. Always allow and encourage your Taurus child to release those emotions; repression can bring a variety of later problems.

Taurus has a very powerful will, although it is not always applied in a positive direction; often it emerges as a defensive reaction against something that the child does not want to do. When the will is fixed, reasonableness disappears, as all the concentrated effort is poured into making that will immovable. All parental attempts at logic, reason and persuasiveness can collapse before that determined face, teeth clenched in opposition. Taurus rarely backs down at confrontations and, even if he has to, will do so with an obviously bad grace, with perhaps mumblings of abuse, snortings of resistance. 'Apologize? Never! The words would choke me . . .' Admitting mistakes and responsibility is uncommon too; part of this probably relates to that lack of inner confidence and security; in a fragile personality, it is too painful to admit being wrong. At best, a parent can only help to build up that child's self-assurance, explain that he is still loved even if he does make mistakes, and hope that as the child matures he will become capable of being more responsible for his actions, and be able openly to acknowledge failures.

Owing to those needs for security and stability, Taurus can often develop regular and repetitive habit patterns in daily life; and will usually reflect those experiences of life that are always enjoyed. Once Taurus establishes those likes and dislikes, a conservative spirit takes over, and they will resist all attempts to change the status quo, preferring the known and familiar to the unknown. Taurus rarely takes risks or acts impulsively. Disruptions in the child's life can have a deep effect, and they will not benefit from regular changes of home and school, and parental marriage difficulties can cause a deep emotional split within them.

When you tidy the young Taurean's room, and you find sweet papers and crisp packets hidden under the bed, you'll know that there's a secret eater in the house . . . Taurus enjoys food, and seems to need more than the regular meals to keep body and soul together. How much is actual hunger, and how much is the sensuality of eating is hard to define, and of course food offers a sense of life security too. Even if you believe that the child is eating enough, when he is out of sight, the sweets come out; most of the older child's pocket money is spent on secret feasts, and if he can combine taking out food when playing in the parks or woods, then his bliss is complete! Taurus boys love fresh air and the outdoors, camping can seem thrilling to him, although they will want all their 'creature comforts' as well. Crawling through the under-growth, playing Tarzan in the trees, whittling wood with a penknife, and running through woods and streams are favourite pastimes.

Gardening can be a suitable interest for Taurus too, combin-ing a creative sense both in designing a garden, and in the cultivation of plants and flowers, and working the earth with her hands is enjoyable in itself. This can help her to develop a sense of discipline and responsibility, so that in looking after her own area of ground, she is required to do certain jobs in the right season in order for the plants to flourish; it also helps her to take pride in her achievements, and encourages her to follow through from an initial impulse to the culmination of her efforts.

Both Taurus girls and boys will enjoy adventurous play and physical activities. Yet as they grow older, many Taurean girls have a tendency to become more feminine, displaying a traditional expression of their emerging role of womanhood. But this is natural to them, and is not something unduly forced on them by dominant social role patterns. However, some Taurean girls who retain strong connections to animals and nature may be less concerned with roles related to traditional feminine behaviour.

Taurus tends to be socially popular and have good relationships with friends, and she can have a fairly unconcerned cheerful temperament. Friends are important to her, and Taurus will gather a small group of close reliable friends around her, almost like a protective barrier. Occasional conflicts will arise, but unless Taurus sets her mind firmly against someone, such disputes will soon resolve themselves. Often the child will emerge as a leader or central figure of the small group, as a natural response to her usual capacity for childhood fairness and common sense, which never seems to restrict their enjoyment. Sometimes Taurus can be accused of being too physically dominant or a little bossy, but her friends will soon sort her out if that happens.

In adult company, they will be shy if a parent expects them to perform, although when in private and feeling secure, young Taurus can be quite an entertainer. There is a more extroverted side to their nature, but it is often restrained through a lack of self-confidence and, as they grow older, through a fear that it may contradict their efforts to appear more mature. In most Taureans, there is a sense that there is a more dramatic imaginative self trying to get out; but this rarely happens unless the controlling personality is willing to move beyond those self-imposed limitations of practical everyday life.

Home life is very important to her, and Taurus can be sensitive to the home environment of colour and decoration, as colours can influence that inner emotional nature, similar to the proverbial red rag to the bull! She will appreciate an attractively designed bedroom, especially one with colourful pictures or posters on the wall, and the teenage Taurean may want to take over the decoration of her own room, as she can be fussy about her private room. A good design sense, or fashion consciousness, is common, and Taurus will put effort into ensuring that her physical appearance is just right (whatever that particular style may be). Even from a much younger age, Taurus has a pronounced body consciousness, and physical appearance assumes a high priority in her personal scale of importance; usually much higher than school work. She applies creativity to her own image, as part of the effort to express her unique individuality; yet Taurus is rarely excessively eccentric. Often her approach is to follow the fashion, to be part of a recognizable group, rather than to draw attention to herself as a visual 'oddity'.

Adolescence can be a challenging time for Taureans, as that assumed stability in life is undermined by the confusing hormonal changes of puberty. They become more emotional, and probably moodier than they have ever been before. Most of this is the response of their sensitive, feeling nature, and the awakening of those sexual impulses of the teenager. Taurus children may have a tendency to mature later than some of their friends, the boys maintaining that fresh and smooth-faced complexion into their mid-teens. The more awkward Taurean traits tend to become dominant, with a surly, tough and belligerent attitude being common; that plus an often unreasonable stubbornness can add to the usual family friction when they go through their teens.

She does not appreciate teasing, and can have a righteous

attitude about herself and life; like most adolescents, she labours under the illusion that she 'knows it all', and often fails to listen properly to adult advice and guidance. Taurus has her own way of doing things, and rarely listens to the possible value of other approaches.

Dealing with the Taurus adolescent can be difficult, and his attitude to school can deteriorate markedly at this time, which with his often slow grasp of lessons can create a downward spiral in his grades. Like most children of that age, he is self-centredly preoccupied only with himself, and his sensitivity to parents and family life can appear to dissolve. Few topics catch his interest, although encouraging him to pick up any threads of artistic talents could help to create a positive release of his self-expression. The problem that most parents face with teenagers is waiting for them to mature past that uneasy phase; some Taureans prefer to remain as long as possible in their familiar childhood attitudes, others can mature in their personality extremely quickly, ready to enter and explore adult life. Taurus is a creative type, and can become quite contrary if he feels under pressure to act in certain ways. Sometimes the only support a parent can really give is to just allow them to get on with life in their own way, to free them to experience life, and to learn from any mistakes they may make. Despite parental wishes, there is no way to transfer wisdom into a young adult, and adolescents are especially resistant to such attempts, and perhaps rightly so too.

THE TAURUS CHILD AND EDUCATION

Taurus is not normally an academic type, and the current approach of many Western styles of teaching is not especially suited to the Taurean temperament. Due to apparent slowness at times, teachers can misinterpret the actual ability of the Taurus child, especially when the child is being slow as a form of resistance to show his or her lack of interest in what is being taught. Laziness is often attributed to young Taureans, and whilst there is some truth in that accusation, most of it arises as a negative reaction to the way in which they are being taught.

A teacher who has no insight into the nature of the child's character (as a Taurus or any other sign), is liable to attempt teaching him from a 'standard approach', which can easily fail because it is not personally suited to that child. Certainly Taurus is one of those signs that is often misunderstood when the teacher is confronted by the child in the classroom.

Taurus is an Earth sign, and the most apt way to involve the child in learning is through an approach that arouses his senses and feelings. An academic, dry intellectual style will just make him switch off. The topic needs to be presented in a way that requires the child to be physically responsive, activating those five senses; perhaps through touching or smelling an object that is being talked about, or by involving him in physical action to experiment and find out for himself. Participation in lessons will work, but passive absorption of words will fail. Asking him to make relevant models, or to demonstrate his understanding through words and pictures should produce a better response, assuming that he paid attention to the initial teaching of the topic! If the teacher loses the child's attention during the introduction of a new subject, then he'll struggle to catch up or find any interest and motivation to do so. Abstract subjects are some of the worst for the Taurean to deal with.

What Taurus responds easily to is physical materiality, where lessons can be translated into a physical result, so that the child is involved in creating something that is the natural point of the lesson. Taurus is a building sign, making real that initiating impulse of Aries, establishing firm roots in the ground, so that the future structure has solid foundations. The inner question that Taurus seems to ask is 'What can I do with this piece of information? How can I use it in real life?'; the answer to that seems to determine whether the child will express any interest and involvement with the teaching. Will it inspire and motivate attention and practical application, or will the child switch off in boredom?

In this context, Taurus is taught best by a teacher who presents new ideas and subjects in terms of the use they have in life, and how that child can take advantage of the information now or in the future. What are the tangible real life examples of that idea? Or how are algebra and geometry relevant to that child? Taurus responds better to simple direct explanations; establish the point which the child does understand, and then slowly work to help him expand beyond that limited grasp. Otherwise, if that personal attention is not given, then Taurus can often slip behind.

Because of an inner insecurity, Taureans are usually modest and unsure of their real abilities and personal value. They need a lot of careful encouragement to draw out their full potential. Emotional support is also vital to them, even though they may not reveal their need for this as they grow older. They are very sensitive to criticism, and this tends to deflate them, rather than serving as a spur to renewed efforts, such as Aries may respond to. For most children, praise is a stimulus, helping to build that fragile confidence.

During school life, the obstinacy of the young Bull often reappears. Whenever either parent or teacher attempts to make Taurus do something that he does not want to do, then the opposition of the immovable object is faced. He can be extremely resistant to all forms of discipline; so fixed is that inner 'No' that it seems as if he becomes deaf to all raised voices of command. This fixed nature of the Taurus mind is one of the sign's more negative tendencies; holding stubborn opinions, beliefs and attitudes means that he fails to listen properly, and often fails to learn from life's experiences. Repetitive behaviour patterns can occur, where the same causes of parent–child friction frequently happen; often these are relatively simple acts that the child fails to perform, and which he is capable of doing. Parents can find Taurean children quite frustrating in certain ways when, through a lack of simple application, they create trouble for themselves.

There is an aspect to Taurus that is anti-authority, and which can lead them towards often futile rebellious action. Direct commands are reacted to with a less than enthusiastic response, or with the question, 'Why?' Most parents respond to this lack of movement with a 'Because I say so . . . ' approach, which rarely seems to convince a sullen Taurus. Whenever 'Why?' occurs, it is because he has no intention of doing whatever he has been told. Parents can attempt more emotionally based manipulation of their children, and this can work more often with a Taurus, but the child may have problems at school or in adult life where direct commands are common in employment situations.

One problem that Taurus often demonstrates is that of lack of momentum and impetus; they can be slow in starting and reluctant to finish, especially when they lack interest, and this will lead them to be marked down in school grades, particularly if continual assessment is the main technique in assessing their standard of education. Taureans may need to become more disciplined in their application, so that they overcome this trait.

Taurus probably will be an 'under-achiever' in educational terms; some Taurus children can be very industrious and serious in their school life, achieving satisfactory results but, more often than not, their eventual performance and results will be lacking. Much will depend on the style and quality of teaching; if it suits them, then they will do well; if they receive adequate attention, then they will prosper; but if through slowness and lack of interest they are 'written off' by teachers at an early age, then they will struggle to gain any incentive to try harder.

How can parents help a Taurean child to unfold his potential? Encouraging him to be creative will help, as Taurus has an ability to work with his hands. This can be through drawing and painting, by developing an harmonious colour and design sense, perhaps, for the older Taurean girl, being taught to cook, sew and dress-make. This may seem a sexist comment, but despite the sometimes tomboyish nature of

Taurean girls, they are usually natural home-makers, and all the female skills of domestic life will appeal to her, and offer a sense of personal satisfaction at the demonstration of her abilities. Taurus is often suited to music, and will enjoy singing or learning a musical skill (if they can generate the initial momentum); although perhaps having a daughter who enjoys singing but is tone-deaf can be a mixed blessing! Quite a few Taureans are very verbally active, talkative and busy in a noisy sense, appearing almost extroverted in such situations. The rhythms of rapping music can appeal to modern Taurean teenage boys, for example. Guide the Taurean male towards achieving practical results; he'll be extremely proud as he demonstrates his carpentry ability. He may make a good builder; he could be a good artist, as long as there is a tangible end product that he has been vitally involved in creating. Being part of an office system of shuffling paper from desk to desk would rarely satisfy him.

TAURUS CAREERS

As Taurus tends to need security and stability, the ideal type of career includes these two aspects; most Taureans stay in their employment for relatively long periods of time, and perhaps apart from their early working years do not change jobs very often.

Working with nature can be appealing, where the rhythms of life and the natural processes can be experienced; farming, market gardening, forestry, plant and tree centres can all resonate strongly with that Taurean tendency. Involvement with food and diet can also touch a Taurus interest.

The security which property and finance appears to offer are very attractive, and careers associated with those two themes can provide suitable employment. Estate agency/real estate, building, surveying and architecture can be channels for those inner Taurean motivations and interests to emerge, jobs which are constants in today's society, and can provide a lifetime career and security. The craftsman dimension of

Taurus can be directed towards the physical building of homes and industrial or commercial construction projects, and can also be used in the creation of attractive furniture and interior design. Taurus prefers a tangible practical result of all efforts made, focusing on the material values of life and ensuring personal comfortable environments.

Usually Taurus can be placed in positions of trust and responsibility, as reliability, consistency and stable performance are character traits; imagination and risk are less common. This helps them to gain positions of seniority, where a cautious traditional approach is preferred, and they can be relied upon to complete their job. Often those types of routine employment where the procedures are firmly established can suit them, such as the Civil Service, banking, accountancy, and bureaucracies. In order to gain stability and security, many Taureans are prepared to accept repetition and routine in a work situation.

Those Taureans that take a more artistic route may be the minority though, yet many of this sign have a real artistic talent and appreciation which may still be hidden. Painting and sculpting are the most common of the artistic pursuits, whilst drawing and design can develop towards more decorative skills, such as jewellery-making. Music and singing can also be a Taurean form of expression, but those taking this more artistic route have to reach an inner understanding of their more conservative tendencies, so that they can move beyond them into the more flowing world of artistic creations. Many Taureans fail to successfully cross that bridge, reverting to a relatively safe and predictable traditional lifestyle.

GEMINI
(MAY 21 to JUNE 21)

Planetary Ruler: Mercury

Element type	Air
Type	Positive/Masculine
Triplicity	Mutable
Symbol	♊
Image	The Twins
Part of Body	Lungs, chest, nervous system
Theme of Self	I Think
Key Qualities	Nonconformist, communicative, intellectual
House Affinity	3rd House

Famous Gemini Personalities: Duke of Edinburgh, John F. Kennedy, Gauguin, Bob Dylan, Ian Fleming, Errol Flynn, Marilyn Monroe, Judy Garland, Kylie Minogue, Mike Gatting, Simon Callow, Arthur Conan Doyle, Sartre, W. B. Yeats.

THE PRE-SCHOOL GEMINI CHILD

Consistent with the mutability of the Gemini nature, Gemini births are very varied. There will be a sense of great energy around, but unlike an Aries who is in a rush to be born, or a Taurus who is more cautious about emerging, Gemini can seem to be considering the situation, evaluating 'Should he or shouldn't he?' Some Gemini births can be start-stop-go again, pending a final decisive movement.

During that first year of life, little Gemini will be a restless child with a naturally erratic pattern of behaviour. Sleep and feeding will be the most obvious areas of this tendency, where despite your wishes, Gemini will be irregular. Establishing successful patterns of sleeping and feeding times can be difficult, but should be persevered with, because otherwise baby Gemini will rule your life. Allowed freedom, she will sleep and feed whenever she wants to, totally disrupting your routines and sleep at night. She'll be a 'wriggler' in her cot, active even whilst asleep, and unfortunately she's likely to be a light sleeper too. Gemini is an alert child, and will demand considerable attention and play from parents; as you'll find in later years, that tendency towards being quickly bored is present, as toys are soon discarded through lack of interest, to make a space for something new to examine. Active toys for the hands are quite suitable.

By the age of one to two, Gemini is enjoying the sensations of becoming mobile. Gemini has become a world explorer, following in the footsteps of Livingstone in Africa; or at least he would if he wasn't limited to his home environment. He has become aware of the world. His curiosity has been awakened, and there is so much to look at, touch, poke, smell, taste in this strange mysterious world. To an adult, a living room is quite common, but to a young child, it is a room of wonders and fascination. What's in that cupboard there? What's under the seat? What do I look like with a plant pot on my head? What are all these wires? What happens if I press this button? He tends to be physically coordinated early for his age, walking quite effectively, loving to climb over the furniture, and apart from his attempts to copy Tarzan by swinging on the curtains, he'll soon be ready to discover a new world that will interest him all his life. Speech. Talking. The thrill of words and being able to communicate his demands. From that previous babble to forming proper words is a joyous step forward for Gemini, and he should learn relatively quickly, taking every opportunity to experiment with his new skill of talking.

Between two and three years, her talking will grow in leaps and bounds, and she will benefit from those conversations with you. She's always got something to say, although early signs of a difficulty in making decisions will be observed.

There may be difficulties with toilet training, which is a major step in the child's development, as true to the Gemini nature, she tends to be unpredictable and irregular. Accidents happen; perhaps too frequently. As with the earlier sleep and feeding patterns, it may help to establish more of a regular pattern with her – not to impose it forcibly, but to observe the times when her motions tend to be after feeding, and encourage her to use her potty at such times. She should improve with repetition.

By the ages of three and four, language and words become more dominant. He likes to perform with speaking, and it can serve as an effective distraction and behaviour control to ask him to recite a short rhyme or sing a verse from a song, or to engage him in a participatory 'discussion' over choices of clothes or food. In fact he is not so good at choosing, but even if you have to eventually decide for him, try to do so in a way that makes him think that it's his choice; this can encourage him to learn how to be more decisive in future. His words may sound impressive, and his vocabulary quite large for his age, but you may need to check that his actual understanding is there too. He can appear to be more mature than he really is, and there is often a hidden emotional immaturity. Simple attempts at early schooling can be effective before the age of five, and free access to books and drawing/writing materials should be developed. Short words will be grasped by him, reading them from books, and helping him to learn to begin writing and counting will suit him. Numbers, words and stories can fascinate all Gemini children, and his interests begin to be absorbed more in that direction. By five, he is a very inquisitive child, and is ready for daily school life.

THE GEMINI CHILD PERSONALITY

When you watch young Gemini in action the quick movements of his limbs, those speedy, nervous gestures of his hands, that inability to sit still for longer than five seconds without fidgeting, then you'll observe the highly strung nervous energy that flows through the Gemini child – not just through his body; his mind is like that too! Restless, active, searching, questioning and wondering – wondering what to do next . . . For those parents who naturally prefer a more leisurely life, who enjoy peace and quiet, and hate having to rush around being fully alert all the time, then a Gemini child may give you a shock. He's a live wire, quicksilver child of the Air, and in trying to keep up with him, he'll help to take a few years off your life, as well as giving you grey hairs sooner. To paraphrase the old Scarlet Pimpernel rhyme, 'You'll seek him here, you'll seek him there, that little Gemini is everywhere!' He's fast; perhaps not in Superman's league of being faster than a bullet, but certainly faster than you. Once he's mobile, you'll think that there's several duplicates of him running around the house; one second he's over there poking at the plant in the window, the next he's crawling underneath the television set, and then he's exploring the cupboards in the kitchen.

Usually you can locate her by the noise; she's a talker, little chatterbox in fact, perhaps one of those children that has to be making noises (any noises) incessantly – you know – those that seem afraid that if she's quiet she'll disappear from existence! Ah yes, I can tell, you've had one too . . . At times, you suddenly wonder if you've gone deaf. It's quiet. Too quiet. Where is young Gemini? What is he doing? Probably something that he shouldn't be doing! It's the silence that gives him away when he's likely to be up to mischief; although let's be fair here, sometimes it is also because he has become so absorbed in something of interest that all his excess energy is taken up in his fascinated inquiry. But be advised; whenever it's quiet, check . . . .

You'll often wonder where he gets all his abundant energy from; you will really want to know, wish that he could share some with you, because he can exhaust you! From the day when he learns to become independently mobile, and discovers the joys of activating his mouth, he rarely seems to stop (certainly never long enough to find the 'off button'). That mercurial mind and brain is always ready to absorb, and despite your frantic efforts to keep him entertained, amused and occupied with toys, games, puzzles, books, and bright ideas, he'll soon be standing there demanding 'More' like Oliver Twist, although it's mind food that Gemini is requesting. Part of the difficulty is that he can soon lose interest, tending to sample each toy or book and then wanting something new again in order to revitalize that waning curiosity. Superficiality can be a Gemini trait, where the focus of attention and concentration is fragmented amongst several spheres of interest. He can turn into a jack of all trades and master of none type. Plus, he has the knack of being able to do several things at once, and this can soon use up parental resources even when Gemini is young. With a broad smile and a happy heart, you'll wave him away into his first day at school.

Hopefully there will be an interesting environment for her, with sufficient variety to keep her attention. As she is basically quite adaptable, she should soon settle into school with those varied lessons, friends, games and books. The school regime of keeping her occupied with lessons should help stave off any tendencies to be bored.

Usually, Gemini is a bright, cheerful and alert child, determined to absorb as much of life as she can achieve in the shortest time possible. She manages this by those invisible antennae on either side of her head that are waving in perpetual motion; much like a proverbial alien, the mission of Gemini is to explore, find and learn. It can be satisfying for a parent though to have such a precocious and enthusiastic child, who seems ready and willing to taste the fruits of life.

The depth of the parental relationship with the Gemini child can vary considerably depending upon the type of parent. Each parent will love their children in their own way, but some may be more suitable temperaments for Gemini than others. Obviously the Air and Fire signs will be more naturally in tune with the Gemini energy, than perhaps will be the Earth and Water signs. The child will need and expect a high degree of response to their mental and verbal attempts at expression and communication, because they are so essential and vital to their nature. They'll require answers to all of their questions for instance, simply because they really want to know; and as most beleaguered parents know, you can get annoyed at having to respond to apparently trivial or pointless questions. It isn't always so easy.

Yet what can suit Gemini are those forms of contact that involve a sense of partnership, of mutual story telling or creation, and perhaps quizzes of questions and answers or word games. These can be fun and beneficial to the child, and help to develop the family relationships.

Often, the main sense of rapport with Gemini is that of a mental relationship, with a more intellectual bias as the child grows older. Emotional and physical demonstrations of affection and love are not really his style, and there can often be a lack of immaturity concerning the emotional dimension of life. Rationality can lead to a certain blindness in being aware of the importance of emotions and feelings between people. Some Gemini can be quite insensitive in relations with others. And yet their own moods can be most irregular and variable; consistency is not Gemini's strongest tendency. Changes of mind and vacillating emotions are more common.

In earlier years, young Gemini's physical constitution and robustness may not appear to be very strong. Often his body tends to be slight and rarely overweight because of that speedy, highly charged nervous energy, and in conjunction with the stresses of growing up can lead to ill health. In later childhood, the body should have naturally adjusted itself to that level of energy, and physically the child will be healthier and stronger. As in later years of adult life, there is a link between the Gemini state of body health and his mental well-being. Conditions of psychosomatic illness as a consequence and result of inner states of worry, nerves or depression can develop. Excessive boredom and frustration of purpose can trigger similar mind–body states of 'disease'. Yet if absorbed by a new interest, or when life takes on a new shade of vitalizing colour, such as new lovers, friends or environment, then sudden remarkable recoveries can occur.

Restful sleep is especially essential to Gemini. With such an active mind, a deep relaxation can be vital, both to store memories and information in the mind, and to recover for the new day. Without adequate rest, Gemini is in danger of burning herself up. Exercise, too, is suitable for releasing some of that excess energy – the type that suits Gemini is that of more skilful sports and games, where some degree of thought and ability is required to be successful. Those sports which are dependent on sheer physical prowess are less likely to attract her. Games involving coordination of mind and hand can become favourites, as the opportunity to exploit quick reflexes is present.

The creative spirit of Gemini can be noticed in that tendency to exaggerate, such as embellishing tales with additional detail and colour, plus an inventiveness that whilst often plausible can still fail to fully convince, but given more years of practice is likely to become more persuasive and realistic. Imagination is a Gemini talent, and is an essential part of his own private inner world. There is a taste for the dramatic – especially with himself in the central role – and Gemini can display signs of being unable to always distinguish such private dreams and illusions from reality. It's not that he deliberately lies, but in mixing imagination and exaggeration the truth of a situation can easily be distorted. Often he fails to realize what he is creating and presenting to others. In cases where the Gemini efforts at communication have been regularly blocked by unsympathetic parents or teachers, this internalized world of imaginative illusion can become more prominent, partly as a form of withdrawal from the external rejection and also as a self-defensive psychological mechanism. Such a state should be avoided as it will create additional problems in being able to distinguish between reality and illusion, as well as creating inner splits in the psyche, which already has a tendency to fragment in the multi-faceted Gemini personality.

Gemini can enjoy performing; hidden within is an entertainer and actor, or at least someone willing to attract attention to himself. Gemini can become raconteurs and wits, tellers of tales and jokes, always having something to say, and they often have a talent for mimicry too. How much this side of them will emerge is hard to say, because it also depends on the other aspects of the full natal chart and the affinity level with the Ascendant. Another factor which could affect their confidence is that occasional Gemini speech problem, where the mind is working too fast for the body/mouth to be synchronized in coordination.

Like the free flowing of the element of Air, Gemini has a great need for freedom to explore and discover variety and novelty. It is best to allow Gemini as much freedom as possible, or else this innate tendency will be repressed and blocked. A search for change and new experiences and interests will be a feature of the adult Gemini.

As he begins to enter his teenage years, puberty and adolescence, Gemini is likely to display signs of more moody behaviour, as those disparate personality tendencies begin to rub together with more friction under the stresses of becoming an adult. He'll often find it difficult to make his mind up about 'crucial decisions', changing his thoughts about his choices with frequent regularity. You'll just have to bear with him; putting any pressure on him will rarely produce any satisfactory results. Sometimes his approach will be to ignore problems, pretending that they do not exist, perhaps hoping that they will just disappear. Future planning is not one of Gemini's characteristics, despite that analytical and logical mind; often Gemini develops his own peculiar style of logic, a 'personal logic' that suits only him.

She'll probably have an active teenage life, being quite sociable and popular, having the ability to make superficial friendships with a large variety of people, but the depth of commitment can often be missing. Keep an eye on your telephone bills. Remember, Gemini loves talking and those minutes tick away so easily . . . and if you cannot stop her, then why not attempt to retrieve some of your money by having shares in the telephone company?

Gemini often experiences 'teenage angst'; in an uncertain time of his life, he often has problems in making decisions, which make him even moodier. Teenage relationships are likely to affect his inner state, although he's more liable to have shorter, less emotionally intense relationships, and his problems may centre around that need for variety. He doesn't like to be tied to one person exclusively, and if that situation begins to develop, he will try to withdraw.

There is a nonconformist aspect to Gemini, potentially a rebel against authority and the status quo. As they need to 'feel different' from others, and assert an individual identity, this can create friction with family, school and the larger community. With modern teenagers, such self-assertion and rejection of what they often consider to be a boring lifestyle of parents and family can manifest itself as an adoption of visually fashionable or different styles of appearance. Essentially, they may decide to become part of a 'new tribe' which has its own identifying clothes, attitudes and behaviour patterns which distinguishes it from the rest of society. Parental opposition to this will only serve to strengthen this phase of alienation, forming more permanent splits in the family relationship; let them go their own way, and they'll probably pass through it in time, unless he is mixing with a more physically violent group, in which case directive guidance is more suitable. At some time in their lives, the 'Gemini revolt' against the traditional attitudes and ways of life will occur; perhaps it may be best to allow it to happen during their young adulthood.

THE GEMINI CHILD AND EDUCATION

Gemini is associated with the element of Air, and is ruled by the planet Mercury, which signifies that the most vital level of activity in the Gemini child is that of the mind.

Curiosity is the key to the Gemini personality, and will be a lifelong motivating force for that darting quicksilver mind. Young Gemini are likely to be very alert, bright and inquisitive. Their minds are liable to be full of 'Why?', 'How?' and 'When?', questions tumbling out almost incessantly. They are like a permanent question mark, which periodically lights up with an exclamation mark when they receive a comprehensible answer to a question.

Gemini is quite capable of learning quickly and relatively easily and, because there is a natural eagerness to learn, can be an enthusiastic member in the classroom. For every answer he receives to his questions, he'll think up several more questions that he must have answers to or he'll burst! Gemini can become a question machine; can his parents become answering machines? Probably not. He has a knack of asking that sort of question which parents find difficult to answer, especially when they are busy at home dealing with something that requires concentration. In the midst of having his car engine in pieces, and struggling to unscrew that vital nut, Gemini will arrive and ask the vital important question that has been tormenting him since yesterday: 'Why is the Earth round, Dad?' Or when Mum is up to her elbows trying to coordinate the cooking for that special evening meal for her guests: 'How did I get into your tummy, Mum?'

Gemini can wear down any parent, and you'll be relieved to see her trotting off to school, and take malicious pleasure in imagining her interrogating her teachers in the same way that you've endured. But, look on the bright side, she's helped to keep you sharp and educated, and since you've had to study all those library books to answer her questions, you've rediscovered the joys of learning, and you're even considering taking college courses now! After all, you've got to be able to keep up with her questions . . . .

His mind is like a butterfly, flying from flower to flower, from each interesting topic to another, as quickly as his attention wanes and his interest is attracted to the next morsel of fascinating information. It's all that highly charged nervous energy moving through him, he can't stop at any one place for long; he's too restless to stay still. As you know, he has to be occupied doing something that really interests him, and his attention span can sometime be quite limited. He needs change, variety stimulates and satifies his restless nature; if all else fails and you're stuck with him at home, and he's bored, take him out for a while as a new environment can shake him out of a bored pattern of mind. Otherwise, he will only cause trouble and be mischievous.

Gemini devours reason and facts, and can often tend to become an 'information dilettante', who uses those fragments of interesting facts to appear witty and knowledgeable in company. Yet sometimes this can be quite superficial knowledge, used only for display purposes in an attempt to impress others. Young Gemini can often give the impression that they know and understand more than they actually do, and that they 'promise more than they deliver'. Anyone with an adequate memory can store pieces of information; understanding that information can be more difficult.

He'll want clear reasons and facts in any answers to his questions, and Gemini absorbs learning through that style of presentation. His memory is extremely good at sorting and filing all information, and his innate mental tendency is to analyse, categorize and apply logic and rationality to everything. It is a mind that can be suitable to scientific and intellectually based interests. Underlying this need to acquire information is a desire to grasp an insight into the hidden relationships of all life, to make some kind of connective, cohesive sense out of all those pieces of information.

Gemini should have little touble in learning how to read and communicate fluently; she is verbally very precocious, talking is probably one of her best natural gifts, which she tends to do excessively and with considerable animated vigour. When young, she can be a chatterbox, when older and with added charm, she can have 'the gift of the gab', be persuasive, witty and entertaining. Yet in some cases, due to the speed at which that nervous energy works in her mind, there can be problems such as stuttering or minor speech impediments, as there is a lack of harmony between the mind and the speech faculty. This should adjust itself over time, but medical advice may be required if it becomes a real problem and affects the confidence of the growing child.

As Gemini also rules the hands and arms of the body, young Gemini is likely to have some talent in using his hands. Often a good form of balance can be encouraged in him through doing projects that involve both his mind and hands working in harmony. This tends to ground that sometimes too mercurial mental energy from rushing through him and being dissipated too easily. This can later lead to skills in mechanical abilities, or even interests in mechanical and electronic engineering. Gemini children are often ambidexterous to some degree, so you may need to monitor your child carefully to ensure that there are no problems with early hand skills like writing and handling. It could be that your child uses different hands for different functions, or can use either hand equally well, or even have difficulty in deciding which hand to use and develop.

One of the 'minor talents' of Gemini is the ability to do several different things at once. Watch the developing Gemini child write her homework, listen to music and watch television all at once. Now, many children try to juggle several such attention demands at once, but few of them actually succeed in doing decent homework, move the body in time to the rhythm of the music, comprehend what is happening in the television programme, and sing along with the music! Gemini intends to pack as much as possible into her life, and somehow she is quite capable of doing so.

Remember though, that the image of Gemini is the Twins; there's at least two of them in there, often pulling different directions too. Gemini can be split, fragmented into distinctly different personality types, which can be confusing for others at times. Sometimes a tendency towards moodiness can affect their school work, perhaps especially during the teenage years, although they will always be tempted towards distraction at school. Concentration and prolonged persistent effort are not often strong Gemini qualities, and the lure of something new or diverting tends to be a temptation that is hard to resist. Whilst the ability to be academically successful is likely to be present, it is probable that young Gemini could always 'do better' if they really applied themselves.

Much will depend upon the teacher's ability to attract the inquisitive nature of the Gemini child; if Gemini turns into a class clown or mischief maker, then you will know that the presentation of the teaching is not suitable for him and, because he is bored, he decides to disrupt the class. Conversely, when he is interested, his attention is extremely concentrated, absorbing every piece of information, and of course, he's likely to be asking more questions!

There is likely to be an attraction towards intellectualized thinking, especially as Gemini grows older. Even at an earlier age, there is a natural grasp of symbolic systems such as numbers and the alphabet, which are the foundation and building blocks for language and our way of thinking. The key phrase for Gemini is 'I think', and in later life this can turn into an ability to be an effective manipulator of words and intellectually based careers. An inventive imagination can also be used to considerable advantage in adult life. However, you will have to be alert to the younger Gemini's clever way with words and excuses; she'll use you to practise upon, in training for the future! And she can be very persuasive and plausible for her age; you say that you haven't noticed? That shows how effective she can be – she also has some skill at being an actor.

There are several points that may help Gemini learn more effectively and easily, which can be applied by parent or teacher. The transmission and dissemination of information and facts is essential to the Gemini mind. A form of presentation that involves Gemini could work well, such as asking him 'Why . . . ?' 'How . . . ?' and 'What if . . . ?'; something that uses a fact to pose a question back at the child, so that he has to think and work out his own answer, and which parallels his own inquisitive thinking process, and enables him to perceive the use and relationship of facts to learning. This encourages him to organize fragments of facts into a practical context, where knowledge and information is applied in daily life. Sometimes Gemini can accumulate fascinating facts like a magpie, but never know what they can be used for; if the child is taught to make use of his knowledge then this will help to balance his nature more.

It should also be recognized that even though Gemini is perpetually curious, that inquisitiveness does not necessarily imply understanding or an ability to do things. Their mental grasp can sometimes be a mimicking of information that they have memorized. The level of the child's actual ability can be lower than it may appear, and he can become frustrated when he realizes that something is beyond his present capacity to achieve. This can display itself at times through that common Gemini tendency to leave things unfinished, apparently as a result of the waning of their interest. Some of these instances can occur purely as a consequence of their inability to finish a project, perhaps as evidence of their lack of understanding. In each case, you may need to establish what the real cause is; a lack of interest, or a lack of understanding. If they haven't grasped the subject properly, then they can be given additional teaching until they do; otherwise, encouraging them to slow down more and to apply self-discipline to complete the task may help them learn to finish 'unfinished business'. This would be a vital lesson for the child, perhaps also preventing such a tendency being carried over into adult life, with potentially negative results.

Gemini is often attracted towards adult company, because listening to and talking with them offers the potential to absorb realms of new knowledge, and possibly new skills too. As a child, Gemini can benefit from intellectual adults, and would be naturally suited to grow up in such a household. Certainly, providing him with books will be a service to him, or ensuring that he sees television programmes related to the subjects he enjoys. These can range from science shows to music and art. He can develop a wide range of interests and talents, and may need some careful guidance in learning how to make the most of them, or how to focus more intensely upon those which could open out into future adult careers.

She may often show signs of being unsure of her choices; she isn't one of the more decisive zodiac signs and, as mentioned before, there are several distinct hidden personality types in the Gemini child, sometimes pulling in different directions. The variations on the 'choices techniques' of Aries and Taurus are not really apt for Gemini; you could be there all morning sometimes waiting for the final decision. If conflicts occur over choices, then apart from telling the child what to do, using reason to explain why she should do something can be effective with her. Communication is a key to young Gemini; it could point the way to adult careers. The ability to think, analyse and reason, and to express this clearly (verbally or in writing) is a most useful talent. The Gemini enjoyment of words can also appear in an interest and ability in foreign languages.

GEMINI CAREERS

Variety is essential to the Gemini temperament. Being desk bound in a repetitive job is not really suitable for them. Employment that offers some scope for variety, freedom and intellectual activity is likely to be preferred. Work with words, communication or numbers in analytical studies could be enjoyed.

Some Gemini want creative types of employment, such as writing books, being critics or television reporters, journalism, printing, publishing, graphic art and design, music and record production. Others are biased to the more scientific side of research and experimentation, academia and laboratory bound. Some prefer to focus more on the verbal communicative skills, like being a salesman or one of those paid persuaders for business/minority interests. Teaching and translating can appeal, and the legal professions of interpreting law, jurisprudence and making court appearances for clients can suitably match intellect and verbal skills. Some Gemini turn into wanderers and travellers, satisfying their needs for variety by roving the world, and then turning their experiences and adventures into films or books. Photography can attract too in this context, merging a technical ability with variety and artistic expression.

Factory and repetitive work is not for Gemini; it would only inhibit their potential, as it does to virtually everyone else.

CANCER
(JUNE 22 to JULY 22)

Planetary Ruler: Moon

Element type	Water
Type	Negative/Feminine
Triplicity	Cardinal
Symbol	♋
Image	The Crab
Part of Body	Breasts, stomach
Theme of Self	I Feel
Key Qualities	Sensitivity, domesticity
House Affinity	4th House

Famous Cancer Personalities: Princess Diana, Rembrandt, Marcel Proust, Ernest Hemingway, Ingmar Bergman, Ringo Starr, Carl Lewis, Barbara Cartland, Glenys Kinnock, Kenneth Clark MP, Edward Heath.

THE PRE-SCHOOL CANCER CHILD

If you are expecting a child due to be born under the Cancer phase of the yearly cycle, then it is unlikely that the baby will be born prematurely, unless there is medical interference. Cancer will not be in a hurry to be born, much preferring to remain as long as possible within the familiar protective and comfortable security of the womb. The inevitable movement towards an unknown world will not be cooperated with, until the point where resistance is undermined by the natural process of childbirth, and the young Cancer emerges crying.

The Cancer baby tends to have a noticeably changeable temperament, where often despite parental efforts, moods come and go; she can be a baby who cries a lot, even though it may not be obvious what is causing discomfort. Then just as suddenly as the crying started, all is smiles again, and the world is a comforting place to be in. Cancer can be encouraged to come out of a crying mood by plenty of physical love, cuddles and affection, or even by protectively wrapping them up to simulate that old favourite sensation of the womb. Feeling secure is essential for her, and probably these unpredictable moods are triggered by deep feelings of insecurity in some way. Cancer can just lie there for long periods of time, nicely wrapped up, passively absorbing all impressions of her immediate environment, eyes wide open, almost in a semi-trance state.

Because of this innate uneasiness with the unknown, and preference to remain in familiar circumstances, Cancer is not usually an early developer in crawling, walking, talking or starting to show signs of independence. He would rather be looked after by a loving parent. There is a fear of new experiences and people, and those progressions in childhood development will only come once he has 'tested the water' and feels reasonably secure in the new explorative step. Water will be a favourite element for Cancer, and bathtime will be greatly enjoyed. An attraction and fascination with water is likely to be a personality trait with Cancer, as it also reflects his turbulent and contrasting inner emotional states; yet it can also serve as a still placid pool which offers a healing quality to him when in need. Cancer children are drawn to pools and water, so great care and attention should be paid to the younger child when they are in such an environment.

By the age of one to two, you'll notice that the sensation of eating becomes a pleasurable occupation for her, playing with food and enjoying the tactile impressions of the food and drink. The sensual aspects of life are stimulatory, as she will respond to bright colours and pictures which attract a developing imaginative quality. Greater independent mobility and the ability to begin exploring her immediate environment take on personal importance and meaning, as she slowly gains a stronger sense of a separate identity. Like the Crab, she'll begin to find suitable hiding places in the home; corners or under tables can be popular, or perhaps behind the curtains, where she can go and be lost in a private little world, along with several favourite toys and dolls. She isn't really the performer-type of child who takes centre stage to entertain the adults. With most adults, she'll tend to be shy and reserved, often clinging tightly to Mother's skirts, peeking out from around her legs, or running away to hide in her special place, cautiously paying attention to the visitor from a safe distance. When she's ready, and feels secure enough, she'll come out of her shell; forcing her to be untrue to her natural instincts will create resentment and a denial of her actual feelings. Acknowledge her overly sensitive spirit, and treat her with gentle consideration, helping her to slowly overcome her fears and inhibitions.

Cancer will be a loving and affectionate child, and you'll probably notice this in the way he handles his favourite toys and cuddly soft animals; he will look after them well, acting like a considerate mother to them. Like their own need for reassurance and security, Cancer children can display a tendency to cosset their toys, often hiding them away in safe containers or secret undisturbed places, out of harm's way.

Between two and three, Cancer can be prone to extreme moodiness; the 'terrible twos' can be emphasized by the fluctuations of the Cancer emotional temperament. Parental resistance to his will and demands can see him rushing off crying in a tantrum behind the chair or curtains, where he'll remain, resisting all encouragement to come out until he is ready, and the mood has passed. He can be touchy and grumpy. In particular, he'll hate changes around him. Security lies in everything remaining the same, repetitive routines offer him protection and familiarity and benefit the Cancerian personality, and he'll become reliant upon the unchanging status quo of his previous experience. Domestic changes will unsettle him, perhaps a new baby in the home will disrupt and upset young Cancer, or a change of house can be seen as traumatic. For Cancer, changes equal the unknown and fear. Even rearranging the furniture and so affecting his special place is disturbing to him. Family and home environment is all that he really knows, and to face the fact that life is not static is a transformative realization for Cancer. Any marital breakdowns at this time (or really any time) with their resulting discordancy and changes in the domestic life will have a profound effect on the unfolding child personality.

Through the ages of three to five, Cancer begins to display a greater sense of individuality, although that sense of insecurity still remains, greater experience of life is forming a stronger foundation for exploration and self-assertion. She is unlikely to be very extroverted, and if anything, seems more clearly introverted now, often preferring to play on her own, imagining her own world and possibly creating those types of invisible play-mates that have their own sort of reality to a child. If she has no real pets of her own, she is likely to create an invisible animal friend to confide in and to share playtime with. Her imagination can be quite active and developed for her age, and she appears to be very comfortable with this type of play. Providing that she does not withdraw totally from socializing and playing with other children, try not to interfere with this personal expression of the young Cancerian; usually it does no harm, and is important for her well-being at a certain stage, and will naturally fade away as other interests take its place.

As always with Cancer, environment is of a prime importance; home and roots are emphasized, and become a psychological support too. There are very ancient links with old tribal associations hidden within Cancer, plus those sometimes irrational fears of the unknown lands around. It is a territorial attitude, fiercely protective of the tribal lands and traditional customs. Tear a Cancer away from his or her roots, and the personality foundations can begin to break apart.

Noise and frenzied activity does not often suit Cancer, and so that form of wild childhood play is not always entered into willingly. Cancer will prefer quieter, sedate types of play, perhaps with a couple of safe, closer playmates. She is likely to make friends with other children who are withdrawn from the main children's group, in the sense that a mutual affinity of isolation and loneliness is present. She will make a firm and reliable friend, although those tidal emotions can make her a little too moody and changeable for some.

By the time he reaches the age of full-time school education, his more withdrawn phase will be over. He'll still be quiet and introverted, but should be able to cope with the varied demands of school life. Cancer is not often a 'modern child', but has a temperament more suited to traditional and conservative attitudes. Basically, he is 'backward looking', a reactionary against the perceived threat of the new, and so absorbs new ideas relatively slowly. He is very receptive though, and both parents and teachers have a great responsibility at this age, because whatever he absorbs he is likely to retain, and in the case of adult attitudes and personal life philosophies that are expressed by people around him will probably reflect them in his later life. In a quiet and unrecognized way, young Cancer is like a 'sponge', soaking up those powerful impressions from parents and teachers, repeating them in later life and believing them to be his own personal attitudes.

THE CANCER CHILD PERSONALITY

As the ruler of Cancer is the Moon, and Cancer is the first Water element sign, your child is a true MoonChild, essentially an emotional being, firmly tied to the home, family and traditional roots. Their life will be inwardly directed and motivated by their needs, insecurities and emotional responses, and unless you are an especially sympathetic and understanding parent, it is unlikely that you will be able to fully fathom that paradoxical and complex personality.

Like the Crab, Cancer can have a misleading outer persona, especially as he grows older and becomes more adapted to the world. That hard protective shell hides the soft vulnerable body inside, and Cancer will always remain vulnerable to

72

being hurt. 'I feel' sums up the Cancer reaction to life; all personal experience is perceived through emotional and feeling responses, evaluated as to sensations of being pleasant or unpleasant, and then these inner tidal waves eventually create overshadowing moods or states of broodiness.

Cancer is a mother's child. She'll be still clinging tightly to you a long time after most children are exploring their independence. In some ways this can be satisfying for mothers, but it also displays the dependency of Cancer. The most powerful influence on her development will be Mother and home, and this is the centre of her world, her retreat and sanctuary from reality. As her psychological well-being is so tightly bound with her home environment, it is essential to have a good relationship with her parents, who provide the only real sense of continuing security and stability in her life.

Cancer is a child that loves to hide. If not close to her mother's skirts, she's squeezed up tight on the chair, or peeking from behind the curtains or from under the table, especially when strangers are there. She needs to be encouraged to come out of that shell and to participate in the adventures of the world. It isn't that she lacks curiosity, but that her deep need for security is always dominant. There is a natural tendency for evasion, a retreat into those private dream worlds rich with imagination where she feels safe and in control. If the child is not drawn out of her private worlds enough, then this ongoing imaginative daydreaming can begin to replace her everyday reality, and this should not be encouraged. When signs of overexaggeration occur and reality and dreams become noticeably intertwined, then you should help her to participate in more peer-age activities with other children, so that the pattern of psychological withdrawal is broken.

It can be a delicate balance that needs to be made. Cancer will love those types of romantic stories of princesses or heroes exploring fantasy lands and having adventures. Imagination and emotion are both engaged, and often (especially if they are feeling lonely) they will create an imaginary friend to talk and play with; this is often common behaviour for children, who tend to inhabit fantasy worlds to some degree, but you must ensure that this does not replace real human playmates.

Most of Cancer's behaviour is derived from those deep needs and feelings of belonging and being safe, protected from that knowledge of vulnerability. Personal insecurity will lead him to look for love and affection from others, making him reliant on them for security. He has a basically gentle and placid temperament, although the tranquil aspect can sometimes be only skin deep as wild raging emotions batter him inside. Usually as a child he'll be reserved and timid, probably finding it hard to make friends, although he will love to play with others, and at times you'll be amazed at how he can suddenly change if he is in an outgoing mood and has compatible playmates around. Then you will see a face of the Cancer child that only emerges irregularly. Possessiveness is another aspect of this dependency. Whether it is the mother, favourite cuddly toys or special friends, Cancer will invest most of his emotions into monopolizing the object of his love.

Rejection is extremely traumatic, often throwing him into introversion, emotional brooding, moods, passive lethargy and disinterest in everything. All forms of personal rebuff or criticism are taken to heart, and are extremely painful, shaking that fragile personality, even when the child has become an adult.

Like the other Water signs Scorpio and Pisces, Cancer is highly sensitive to impressions and atmospheres, both of people and places. As a child, she will not be able to explain or express her feelings very well, she has an ability akin to a psychic intuition, a sense of knowing without a rational explanation. She 'just knows'. If Cancer learns to trust that intuition, then she should be able to discern the real feelings and intention behind people's words, and so should not be deceived. If there are arguments at home, or something is not quite right in the family, then she will unconsciously absorb the energy and tension in the air, which will have a corresponding impact on her own behaviour. Even though she may seem to be a quiet, self-contained child, don't assume that because she isn't saying much that she isn't experiencing deep confusing feelings. Wrapped tightly in her inner cocoon, she finds peace and strength in solitude.

Emotions and fears can have a direct influence upon their health. Those shifting sands of their emotions, and that tendency towards developing obsessive fears all conspire to erode their physical well-being. They can easily become a nervous worrier, repetitively churning around the dominant fears of the moment, which inevitably reflect those fears of personal insecurity and problems with confronting and coping with the new and unknown. Entering new stages in life can trigger such fears. The physical area of the body that is often most affected is the stomach. Nervous reactions, excessive 'digestion' of powerful emotions, can create stomach disorders, digestive and gastric problems. This is also associated with food intake, where there can be ambivalent or extreme reactions to eating. Food can be seen as a form of life security, essential for health and well-being, and some Cancerians can take this to an extreme, using food as a substitute for emotional consolation, leading to weight problems. Alternatively, and this can occur especially during adolescence, the young Cancer girl could become obsessive about her appearance, imagining herself to be ugly because of overweight. As Cancer has a developed sense of personal vanity, and being neat, tidy and attractive is an essential part of feeling personally secure, this can develop into the psychological obsessions of illnesses such as anorexia nervosa, the 'slimmers' disease'. Being aware of your teenage daughter's eating habits is advisable, especially if she is a Cancer type. Generally, the child's health will be mixed; much will depend on the child's ability to process emtional energies through their system, although there can be a tendency to suffer from colds, fevers and chills.

For the supportive, caring and understanding parent, helping your child to grow out of certain unnecessary fears is important. Building up that personal confidence and self-assertion can be the key to strengthening the Cancer temperament to deal with this world. Teasing or ridiculing the child's fear is not the right way by parent or teacher, and this can damage young Cancer, who tends to withdraw under that sort of response and pressure. A patient and supportive guiding hand of encouragement will help young Cancer warily step towards new experiences and challenges. With that natural tendency to retreat into the familiar, most forms of growth and new discovery can feel painful to Cancer, although once she feels certain that there is no hidden threat, she will soon embrace that new facet of the world to which she has now opened herself.

His general behaviour will usually be good, and he will respond well to parental or school discipline; this is partly due to a non-confrontational character, and because he wants the constant approval of his parents, and doesn't want to give any reason for their love and affection to be withheld. Cancer can be very considerate, thoughtful, loving and conscientious, and will rarely deliberately intend anyone else to suffer emotional pain caused by his actions. The only times when his temperament is disturbed is through those deeply unsettling mood changes, which can suddenly descend upon him. It is possible that these could be associated with synchronicity to the Moon's activity, both with its influence on the tidal flows and in its waxing and waning pattern, or as the transiting movement of the Moon (orbit of the satellite Moon around Earth) activates by aspect the planetary positions in the full natal chart. It may be useful for an adult Cancerian to take account of such possible influences if they are especially prone to sudden uncontrollable mood changes; astrologically such patterns, and time dating of Moon activity can be useful as a reference to observe if the moods follow a recognizable pattern.

Cancer may need to find a key to this inner emotional tendency. Bad tempers and irritability can flare up, or the young may resort to periods of grumpy silence, brooding heavily. By the mid-teenage years, Cancer will see the need for a greater degree of self-knowledge and a grasp of the nature of these fluctuating emotional waves, or else he may be a passive victim of them all his life. He will require a more realistic degree of personal perspective, so the tendency to create obsessive patterns of behaviour does not dominate.

The absorbent quality of the Cancer emotions is likewise a feature of her mind, which is also very receptive and retentive, although what tends to be more effectively retained are experiences and teachings which have connections with vibrant feelings and motions. Her mind is attentive and observant in nature, tending to have a recording quality which processes whatever has been seen, heard, and experienced in a relatively undiscerning manner. The problem can lie in making any use of this 'raw data', and Cancer lacks the ability or interest to draw these fragments together in an attempt to derive knowledge, unless the impetus to do so is arising from an emotional need. Certainly just giving a word description and explanation to Cancer is often not sufficient, and she will fail to grasp the information or message being presented by parent or teacher. Her ability to intellectually understand is dependent upon an emotional affinity with the subject.

Cancer often tends to surround himself with interests, collections, personal treasures and meaningful memories of the past. There can be a hoarding of possessions, because such activity is felt to offer security to him. A private room is very important to Cancer, and parents should ensure that it becomes his own domain, making him responsible for its tidiness and cleanliness, and certainly not throwing away any old toys or clothes that you may decide he has outgrown. They may be treasured possessions, full of important personal memories for him. Let him decide when to release old possessions; or discuss the need for a springclean with him first. Cancer can have faddish interests and preoccupations as he grows older, although these often have a quality of over-enthusiasm about them, and can suddenly stop almost as quickly as they started.

Nature can attract Cancer, and water is a favourite aspect, with ponds, pools, lakes, rivers and seas being especially fascinating. Encouraging the child to take an interest in gardening can be useful, and giving her a small area of ground to be responsible for can be very beneficial, so that she can care for the plants and flowers that she can grow and nurture.

Adolescence can be a difficult phase, with their emotional lives even more shaken by the hormonal and puberty changes occurring. Cancer may often seem quite irrational and sullen in a moody sense, and friction with parents is to be expected. Emotional outbursts are common, and they are likely to withdraw into their rooms for hours at a time, rejecting personal contact and preferring to remain on their own, perhaps listening to music or reading. Music is important to them at this time, and they will be very receptive to its influence and lyrics.

Their imagination will be very active, and that fantasy life will be quite potent. Teenage crushes and relationships can be emotionally fraught, and often perceived with little sense of proportion, and personal appearances and clothes will begin to take a high priority. Cancer can become a rebel without a cause, anti-everybody and everything, thrashing around emotionally, a pawn of inner conflict and confusion. Beliefs tend not to be rational or logical, but are extensions of powerful emotions; it is futile to disagree intellectually with Cancerian beliefs, because you are trying to relate across two different levels of communication. Try not to directly contradict and clash with them, but allow them time and space to evolve through this phase of life, and to develop their own attitudes and ways of thinking. Over time, Cancer can develop as an individual and independent thinker, and not just reflect the mass mind. Whilst it might be a surprise to you, your Cancer child may develop into a talented creative artist of some kind, and may also display a flair for business and financial speculation in later years, as those needs for security and stability become translated into ambitions to gain a social or business position of authority and prosperity.

Hopefully, that shy Cancer can have an early upbringing that gives him confidence to become more assertive and to display those talents that are hidden under that reclusive shell.

THE CANCER CHILD AND EDUCATION

Those early days at school can be traumatic for some Cancer children, especially those that haven't had the experience of being separated from their mother for a few hours. The typical Cancer child might be like a shrinking violet in the classroom. The one that sits there in the corner, quiet as a mouse, trying to be invisible is probably a Cancer. He'll acknowledge his name at roll call almost reluctantly, in a soft, timid voice, hoping that the class attention will fail to be directed at him. Sitting in an unknown school environment, probably with a group of children that young Cancer does not know and away from the protective embrace and presence of Mother, leaves Cancer with only one realistic option – to retreat into his shell.

Through most of her life, this tendency will be a natural reaction to times of stress and tension, a response to unpleasant experiences. As a parent, you've probably observed this many times before, as well as knowing her need for close physical contact with you, and that personal dependency for protection. The main task for a parent with a Cancer child is to draw her out from hiding in her shell, to help her to become more independent and self-assured, and this is what any teacher will have to achieve too, if the child is to have a successful education.

That early experience of school life can be very formative in the later development of the Cancer personality. If all goes well, and he is with a supportive teacher with whom he can feel reasonably safe, and can make a few close friends amongst the children (perhaps those whom he may know from a previous playschool group), then he should begin to relax quickly into his new daily school experience, and feel more strengthened in his ability to survive and cope with independence and new environments. This can build a foundation within him that enables him to explore new situations with sufficient personal confidence. If, however, he is basically ignored or treated with a lack of sensitivity in those early days, either by the teacher or by more assertive and physically boisterous classmates, then the natural pattern of responding with withdrawal into a private shell will be reinforced. It may be essential for a parent to check with the child how he is finding school life, particularly at that early stage, although periodic checking is also valuable to ensure that the child is still participating correctly. If the child is not especially forthcoming about his experiences and feelings, then it may be wise to ask his teacher about how he is responding, before any possibly more negative patterns of withdrawal become too dominant. Many children are effectively 'written off' by educationalists even by the age of six, as being unsuitable for that style of state teaching.

The withdrawn type of Cancer child could fall into this category. It isn't because they are unintelligent, although, to be honest, traditionally they are not necessarily the academically brightest children around, but that their natural talents and personality needs to be greatly encouraged to emerge. Often, in state schools, teachers rarely have the time to devote to individual children when there are so many others in the classroom. With standard techniques of education, some children fall by the wayside, because the particular approach does not 'speak ' to them in a way that they absorb learning.

A more suitable approach for a Cancer child is to recognize that she'll learn through having her feelings activated and stimulated; if her feelings are not engaged in a subject, then a lack of interest will be displayed, and the child will fail to grasp and retain the content of the teaching. In becoming a 'failure', that tenuous sense of individual ability and personality stability becomes more weakened. Ideas and concepts which are presented to her in more abstract or intellectual terms tends to confuse rather than illuminate. Cancer has a natural affinity with the more intuitive, sensitive and artistic dimensions of life, and it is that part of her that needs to respond to any teaching if it is to become effective. Whilst Cancer is not usually one of those physically aggressive and boisterous children, she will respond to teaching in terms of physical sensations, where the five senses are engaged and the teaching becomes more real.

For Cancer, sensations evoke corresponding feelings, and it is that process that awakens their interest; for instance, history lessons. These can be presented in a bookish or abstract way, lacking any real identification by the children with the subject. Yet if it is done by helping the child to contact something that is still present and associated with that particular time, such as old clothes, coins, houses, paintings, armour, machinery, etc. then it is more likely that children like the imaginative Cancerians will respond positively. Similarly biology or science lessons could be presented with an emphasis on physical objects and applicability. Becoming personally involved with the teaching in some way is the approach to grasp the Cancerian attention; pure mental curiosity and questioning is not the natural style of the dreamy Cancer child. Yet if a subject gains their attention, then their imaginative faculties begin working and weaving brightly coloured webs around it. This 'embroidery' can be incorrect and exaggerated, yet a wise teacher should gently correct the child whilst ensuring that the inner process is protected and the interest maintained. It can be the seed for future adult creativity, and Cancer tends to carefully 'store' such interests, expressing them wholeheartedly for long periods in later life.

Usually Cancer is too absorbed in her own little private world to be overly studious as a child although, once entering the adult world, may seem to wake up, and begin to apply herself diligently in study and further education. Cancer can be the proverbial 'late developer' in several respects, as the temperament is not to rush into new situations until they have been carefully evaluated. The only exceptions to this lie in those occasions when her imaginative emotions have been so

81

stirred by something that she has to move rapidly in that direction, and then she will move extremely quickly to achieve and experience her aims.

Learning is a deeply personal matter for Cancer; as are the relationships that develop with those who are attempting to share and teach knowledge to the young child. The development of a Cancer child is often very dependent on the quality and sensitivity of those who are in close contact with the child, and who have a formative influence upon him. This need for personal dependency is a Cancerian theme, and he will respond well to any adult who clearly displays a confidence in his abilities and attempts at self-expression. Personal affections can develop with a teacher who takes time to ensure that he is integrated into the class group, and guides him into more socializing activities with the other children, like games and class projects.

Cancer will always respond to encouragement and support, praise and confidence will lighten her temperament and build a sense of personal ability and self-worth. As the Cancer child needs approval, she is rarely a class troublemaker, and usually tries to do everything to the best of her ability, as she soon discovers that this is an effective way to gain the 'love' and commendation of others whose approval she is seeking. Entrusting her with responsible tasks can work well, both in her discharge of responsibilities and in that positive boost to her self-esteem. Supporting her in learning to become more independent and capable is of great value; but allowing excessive dependency is an action that does Cancer no favours. A gradual weaning away is essential.

Cancerian children need valuing and reinforcing, so that sturdy personalities can eventually emerge into the light of day. It isn't that Cancer is 'weak', but that the sensitivity and often psychic-like intuitiveness of the child can be damaged by the sometimes harsh reality of this world. Cancer has a temperament that is like a 'bridge between the inner and outer universe', and which prefers the sanctity of the personal, imaginative and dream world of beauty and harmony. Like the Moon's effects on tidal flow, Cancer's emotions ebb and flow directing attention inwardly or outwardly, and defensive inner walls are established against the emotional tides. From young Cancer could develop a future artist, musician, or writer, if the early life has been carefully guided. In today's world, imagination is a valued quality to possess and, along with a talent for artistic creativity and craftsmanship, is part of the intrinsic talents that Cancer can express.

CANCER CAREERS

The ideal type of Cancerian career is to find employment where those qualities of emotional sensitivity can be useful. These include the 'helping professions', where compassion can be constructively expressed in supporting and healing people with problems. Health care, like nursing, is one example, charity organizations is another, or social aid to help disadvantaged minority groups. The main point to be noted here is that if Cancer decides to enter such an occupation, then they do need to be reasonably emotionally balanced themselves, and to be aware of how their emotional empathy with others is affecting their own state of well-being. Being involved with nature or the sea is likely to be attractive, such as garden centres, landscape gardening, nature conservation, ecology, shipping, fishing, marine science or research. Also of interest are careers associated with roots, foundations and homes, such as estate agents, hoteliers, publicans, interior designers, architects, or those involved with restoration of old houses, furniture, etc. Work with history, research, the fascination with the past traditions can appeal. Photography and records of personal moments of significant memories is a Cancerian interest. Music or artistic/craftsmanship can express that inner sensitivity, or business where innate financial shrewdness and caution are valued, such as stock market speculation (in its more defensive portfolio aspect!).

LEO
(JULY 23 to AUGUST 22)

Planetary Ruler: Sun

Element type	Fire
Type	Positive/Masculine
Triplicity	Fixed
Symbol	♌
Image	The Lion
Part of Body	Heart
Theme of Self	I Will
Key Qualities	Vitality, power, authority
House Affinity	5th House

Famous Leo Personalities: Napoleon Bonaparte, Benito Mussolini, Fidel Castro, Princess Margaret, Carl Gustav Jung, George Bernard Shaw, Percy Bysshe Shelley, Alfred Hitchcock, Cecil B. de Mille, Queen Mother, Dustin Hoffman, Robert De Niro, Kate Bush, Mick Jagger.

THE PRE-SCHOOL LEO CHILD

Leo likes to make an impressive, dramatic entrance onto the stage of life, so a child born during that phase of the astrological year may emerge with an aura of drama surrounding them. It may be a sudden birth, catching people unprepared, or in attempting to reach the maternity hospital the baby decides to emerge whilst the car is waiting at the traffic lights! In some cases, medical difficulties can be the source of drama. Such an entrance is not inevitable of course, and many Leo children are born safely at hospital, but being prepared for that Leo tendency could be useful.

The Leo baby tends to become the 'star of the show', demanding the maximum amount of parental attention. Before his birth, you probably had a free and quieter life, able to do whatever you chose (assuming that there were no other children); now that Leo's here, that time becomes just a memory. Like a magnet, he'll attract all of your attention, filling your mind with thoughts of him, organising your whole life around baby Leo's needs and demands. He has taken control of your life . . . and he loves it! He is generous though; from time to time he may fall asleep, and so his demands for attention lessen, but you'll still have to do all the work that revolves around the baby's needs, like preparing food, washing clothes and sorting out the nappies. And then, just when you've sorted everything out, and decided to have a quiet few minutes with a cup of coffee, and perhaps read a few pages of the novel you started several weeks ago, he'll wake up with a loud cry, demanding your wholehearted attention, because his nappy is wet . . . .

Even at an early age Leo wants company, and seems to flourish on the adoring gazes of parents and grandparents, smiling contentedly at the collection of faces above her. She needs appreciation almost as much as she needs food to grow and develop; that more subtle transfer of energy is absorbed by her sunny disposition, and she'll seem to glow at times, radiating out benevolence. She's very lovable, although sometimes you may secretly wonder if that is just a ruse to receive attention and get her own way, especially when she tries to command through loud and violent screaming during those times when your response to her needs is not quick enough. Certainly the mother sees that little dictator in the crib! She prefers regular fixed rhythms of feeding, sleeping, bathing, and should soon adjust to the imposition of them; they offer a sense of support and a pattern which aids the adaptation to life for the young baby.

By the ages of one to two, you'll know that you've got a little performer on your hands; once he's more mobile and independent, he'll try to be the family entertainer, lapping up the applause and laughter at his antics. Watch him practise his bows! A few signs of his individual will developing are his tendency to have an energetic tantrum when his will is thwarted by a resistant parent, and in a growing reluctance to go to sleep so easily. Part of this is a reaction against losing company, and feeling isolated and alone, which he doesn't like at all. If you place him down alone in his bedroom, then expect cries, yells and calls for Mummy. When you arrive, he'll smile at you quite engagingly, and you may feel tempted to lie down with him until he goes to sleep. This would work, but may also establish a pattern of sleeping behaviour which requires you to be there every night with him until he falls asleep. It's your choice! Resisting his cries may be hard to stand initially, but in the long term may be more beneficial to both you and him, as he'll learn to be alone.

Leo likes food and sensuality of its taste and texture. You'll notice this as they prefer to eat with their fingers, messily spreading it around. They are not the most delicate or fastidious of children, but they certainly enjoy themselves.

By the age of two to three, she's still liable to throw those dramatic temper tantrum performances; as she thrives on applause and attention, why not try just ignoring such actions until she runs out of steam. After several performance failures, she may begin to sense that it is pointless to act in that way, because she still doesn't succeed in getting her own way; but it often takes many children a long time to learn that lesson, and many adults still haven't!

What about toilet training? A major step in childhood development, and one that Leo can usually take quite easily, assuming that the start of the training is not attempted too early. As Leo likes regularity and fixed patterns, careful timing can be established; the main point to encourage them to learn is obviously to appreciate every performance, so that they receive approval and pleasure at their success. Applause is the lifeblood of a Leo, and they'll soon get their act together.

The issue of choice and free will begins to emerge, with the young Leo trying to assert his will against yours by the age of three. Whilst some direct clashes are inevitable, as the daily running of a home means that most children have to do whatever the parent is doing, like going shopping, it may be better to ensure that he is given a free choice in unimportant situations, such as clothes to wear, a choice of cereals to have for breakfast, etc. This helps him to evolve his own decision-making faculty, and to feel that he has some power and choice in his own life, and begins to modify his dependence upon his parents.

Playtime can be highly energetic and noisy with Leo, who seems intent on making everyone aware of his nearby presence. He rarely plays quietly; even if he is on his own, he's making a variety of noises as part of his game. He much prefers to be with other children though, playing those aggressive, physically adventurous games. He seems to shrink when he's alone, needing the spark of company to vitalize him into action. Pets and nature can start to attract his attention now, and a personal pet would become a close companion to him, and one which he would love deeply. Resistance to his will can draw from him that look of imperious royalty – 'How dare she say no to me?' – and he may stand there attempting to summon up all his physical power and will, trying to decide whether to challenge or not. He's not a coward, but just being aware of the size difference may tip the decision.

Between the ages of four and five, she becomes a more dominating and confident Leo, full of her own self-importance. After a little wobble in her level of confidence between three and four, she feels ready now to dominate the world. This personal confidence is often exaggerated, but she believes it, and she attempts to exercise her regal power over her playmates, often with success as she becomes the leader of the pack. Yet she still needs adult approval and attention, and can be irritating as she tends to interrupt and perform in an attempt to gain adult attention. She may need to be taught social manners, so that she realizes that there are more suitable times to receive the attention that she desires.

He tends to be aware of himself growing up, and takes great pride in his unfolding physical prowess and abilities. He has considerable physical vitality, and an overflowing of this without conscious control can lead him into problems caused by over-energetic behaviour, perhaps being too rough with other children, or too noisy, acting like a whirlwind passing through the house. Cheekiness and obstinacy are likely too, as he flaunts what he believes to be his supreme power; he can have an exaggerated sense of himself. Underlying these tendencies is a more simple soul who just wants to be loved, and one of the best ways to get better behaviour from him is to encourage him to please you, and not to behave badly because that upsets and disappoints you.

Before she ventures out into the big wide world of primary school, it would help her to feel more secure if you began to involve her more in the running of the home. She will probably respond to taking responsibility for some small simple chores, perhaps based on her own room, like tidying her toys away, or taking some role in looking after the family pet. As she is soon to be more on her own, making her aware that she is a part of the family helps her to feel more rooted and important. By five, she's ready for school. It's a new stage to perform upon.

THE LEO CHILD PERSONALITY

Standing in the spotlight of centre stage, the perfomer takes a deep bow, acknowledging the rapturous applause of the cheering audience. He basks in the warm feeling of being appreciated and enjoyed; his talent has been recognized. The applause goes on and on. The audience will not let him leave the stage. He waves and smiles regally at his adoring fans. This is what his life is about. Recognition, fame, applause and appreciation. He has found the Leo's heaven.

This key unlocks that secret hidden door to the Leo character. Well, perhaps it isn't so secret after all; once you've seen your child as an entertainer and performer, noticed his glowing inner bliss in such a role, then you'll know what private dreams he has of himself. Think of images associated with kings and queens, television and film stars, famous rock musicians, authors, politicians, and you'll get a sense of what will secretly appeal to young Leo. He might never achieve such status, he might never admit it, but there's a deep underlying, motivating drive in Leo to reach 'the top', for people to know of his success, and to admire and respect him accordingly.

When you see him amongst his young friends, issuing orders, directing the games, you'll observe the born commander and leader at work. He's very serious too about this role. If his playmates reject him and his attempts to dominate, he's liable to slink away like a defeated lion, choosing to sulk out of sight from the others. He isn't satisfied in being just one of the crowd, he has to be the centre attraction, the one who draws the crowd to him, the one with the best ideas for hours of fun. He can be bossy, attempting continually to assert his will and assumed dominant position as leader of the gang. Being a follower is not his style. If his friends prefer to have someone else to organize them, well, young Leo is just going to have to leave and find another collection of friends who do want him, as leader.

Leo tends to be an active child, a bright, optimistic and enthusiastic spirit, much like their planetary ruler the Sun. They have an innate personal confidence – no shrinking violet is Leo – and this enables them to approach life with an exuberant leap, sometimes perhaps too energetically and impulsively, and without careful consideration of their choices and possible consequences.

He tends to have a lot of physical vitality, and in early life he certainly enjoys outdoors play, whether it is organized sport or having exciting and dramatic life or death struggles with the Red Indians out in the trees and bushes. The Leo boy has a marked martial temperament, physically assertive and often reliant upon physical strength. Adventurous war games suit him, and in later life that tendency plus the competitive spirit to be number one can lead him towards martial arts training, or skills to express the 'machismo' nature, such as becoming a businessman.

So, what do you do with your little 'king or queen of the beasts'? How do you deal with their ways, so that they eventually mature into successful human beings? Sometimes it's a careful balance that needs to be developed. Obviously that domineering tendency may need to be adjusted, because many people react against anyone who assumes a sense of superiority (especially those who do so and are certainly not 'superior' in any way). Many managers fall into this category, and Leo likes to manage people. Asserting superiority in certain ways rarely attracts friends and is more likely to create enemies. Leo wouldn't want this to happen, as they need the genuine support and applause of people.

What probably needs to be encouraged and developed in him is a real respect for others, so that his relations with them are based on a mutual respect for each other's individuality and personal rights, in order that the more dominating Leonine power does not become too oppressive and dictatorial. He has to learn that the world and other people are not just there for him to impose his will upon. Leo has to be socialized, for his own good. He might be a leader of men, but that is no use if everyone is turning against him. To be a successful leader, you have to rely on the support of others, and abusing that position of responsibility is a sure way to lose that position sooner or later. He may need to learn about honesty, justice and fair play for everyone, so that people can live together in peace and cooperation; that ideal is likely to appeal to the older child, because it also taps his more romantic and idealistic spirit, where his essential optimism and sense of well-being is expanded to include the whole world. If you can succeed in getting young Leo to see that vision, then that will begin to transform those qualities that can be applied negatively in life into positive qualities.

In several ways Leo has an unconscious self-centredness; he is often genuinely innocent of how his personal power can inhibit the personal expression and assertion of another. This isn't his intention, but is a by-product of his impulse to be a leader; he has to create followers. If possible, he needs to realize that genuine affection and respect from others based on the way in which he expresses his benevolent nature, is the only certain way to earn the appreciation that he desires. The issue of power will confront Leo as he matures. Most Leos attempt to gain power over people, but the safer and more effective way is to become a powerful personality, one who is secure in their own sense of identity and does not have to resort to dominating others. Otherwise, future clashes of will and authority will affect his life; a Leo who has always got his own way can have future marital or employment problems. He may need to learn how to consider more carefully the future consequences of his decisions on himself and others, and not rush ahead spontaneously on impulse.

Leo loves to be the centre of attention, an extroverted child who is a natural performer and somewhat of a show-off. An unleashed Leo is a character who is 'over the top'; colourful, an aura of dramatic flair and imagination surrounding them, making extravagant gestures as they wholeheartedly perform their role. Fantasy and mystery attracts them; the young child lives easily with her vivid imagination, and this is one of the reasons why she can become so popular – she creates the best games! If you dress either the Leo boy or girl in flamboyant clothes, then watch that actor's transformation slide over them, and see them strutting around the room. The boy will become the courageous proud hero, and the girl will be regal and ladylike.

Leo hates to be ignored. He won't allow it. He can become a very demanding child for parent and teacher, and his presence can become disruptive as he strives to gain their attention. Recognition seems to vitalize and strengthen his sense of personal uniqueness and affirm his existence. Lacking attention, he seems to shrink and become that scraggy old rejected lion, whose time as king of the pack has ended by being replaced by the new, younger virile model.

91

Often he can become annoying when he asserts this need, perhaps by interrupting and interfering as a prompt to remind you that he is still there – as if you needed any reminder with him stalking around you, broodily waiting to catch your attention. The younger child is liable to create emotional scenes – dramatic and effective – in his search for attention, or possibly become more aggressive with other children as a release for the pent-up emotional energy. If that occurs, it may be worthwhile evaluating if it is because you haven't given him sufficient personal support, especially if there has been a new brother or sister in the family.

There's a tendency towards boasting and exaggeration in a Leo, partly because of that need to invest life with a bit more colour and glamour, but you may need to see that your young Leo does not take this to an extreme, and perhaps begin to correct this trait if it becomes a problem. Encourage the expression of this characteristic through other channels, like writing adventure stories or doing drawings, so that real life does not get confused with imaginative excess. In fact, Leo has a need to be creatively self-expressive – as do the other Fire signs, Aries and Sagittarius – and it is likely that there will be a talent there waiting to be released and exploited. You've already noticed their inspirational play ideas, so perhaps helping them to direct and discipline that gift may be quite valuable in later years, and help to form a suitable career.

Leo ideas tend to be on a large scale, vast extravaganzas and concepts; 'draw a ship' is turned into a full-scale pirate battle, a 'house' becomes a castle. He enjoys expanding such ideas, and has a fertile mind. His main difficulty can lie in overconfidence in respect of his actual ability to turn his ideas into reality; over-stretching himself, and seeing that what he has produced is much less than his vision can depress him for a while. Helping him to discipline this tendency so that he achieves something of value but with a less broad scope (just creating a country instead of a world!) can be beneficial to him. From a point of realistic achievement he can then learn how to expand his talents; but overreaching and failing will become too discouraging, eventually resulting – if regularly repeated – in a loss of confidence and a rejection of the potential of his personal talent.

The roots and foundations of family life are important to Leo, and she will have a deep emotional attachment to that basic relationship. Whilst it may not be too obvious, Leo does need to rely on parents and family to provide a safe and supportive environment for her to grow within, one that is warmly appreciative of her efforts at entertaining and with whom she can display her love and affection. Beneath those sometimes egotistic performances, Leo has a very loving heart, although she can feel insecure about demonstrating this; as Leo is a fixed sign, once her emotions are engaged with a person, then her love is steadfast.

The Leo temperament is encouraged to flourish by the attention of parents and brothers and sisters. It is important to receive that family approval, and his confidence will grow in leaps and bounds when it is given. As Leo intends to become 'king' when he matures, he tends to study his parents as role models of power, so that when he arrives at his destined place, he is fully prepared to perform his role. He needs to be able to trust and respect his parents, so it could be appropriate for you to set him an example, by providing a role model that is a shining example of a loving, considerate and thoughtful human being. He'll take that as the way to be, and this will help to modify any of his overly assertive tendencies with people. Don't force such an image, if it is not real for you; after all, surely you're willing to change for the benefit of your child? He'll perceive you in a glowing light, and isn't that worth the effort?

There are bound to be times when family friction occurs; that Leo will can be very obstinate, but basically, Leo wants to feel secure in receiving the love of their parents, and hates to believe that they have disappointed anyone. Arguments can be more successfully resolved by appealing to their feelings, family loyalties and responsibilities, rather than by a direct confrontation of will to will. Leo does not like to submit very often. If they are forced to do so, by equally dominating parents, then they can turn into that rarer breed of Leos that are repressed, quieter, even timid and shy of people. If so, then some real damage has been done to the Leo temperament, which inhibits their real personality shining through in the normal manner; the more cheerful, easy going, extroverted, generous and friendly Leo with which most are familiar. Sometimes a strategy to persuade them to do something that you want, and which they have been resisting, is to imply that it is beyond their capabilities, and that you understand their reluctance; the odds are that they'll take this as a personal challenge, and assuming their heroic armour will take to the quest to prove that they can do it, if they choose to, and that you were wrong in implying that they couldn't. They will then preen themselves with self-assured satisfaction. But secretly, you have won too, and so have they, with another confidence booster . . . .

During puberty and adolescence, these character traits start to come to a head, and they'll be even more noticeable. Those teenage years are likely to be volatile, especially as she struggles to make some sense out of swirling emotions overlapping and energizing that personal temperament. Self-centredness becomes more amplified, mixed with phases of insecurity and confusion, especially if she becomes involved with teenage romances, which are fragile things anyway, and fraught with heartbreak and dramatic gestures. She'll soon wake up to the attractions of the opposite sex; but like many adults, she'll realize that they are hard to handle, and having a vulnerable heart and a need to be loved is a dangerous target to possess. Being so friendly, she'll enjoy socializing and parties, preferring to be loud and noticed, rather than hiding away in a corner out of shyness. For Leo, life has to be enjoyed in company; unless there are other strong astrological influences at play, or Leo has arrived at a very mature adult perspective on their unique identity, then Leo performs to their audience. A Leo standing alone is a man or woman adrift, as their identity is so tied up with the reflections coming from others' eyes, that it tends to deflate too much when isolated. In fact, one weakness of Leo is an inability to be on their own, and to feel personally comfortable in that situation.

The Leo adolescent can be a touchy beast, so proud, haughty even at times, having a touch of vanity as he struggles to create the right image to project at the world. Any criticism or humiliation really rankles with him, and he can brood deeply over such hurts, possibly breaking off friendships if someone has said something that penetrated through his egocentric shell into that soft heart underneath. Leo is not that tough after all, he's more a cuddly cat really. He hates being ordered around, and won't become the most passive employee. That sense of pride and dignity is offended by teachers and parents who are dictatorial, and he is likely to react against any chores which he considers to be beneath his royal position. Like a lazy lion, he can tend to treat doting parents as royal slaves, commanding them with an imperial style to do this, or that. As his parent, never fall into that relationship trap, it will do him no good at all; when he does that, ignore him. Soon, he'll get the message that unless he does things himself, or is more cooperative, his demands will be frustrated. Neither parents nor children are slaves, and he'll learn that mutual respect and working together in order to achieve results is the best way in life.

Supporting that lurking inner image of 'kingship' and placing the child on a pedestal is not really the right approach. It can be hard to fall from that height, and in later years demanding attention and subservience from others is a recipe for the collapse of good human relations. A balanced approach to the efficacy of their will is better where they know that some degree of failure is inevitable, and that they shouldn't tie up their ego's well-being so tightly to its total success. It can be a lesson well learnt, one which prevents them later from trying to be too dominant with unsuitable people, who may enjoy putting them firmly in their place.

It's unwise to try to restrain his natural energy, and attempts to discipline it by forcing it to move down certain paths is liable to be a failure. In many ways, Leo finds it hard to be self-disciplined, as that tendency to act impulsively and intuitively is so strong, and especially so where he believes that there is pleasure to be achieved. Parental guidance based on his love and affection is the best route to take, where by using a softer and more persuasive style, he sees the reason for your concern about his behaviour. Usually he will try to improve, unless the clash is about something that holds great personal meaning for him, and then his will is likely to be fixed. If it's about his personal appearance, then let him have his head, and if he chooses to go out 'looking like that!' then it is the image he wishes to present, and is of meaning to him as a sign of a unique identity. He'll also want plenty of freedom to roam around, and reining him in will probably not work very well, making him stalk around the house like a caged lion, waiting for an open gate to escape through.

Money can burn holes in her pockets, and she may not be very prudent with her pocket-money; saving is a word rarely found in a Leo's vocabulary, as she prefers spending to enjoy life today, rather than to postpone it till tomorrow. He can be overly reckless at times, and may need to be careful when he reaches an age to have motor cycles or drive cars. In relationships, he can be a little too direct and outspoken; there is sometimes a lack of subtlety in Leo which some find refreshing and others offensive. Perhaps surprisingly, a Leo who has had good family relationships is often reluctant to leave his home to become independent; he feels those strong emotional umbilical ties, and, despite his bluster and assertive style, can find entering a real unknown a disconcerting experience; the supportive environment is lost, and he has to be totally self-reliant. Yet if he has had family friction, then he can be as eager to leave and to assert his own will and freedom as soon as possible.

If your Leo is female, then these basic traits may be a little modified and less on the surface. Don't be misled though, as she will have a very strong will and desire to stand out in the crowd too. It's just that her way of doing this may be more subtle. She'll probably pass through a tomboyish phase, but her attention will become focused on her image. Attractive clothes and admiration vitalize her, and she may develop an extremely flamboyant sense of dress if she feels comfortable about deliberately drawing attention toward herself. She'll probably contain her extroverted nature better than the male Leo, for reasons of social acceptability, but it's there alongside her will; in a quieter manner, she tends to achieve whatever she has set her heart upon.

THE LEO CHILD AND EDUCATION

Leo children are often bright and alert, although they may fail to fulfil their potential at school due to a lack of continual application, and by being sidetracked by their own powerful personality needs. This can occur especially during adolescence, when this coincides with those crucial years leading up to examinations.

With that love of performance and the applause of the crowd, young Leo can find his audience amongst his school friends in the classroom. He isn't too fussy about how he gains people's attention, and he can develop into a class clown, or be the ringleader of a small group of children who are mischievous. At worst, he can become a distracting influence at school, especially in any lesson which fails to interest him, and then he'll decide to liven it up. Leo will love people laughing at his actions, but would hate anyone laughing at him, because that deflates his ego. Some Leos may be tempted into testing their power against the authority of a teacher, especially during the teen years. He's sensible enough not to choose one whom he recognizes as having personal power, but one whom he feels is weaker. If it isn't a teacher, it'll be one of his parents, as the young lion decides that it's time that he begins to make his presence felt, and starts his campaign to seize the crown of power and authority.

One of the keys for a successful education lies once again in that need for appreciation and compliments. If young Leo feels valued at school, and that her efforts are 'rewarded' with approval by her teachers and parents, then she will strive even harder to win more plaudits. At the heart of a Leo is a lack of self-confidence, and a need for social acceptance, which is often unrecognized due to her extroverted style. Another approach to draw out her real potential is that appeal to her vanity, wherein you encourage her to do better because 'you know that she can do it'; as she will prefer not to disappoint you, she'll try harder and probably succeed.

With that basic intellectual ability, Leo can do well at school, especially if he decides to be an achiever to justify that image of standing out from the crowd, being number one and respected by others. If that inner motivation takes root, then that aspect of his character will begin to replace the entertainer, and the serious Leo will emerge with his eyes fixed on his objective. With his willpower and natural talents, he is likely to achieve his aims.

Much depends on the personal choices that Leo makes; some become relatively lazy and apathetic at times, preferring to coast along relying upon their 'charisma, charm and personality', to get them through. For a lucky few, this may well work, but probably for the majority a resounding failure will occur when they come face to face with the adult world.

If Leo so chooses, he can absorb his lessons reasonably easily and fast. As he can tend to be lazy, helping him to develop better application and discipline is very important, so that consistent progress is made, rather than an erratic effort derived from occasional teacher pressure. Leo has a reservoir of physical and mental energy waiting to be released and this needs to be directed towards suitable channels which are beneficial to his well-being and education. Deciding which channels are suitable is the problem. Obviously, any subject that he has a real interest in will be one route, because everyone applies themselves when there is a personal interest. Establishing a definite direction for Leo – in accordance with his own decisions – is the best way to release and exploit his own potential. Self-expression, creativity and positions of responsibility are general routes to explore. If Leo has no obvious objective to aim towards, then his potential stays locked within him, and his personality begins to take on an edge of dissatisfaction and frustration.

Leo likes to generalize instead of focusing on specific details, and prefers those subjects where there is a broad scope for their interest. Their mind works best in grasping a 'whole picture', and this is associated with that intuitional fire element which is geared towards large-scale projects or empire building. Unlike a Virgo, for example, they have little interest in the component specifics of a project or idea, and they have no interest at all in 'dotting the i's and crossing the t's'.

Leo learns mainly through a questioning mind, asking those pointed and relevant questions which, when answered, contain an expansive impression of all the main points of a topic. She rarely likes to collate masses of information which then need to be memorized in order to be useful. Her approach is to absorb the whole picture, ensure that she understands that, and then the relevance of the pieces becomes obvious. Reason is important to her, and she needs to grasp the logic of an instruction; so she's likely to question commands out of an attempt to understand rather than by being awkward and non-cooperative. Being aware of that inner need can stop certain misunderstandings occurring by teachers and parents, as she is likely to question commands and instructions through a genuine need to comprehend.

He likes to demonstrate his understanding and knowledge to others, as this gives him an aura of authority, and people have to look up to him. In fact, he'd often prefer to replace the teacher in the classroom with himself, privately believing that he could give a much better performance. Sometimes when the teacher's back is turned, or the teacher has left the room, young Leo cannot resist the temptation to prove his belief.

He will be attracted towards the social aspect of school, and will probably become involved in several interest groups, perhaps even discussion or debating groups, where his love of being in the spotlight and his fixed opinions can be displayed. Theatre performances can attract him, or music. If there is a school magazine then he may be a contributor through choice, and participatory school councils may be a forum for a Leo performance. As well as following genuine interests, such associations also satisfy his need to express 'leadership, dominance and organizing abilities' as an assertion of personal power. Similarly, if he arrives at university, these other interests are likely to distract him from focusing on his studies; yet in them can lie the seeds of future careers and work satisfaction too.

LEO CAREERS

A suitable career for a Leo is one where those main personality characteristics and needs are satisfied. Leo needs a career where there is enough space for him to demonstrate his talents for leadership and organization, or where self-expression through creative channels is the chosen route. They either need to be independent and free to create their own lifestyles and creative paths, or else to be dominating figures in top hierarchical positions. Being a mere employee is not a favourite role of the Leonine temperament; just being one of the pack is not satisfying, and the likely result is antagonism with his superiors.

Business and managerial roles are attractive and fit the Leo character, reflecting that inner kingship image that can dominate his life. Owning his own business would be especially favourable, because even as a manager in a company, there are people more senior to Leo.

If Leo has absorbed some strong social ideals during their development, they could decide to work with social betterment schemes. This could satisfy an awareness of others' needs, and be a reworking of that pattern of leader–follower, where they receive the knowledge of helping others, and the satisfaction of that sort of approval.

Drama, theatre and music could appeal to their extroverted

self, as an actor's life is perpetually in the spotlight. Self-creativity through literature and art can be favoured, where they can become self-preoccupied as an 'artist', influencing people by their creations and hopefully receiving the approbation of an admiring audience.

Another aspect of those social ideas and principles being applied could be through a more direct social involvement as a campaigning journalist, or involvement in local or national politics. Yes, that's right, he certainly could imagine himself as Prime Minister, solving all the national problems and receiving the adulation of his supporters. Whether it would be good for him is another matter! Leo will only be satisfied if he either achieves his high personal aims, or if he makes a mark on society. The worst response that a Leo can have is to be ignored. He should strive to succeed, and then his talents will flourish.

VIRGO
(AUGUST 23 to SEPTEMBER 22)

Planetary Ruler: Mercury

Element type	Earth
Type	Negative/Feminine
Triplicity	Mutable
Symbol	♍
Image	The Virgin
Part of Body	Abdomen, intestines
Theme of Self	I Analyse
Key Qualities	Discrimination, service, methodical application
House Affinity	6th House

Famous Virgo Personalities: Goethe, D. H. Lawrence, Greta Garbo, Sophia Loren, Peter Sellers, Lauren Bacall, Roald Dahl, Lenny Henry, Stephen Fry, Larry Hagman, Richard Gere, H. G. Wells, Agatha Christie, Sean Connery, Robert Redford, Jeremy Irons, Raquel Welch.

THE PRE-SCHOOL VIRGO CHILD

The ideal type of Virgo birth is one which is similar to the 'textbook example', where everything goes according to plan, is extremely well organized and correct, and proceeds naturally without undue drama or fuss. Virgo births are often controlled affairs, with very little scope for anything unusual to occur, and are normally associated with efficient professional skill which is capable of dealing safely and effectively with the situation.

During the first year of life, baby Virgo is likely to cause several sleepless nights. She is often a light sleeper, reacting quickly to any local disturbances and noises around her, and waking up several times. She can be erratic with her feeding, whether it is breast or bottle milk in those early months, her body shows signs of minor difficulties in adjusting to the feeding process, and stomach or digestive disorders can occur from time to time. She can suffer from minor allergies, such as oversensitive skin and rashes, caused by her clothes.

The impression is that they are serious babies, assessing the unknown world into which they have suddenly emerged, and making up their minds whether or not they like it. Caution and slow deliberation is their style, wondering how trusting they can afford to be; they are not the most smiley and responsive of babies, especially if strangers are around.

Between the ages of one and two, growing familiarity with his body and the world, together with physical mobility, leads him to become more curious and active in exploring. He can still display some reluctance for physical contact, and seems to get less pleasure from cuddling than many other babies. What he does enjoy is human communication, and talking to him usually gains his attention even if he does not really understand what you are saying. Over this year, he begins to show clear signs of grasping word meanings and, through words and pointing at objects, begins the process of association and classification which Virgo enjoys. It is likely that he will begin to talk early, and will show that he is understanding basic language; his efforts bring him great delight. Those simple word and picture books fascinate him now, and his development can be encouraged by sitting with him and looking through such books, until he can name the pictured objects. Repetition and familiarity is the key to the early phase of learning.

Virgos may find it difficult to sit still without wriggling, and will generally always want to be active or involved in something. Toys which require manual dexterity attract them, especially those which also need a little thought and working out, such as shaped pieces which have to be placed through the right holes into a container.

103

By the age of two, her attempts at talking are greatly improved, and you'll realise by her responses that her comprehension is quite advanced for her age. Toilet training, which should not really be started until between eighteen months and two years old, can pose difficulties. Like the other Earth sign, Taurus, anal retention may occur, and constipation can result. Try not to place pressure on the child to perform or become angry when mistakes happen, because this can make the child 'tighten up' through fear, and resist the natural process. Also, the Virgo trait for cleanliness and hygiene may make her associate the toilet with being 'dirty' and she may react psychologically against that body function. Try to emphasize its naturalness, support her efforts, and attempt to establish a regular routine and time, so that the body mechanism begins to act automatically.

Virgo tends to develop habit patterns as a means of organizing and imposing order on the world, so signs of this begin to occur. For instance, favourite toys have to be placed in certain places, or hiding spots are established. This is another common factor with Earth signs, where life has to become structured, and feelings of stability and security are generated. An early indication of tidiness may be noted, mess is not tolerated, and young Virgo may go around the room attempting to tidy and rearrange. Her own private room can become important, both as a retreat and a personal play area, where she can indulge in her own little world without too many distractions, and arrange her toys in her own special way. Personal untidiness and mess are disliked, and she'll often come to you wanting to be cleaned up if she's noticed that her hands or clothes have become dirty. She'll take great pleasure in being bathed and emerging nice and clean, and will probably soon want to do it all herself.

Through the third and fourth years, Virgo can seem to be quite self-contained and independent. His caution and need for regular routines is still present (as it will be for all his life), otherwise he can become unsettled and worried if changes occur in his predictable life. The absorbing of new life experience and knowledge through daily living, and perhaps play-school attendance, can lead to a phase of uneven sleep patterns, as his brain attempts to absorb, classify and understand his experiences. Sometimes caution and evaluation of options can create difficulties in the act of decision-making, and you may need to offer him some help at times. He'll enjoy playing on his own – even when with other children at playschool – and what will focus his attention are games which are active yet also require some mental effort. Simple puzzle books, or finding hidden animals in the pictures, Lego construction bricks, dolls' houses and furniture can all appeal to the Virgo nature, as can any games which require observation skills, Virgo can be extremely good at those.

Most Virgo children are well disciplined, and you are likely to have fewer tantrums with them than with other children, At playschool, she's liable to keep to herself, not mixing easily with all the children, but preferring to occupy herself and over time learning to play with a couple of intimate friends with whom she feels safe and can trust. She isn't very assertive, and you may need to help her to build self-confidence, rather than criticize her at times. Food can be an awkward area, and her fussiness will still exist, so open confrontation is not advised. Accept it as part of her nature.

Between four and five, his questioning mind becomes more prominent, and he is ready to devour any and all sorts of information that he can grasp. What may puzzle you are the details and apparent trivia that he seems to need answers for, and you're liable to be asking him 'Why do you need to know that?' He doesn't really know why, and is equally liable to reply 'Because I do!' There's an information explosion going on in him, and his mind becomes a melting pot of facts and observations; what he is able to do with it is another mystery, but it satisfies that inner need. He will like to build collections now, and over the next few years will probably spend much time in being a collector of various intriguing or meaningful items, which he will take quite seriously – woe betide anyone who disturbs his collection.

She can be a chatterbox at this age with parents or people that she knows, although she can be stunned into unhappy silence if she is told off for any misdemeanour. She hates to fall short of parental expectations, and takes any criticism to heart, probably brooding too much on those admonishing words. Direct discipline is often too harsh for her, and threats only make her more fearful and withdrawn, whereas talking with her in a reasonable way about her behaviour and encouraging her to improve in specific problem areas will often gain the required response and improvement from her. She isn't a naughty child by temperament, and only wants to be liked, so more subtle approaches are the most suitable. Now she'll be ready for full-time schooling, and once she's adjusted to the shock of the new environment and the classroom full of children, she'll be looking forward to absorbing all that new range of knowledge.

THE VIRGO CHILD PERSONALITY

None of the Earth signs are ebullient extroverts, and young Virgo is no exception, having a friendly but essentially serious temperament. There can be a feeling that Virgo is older than their actual years, and that more adult concerns seem to weigh them down, restricting that degree of unconcern and preoccupation with play and fun that most children display. What creates this impression is a natural reserve, an active mind and a tendency towards nervous worrying.

Having a Virgo child can seem relatively easy for a parent, because he or she is usually well behaved, independent, reliable and socially well adapted towards the requirements of daily life. Yet that natural reserve and distancing of themselves from others can make it difficult to really begin to get close to Virgo children, let alone understand their inner nature, unless you too, are a Virgo. Much of the real Virgo is privately locked away from open display, and the key to that padlock is rarely given to anyone else to open, even in adult life. It is likely that despite a natural parental love for a child, a communication gap with the young Virgo will develop over time, which, whilst seeming to be there on a superficial level, will operate on a deeper more meaningful level in the relationship. Attempts to bridge that gap can be difficult, but mutually rewarding; the first step is to acknowledge its existence, and to recognize that it isn't deliberately done by the child or by yourself, but is a natural consequence of that Virgo temperament operating in relationships.

Underlying this self-contained nature is an inferiority complex, where a lack of personal confidence and that cautious, shy tendency tends to inhibit an exploration of life. Virgo has a personality pattern operating that is afraid that others do not like her, and this acts to repress her own assertion of her nature and talents and diminishes her self-esteem. Yet Virgo has a basic optimism, despite that cautious approach to life and decision making. She certainly needs to be encouraged in personal assertion and a more positive form of expression; if that can be achieved, then the young Virgo will blossom, demonstrating those latent gifts and qualities of personality that had been hidden away. Once that self-confidence is established, then several of the more negatively influential Virgo traits will dissolve away, and that pattern of worrying and mental agitation will begin to fade.

Understanding the Virgo character is essential to help the child develop in a positive way. The more obvious Virgo emphasis is with the mind, but this is often at the expense of a balanced expression of the emotions, and the resulting combination can stimulate health problems, especially in later adult life. The Virgo mind has to be active and busy, continually engaged in a process of analysis, classification, categorization and assessment of people and situations. The hidden motivation for such restless activity is a deep need for security, stability and certainty about existence, which is usually a common desire with the other two Earth signs, Taurus and Capricorn. As the key theme for Virgo is 'I analyse', looking for an inherent logic and rationality in everything is the basic quest of the mind. Unfortunately, life does not easily conform to providing such clearly defined answers that Virgo wants. Whilst humanity tends to attempt to impose such order and stability on itself and the natural world, there are a multitude of ways in which that superimposed façade of conformity breaks down. This disturbs Virgo, who is faced with attempting to satisfy an impossible inner demand.

Perfection, idealism and order result from this personality pattern and with the Virgoan tendency towards excessive scrutiny and self-criticism applied both to themselves and others, this tendency can serve to create personal inhibitions and misunderstandings with others. Any sort of personal criticism is taken to heart, and used as a focus to confirm that sense of personal inadequacy that sits deep within the Virgo nature. Failure in even trivial and minor matters tends to deflate that fragile confidence, and all disappointments are inflated beyond their real importance. Eventually, if this experience pattern persists, then young Virgo can feel afraid to attempt the challenge of new phases of learning and unfoldment, or applies themselves in such a way that relative failure becomes inevitable, thus reinforcing a vicious circle. What is needed here is for both teachers and parents to understand the child, so that their own responses to them do not activate such a process. Virgos should be encouraged to allow themselves to accept that sometimes they will fail to be perfect, and to turn that into a spur to learn and achieve, and also accept that sometimes they can make mistakes. Help them to realize that everyone makes mistakes when learning, and that there is nothing wrong in doing so; support them closely when showing them the right way to do things; reassure and openly praise them for everything that they are doing well. This all helps to boost their confidence and readjust that perfectionist tendency so that failure is not another blow against a fragile personality. Virgo often needs closer support than is apparent, and parents can greatly help by consciously modifying their relationship with them so that it becomes more positive and constructive in the forming of their unique identity.

Virgo's health will be affected by the state of her inner self, and that is why adjusting those tendencies of the Virgoan mind is so important, as they often live on nervous tension, which has a negative body reaction over a prolonged time. What often results is nervous tension in the body, and this usually finds its release through stomach discomfort, intestinal upsets and sickness. Virgo can develop a preoccupation with their own physical health – another source of worry for the mind – and signs of hypochondria can be evident, especially if the child has been worrying over something for some time, or is acutely disturbed by some failure or disappointment. Whilst there may be something really wrong with the child's health, and this should obviously be checked, it may equally be the result or symptom of an inner worry or emotional repression, and can provide an opportunity to discover what is really disturbing the child. Allow her to open up and to talk about any problems, releasing any emotions that she has been damming up inside.

Most Virgos are fussy about food, having a fastidious selectivity that can be difficult to understand; you are likely to have several battles with them over the issue of food. Sometimes the problem is associated with the cleanliness of certain foods; particular food is connected with being 'dirty', whether through colour, texture or general appearance. Instant dislikes are common and, irrational though they may appear to be, Virgo is determined not to touch that food! Such instinctive reactions are often opposed by parents, who, for reasons of economy and effort, often insist that their children eat whatever is placed before them, and mealtimes become a common battleground in many households as will opposes will. With a Virgoan child, it may be more advisable to acquiesce to their demands, mainly because self-assertion is not their strongest asset, and a repetitive breaking down of their will at mealtimes can only have a negative reaction. As children grow older, their personal tastes change and develop naturally, expanding to take in a wider range of foods. Forcing food on a younger child despite tears of opposition may not be the most appropriate way of proceeding.

As Virgo grows older, he may amaze you by his natural gift for absorbing information and facts, which he manages quite effortlessly. He is usually very observant, especially about details which many people fail to notice, and he succeeds in storing away all facts for future reference; he tends not to differentiate between relevant or irrelevant facts, to him a fact is a fact and that's sufficient! He has a quick mind, more naturally attuned to reason and logical progression than more imaginative leaps of creative connectivity, and will always need clear explanations of everything. This helps him to feel in control. By 'knowing' about something, it becomes fixed in its rightful place in his world; his ideal is to see everything categorized, so that stability, order and a sense of emotional security can then be felt. Allied to this is his tendency to develop fixed lifestyle routines and predictable regular habit patterns.

This need reappears in reactions against changes in her life. Virgo will hate disruption, as it dissolves her carefully constructed reliable patterns of living within a familiar world. Her emotions – which are a weak unintegrated area of her life – are highly agitated by change which is seen as being quite traumatic in impact, such as changes in school, home, in the parental marriage, or in the arrival of a new member of the family. Virgo can grow very confused and nervous if she finds herself in a chaotic situation or where everything has not been properly organized. Usually though, when she is established in her new situation, then she becomes emotionally settled. If change becomes inevitable, then it is best to spend time reassuring young Virgo and explaining to her why things are changing, what they are changing to, and what she is likely to find in the new situation, and then closely monitor her reactions. This can help to give her some security in the situation. Quite often though, adults are preoccupied with reorganizing for a new situation themselves, and often fail to pay full attention to their children's needs and sense of disturbance.

Virgo tends towards being 'materialistic', in the sense of

interest in the physical world and in being practical, efficient and organized. They will have the ability to be a hard worker, reliable and conscientious, particularly enjoying seeing the tangible results of their efforts, which gives them a sense of achievement. They may lack an inner fire and an enthusiastic imagination, as they are too earthbound, and that streak of realism may make them less receptive and fascinated by traditional childhood stories of myth, legend and fairy tales. If they could open themselves to such fanciful evocative worlds, then it may begin to transform that often stark, emotionally dry, inner life of many Virgos, where the earth is cracking through lack of water. It can be rare to find a sentimental and emotional Virgo; but this is only because the emotional dams have been erected and established over years of self-protection. A Virgo who has come to terms with that emotional level is much more relaxed than one who keeps it firmly under control.

Virgo can have an ambivalent attitude towards socializing and playing with young friends. She tends to be cautious in forming friendships, and at initial meetings can appear to be withdrawn and distant, until she feels that she now knows a new playmate and then she opens up more, often becoming surprisingly chatty with an accepted friend. When in adult company, she can be very quiet, rarely making noticeable demands for attention. Underlying her friendships is a real fear of not being like by others, which arises from that sense of personal insecurity. As she grows older, and perhaps especially by her teenage years, her critical and fastidious nature can result in upsetting several of her friends, as she is liable to make tactless remarks at which other take offence. Often her aims to please and her good intentions collapse in failure due to this tendency to be so direct and honest, and her friends misinterpret her lack of subtlety and diplomacy as unnecessarily hurtful. Such confusion in relationships will cause her pain, until she perhaps learns that some friends will not welcome her precise honest comments, and recognizes those who can value her honesty. The likelihood is that she will have a small selection of closer friends, who will probably have compatible tendencies, being relatively conservative, traditional and with a pragmatic intelligence. She will feel less easy with those who are rebellious or extroverted, because these bring the winds of change into an ordered, settled life. Virgo evaluates people on their actions and tangible achievements rather than on what they say or intend to do. For Virgo, being a part of society implies responsibility, duty and order, and most Virgos take their place in society easily, rarely questioning or subverting the created social structure.

The adolescent phase of the Virgo childhood can be quite touchy, where those undercurrents of emotional and mental change seem often at cross-purposes with the physical maturation which is occurring. Signs of this maturation often come earlier then average, especially in the adult attitudes of responsibility and reliability, and many young Virgos show signs of a common sense which is in advance of their years. Encouraging them to help more in the house is useful, both as a form of household training for them, and as an outlet of that natural impulse to be of help to people. Ensuring that the house is tidy and clean will certainly satisfy that Virgoan need for an ordered environment. Their own room will probably be well looked after although rumours have it that there are a breed of Virgoans that can exist in a state of organised chaos, where everything looks messy but Virgo knows precisely where everything is to be found. This breed is in danger of extinction from parents who insist on children's rooms being tidy, but probably a few slip through the net to emerge as adult Virgos!

Appearance will be important to the teenage Virgo, and part of their self-confidence will be strongly tied to their clothes and visual impression on others. Cleanliness and personal hygiene should not pose any problems, as Virgo will be very fastidious, perhaps excessively so at times. Difficulties may lie in their emotions and those early relationships with the opposite sex, because rampant emotions dissolve those barriers of mentally imposed order, and sweep them into inner depths that are too deep for them to swim in. Emotions will send them on a rollercoaster ride, and you may see them becoming strangely moody and changeable, in contrast to their normal temperament. They'll also be very touchy if you probe into their emotional well-being at this time, rejecting your advances of support. It's best just to reassure them that you're there if and when they need you to confide in, because it's better if the impulse to share comes naturally from them and not from your persistent inquiring. Try not to tease them; they will not like it, and will probably cut off from you more. It's still a time to support them and to encourage their own identity to emerge; that lack of self-confidence will be emerging again, and they will often perceive themselves to be quite boring and uninteresting when compared to those socially extroverted types. Point out to them all those qualities they have that are positive and useful, and help them to gain esteem and self-value.

She can feel uncomfortable with close physical contact and cuddling, as it can stir emotional depths that she is uneasy with, so if she seems to avoid that with you, then it is not a rejection of you but a symptom of her own lack of emotional integration. Yet if she has a small animal to care for, she will give it much love and attention, protecting and caring for it with great affection, because this taps her talent for serving others, and is a situation where others can rely and depend upon Virgo to fill their needs. Being dependent on others makes Virgo feel insecure, and this adds to that ambivalence with relationships.

THE VIRGO CHILD AND EDUCATION

Virgo children tend to settle into school life easily, and are quite suited to the type of education that they will receive over the years. In several ways, Virgo is one of the signs that is more receptive to current teaching techniques, and the child's personality is one that is normally well behaved and so doesn't create problems in the classroom, unlike certain others that are more disruptive, demanding or mischievous. This isn't to say that young Virgo is incapable of such actions – any child is, in certain moods and encouraged by school friends – but that it isn't a dominant feature of their nature. They will usually respond quickly to a teacher's discipline, and certainly would not be regular offenders.

Virgo will become a conscientious student, who is capable of application and good work; school work seems to genuinely interest her, and those natural talents of an alert and keen intelligence will begin to shine through as her abilities continue to develop. Because she actually pays attention to the teacher, instead of being sidetracked into comedy routines, daydreams or chatter, she grasps the information that the teacher is struggling to communicate to the class. This should ensure that her schoolwork rarely becomes poor or a problem to her. She may not be the academically brightest in class, but she certainly will not be amongst those with the lowest marks.

The only aspect of school life that can negatively affect Virgo is in the relationship with the teacher, and the fact that the Virgo mind tends to create habit patterns of repetitive worrying, almost obsessively or compulsively so at times. Virgo has a tendency to create or imagine negative scenarios, which then become a focus for the mind to whirl around, repetitively circling an issue which may not actually exist, yet has somehow been identified as a real problem. Because the Virgoan's mind has to be constantly active, false or pseudo-dramas are established, triggering off a mind loop. Such triggers can be the experience of a small disappointment in life, perhaps a low mark in a school test, a lack of personal ability somewhere or a remark by a teacher or parent. There may be a lack of personal confidence in the Virgo, whose modesty and relative lack of self-assertion can need drawing out. These triggers are taken very seriously, giving an inner opportunity to fret away and try to analyse the problem, but in a way that fails to resolve the issue; it just gnaws away inside.

The actions of a teacher can be very influential on the private life of the Virgo child. The sensitivity of Virgo is such that public humiliation and criticism in the classroom can cause a severe personality trauma. The child reacts by withdrawal and silence, and by a lessening of interest and effort in their school work. As Virgo has a more serious self-image, public mockery and a rejection of their efforts and abilities as not being sufficient or worthwhile is not the appropriate way to deal with this child. It isn't just teachers who can be at fault; parents too are equally liable to damage their child by insensitive actions and words. Virgo is extremely self-critical anyway, and external criticism just adds fuel to that psychological fire, so that those worry loops become established as part of their personality, and can possibly develop to create serious nervous problems as an adult, or at least an extremely restless type of analytical mind.

The most suitable way of handling young Virgo is through a process of conscious, deliberate reassurement and encouragement, praising everything that they do, which will help to develop a more positive self-image and confidence in herself over time. Whilst the child will obviously make all sorts of mistakes, both at home and school, her temperament is such that she is always willing to learn, and so such mistakes should never be overstressed or turned into serious errors. A few quiet words with her, showing her how it should be done, will be more effective. Virgo will respond eagerly, as she has a perfectionist streak and will want to correct her own mistakes and ensure that she does not make them again. Personal criticism and humiliation should never be used on her, because it adds to that inner self-doubt and inhibits her approach to life.

If anything, conscious effort may need to be made to communicate the fact that most trivial mistakes do not really matter, and that they can soon be successfully amended. Virgo tends to overexaggerate any failures, blowing them up out of all proportion, due to that overly critical and perfectionist attitude. A more relaxed attitude needs to be encouraged.

The Virgo mind is a naturally enquiring one, operating

through a logical and rational perspective. Of the Earth signs, Virgo is the 'thinking one', although it is a very earthbound style of thought, based on analysis, criticism and detail. Information is easily received and stored in their memory database, and the emphasis is placed upon the ability to turn that information into a practical application. Facts and questioning are the keys to such enquiries, and 'why, what, and how' are favourite words to commence their search for knowledge. Order and a methodical approach suits the Virgo temperament, and they will try to organize their knowledge and eventual lifestyle accordingly. Completeness and neatness will be the Virgo ideal; attention to detail is a necessity to them. Sometimes they may need several attempts to succeed in learning something, but with the right sort of encouragement, they will eventually achieve their aims.

At school, receiving information in a passive way is common. What Virgo needs is to see the end product or use of that information too; it completes the process for him, and enables comprehension. He may become a little too fixed on the end result, that tangible culmination of thought. Showing him all the sequential steps that need to be taken to achieve that end point will be fascinating to him, as it can satisfy both his type of mind and his need for an objective result. Yet more abstract subjects can gain his interest too, even those subjects like science and maths with which many people have difficulty. These appeal to his analytical mind and, if the results of formulae are also demonstrated, can fulfil his Earth's need for material results. Virgo can also be quite adroit at modifying, adapting or inventing new ways of performing daily functions, at home, work or school. There can also be a more creative dimension to Virgo, which is that of a perfectionist craftsperson, making either beautiful or perfectly functioning items.

A good education is vital for Virgo; it is an essential part of the process of moving beyond the self-doubts and inferiority complexes that many a Virgoan secretly has. Building up their confidence in their own ability is vital, so that they are able to realize their full potential, both during school life and as adults. Regular and consistent support can reap great dividends in unfolding that modest and unassuming character, so that those natural talents can be properly applied.

VIRGO CAREERS

The ideal Virgo careers are those which take advantage of Virgoan talents, such as that analytical, discriminating mind, with its ability to categorize and classify. Working closely with detail in a well-organized routine is often favoured by Virgo, and so the civil service and bureaucratic structures can appeal. Few are as capable as 'following the book' as Virgo. Being an administrator or organizer could be ideal, as could an examining inspector of goods or materials, where that Virgo knack for detailed observation would be very valuable to a quality-conscious company. An efficient secretary or personal assistant could display those natural talents too, because we all know that a manager's office is only as effective as his secretary!

Working with numbers and figurework, such as accountancy or statistics, could reveal Virgo's attention to detail and that reliable efficiency. Science too can attract, especially the fields of research, experimentation and theory, or analytical science; but here the suitable emphasis would have to be on mainstream science, and less on the exploratory aspects where imaginative leaps open new doors to scientific investigation. Virgo is suited to the more regular scientific work, or where large periods of time are required in testing hypotheses or new pharmaceuticals, etc. The social awareness of Virgo can find avenues of expression through teaching, nursing, health and hygiene care, or through community work to improve the standard of the environment for everyone. With their fascination for the mind, some are attracted towards the area of mental health, such as psychology, but here the more traditional approaches appeal most.

LIBRA
(SEPTEMBER 23 to OCTOBER 22)

Planetary Ruler: Venus

Element type	Air
Type	Positive/Masculine
Triplicity	Cardinal
Symbol	♎
Image	The Scales
Part of Body	Kidneys, lumbar region
Theme of Self	I Balance
Key Qualities	Relating, harmony, socializing, partners
House Affinity	7th House

Famous Libra Personalities: Dwight Eisenhower, David Ben-Gurion, Mahatma Gandhi, Margaret Thatcher, Nietzsche, Oscar Wilde, John Lennon, T. S. Eliot, George Gershwin, Julie Andrews, Brigitte Bardot, Martina Navratilova, Charles Dance, Steve Ovett, Matt and Luke Goss (Bros), Duchess of York, Christopher Reeve.

THE PRE-SCHOOL LIBRA CHILD

Most Libran births are stylish, beautiful and ordered, unlike the more traumatic or dramatic births that can come with Leo or Scorpio children, and not usually having the sudden rush with which Aries can enter the world. A Libra birth attempts to be harmonious, with everything in order and in the right place, although it may be slower due to that need to evaluate 'situations' before proceeding, and can appear to be indecisive to the mother, who may have to endure several false starts before the final decision to emerge into the new world is made.

The child that emerges is often a very attractive baby, with appealing Venusian features and a lovable expression. Over time, many Libran's develop quite distinctly cut facial features, which have a look of refinement or delicacy about them, focused sometimes around a dominant nose.

Developing an ordered, rhythmic pattern of feeding and sleeping will suit the inner needs of the Libran baby, offering that sense of support and attention that the child needs. Over that first year of life, establishing order in the parent–child relationship will build a foundation of security that he will be able to develop from; if that is achieved, then it is unlikely that you will face many problems from an upset baby. You'll fall in love with his bewitching smile and charming nature, and feel very proud of him. He'll love being the centre of attention and admiration, absorbing all that adult focus and interest that he is being shown; he's likely to smile contentedly at every face that appears above him in his cot. Libra is a child who will need a lot of attention and almost constant company, and can become upset mainly through suddenly becoming aware that there is no one there within view; then he'll cry out, summoning you back again. At times this can become a little wearing, but it is best if you just acknowledge his need for company, and try to adjust your daily rhythms and routines to accommodate this need. Keeping him in a postition so that he can see you should be sufficient to keep him happy.

By the age of one to two, she's becoming mobile and more independent, although you can't relax yet because she's still demanding your immediate company; what distracts her now is that mobility, and the fact that she can begin to explore her environment on her own. If she hears music now, she's likely to respond quite energetically, enjoying her attempts to dance as well as gaining your applause and appreciation for her little performance. With her growing interest in colours and drawing, and her developing speech by the age of two, there are a few embryonic signs of what could become more prominent interests and talents as she grows older. She'll enjoy her toys, but what you may notice is a fairly short attention span and an inability to settle with one toy, especially if there are several scattered around. Choosing what to play with is difficult for her; she'll pick up several before quickly discarding them to go in search of another.

This indecision will become clearer between the ages of two and three, as his life enters a stage where there are increasing amounts of minor choices to be made. Helping him to choose, or limiting his possible choices of toys or kinds of food, can help him to focus more easily on his decisions. There should be no major problems with his toilet training, although establishing a pattern of regularity will be beneficial, and he'll want to perform successfully so that he receives your approval; so try not to admonish him too harshly when he makes those inevitable mistakes. These usually happen when the child is out of his familiar environment, such as in other houses or on shopping trips.

His artistic tendency will emerge more strongly as he spends time drawing, painting, or colouring, and he may begin to display a talent that is a little beyond his tender years, with a sense of colour harmony. Bedtime may become an area of trauma, mainly because he still hates being left alone, so be prepared if he fails to settle on his own, and creates all sorts of reasons to call for your attention or to get out of bed.

She's usually a well-behaved child, who will mix and socialize well with other children, as at playschool, which she'll be ready to join by the age of three. Taking that step is a crucial one for her; becoming independent from mother, being alone – even with a group of noisy, active children. Those first few times may be difficult, and she can become upset, but with perseverance and increasing familiarity with the new environment, together with recognizing that Mummy will come back to collect her, young Libra will begin to settle down and enjoy playing with the other children.

Between three and four, she may become more moody and changeable in temperament, perhaps becoming less acquiescent to your domination, and trying to assert her own will more – if only as a negative reaction against doing something she doesn't want to do. Libra can experience this phase a little later than some children, but it marks a turning point in her development; her own individuality grows stronger, and she becomes less of a reflection of you. Try not to attempt to dominate her so much, but allow her own nature more space to emerge, as she needs to assert her own identity before she starts school in a year or so. Even whilst you see her begin to draw away from you, she still needs plenty of love and support, although she may not openly display this need; so try to ensure that you give her lots of physical affection and reassurance.

Between the ages of four and five, it will become obvious that he's a child who comes alive when in company, and he plays easily and naturally with mixed groups at playschool, often acting as a harmonizing factor when childish disputes erupt. He's more suited to play which is supervised by adults, and can be unable to decide what to do if the playing time is free form and spontaneous; deciding for him, and ensuring that he is organized brings out the best in him. At times he can be quite argumentative, especially if he's experiencing a swing in moods; if he becomes too uncooperative, and if reasoned dialogue fails, a short spell of isolation can be effective in triggering off a more contrite and agreeable temperament. His interest in artistic pursuits is likely to intensify, and he will become very interested in the different environments that he experiences, evaluating their relative harmony factors and visual attractiveness. The beauty of animals will greatly interest him, and he may begin to want his own pets to look after. At the age of five, he can seem a little precocious in his attitudes, and will certainly be concerned about the impression that he is making on other people. He's quite adept at conversation, has good manners and is polite, seeming to be a little gentleman; although that will probably wear off after a few years at school! He has a more dignified style of personal assertion, and is entering a phase where he is obedient again.

THE LIBRA CHILD PERSONALITY

The inner quest which faces the Libran child is the ever-present search for balance and harmony in life; it is a difficult if not impossible challenge. Their motivating impulse of Libran children will be to balance the relationship between themselves and others, and in that process, they'll swing like pendulums between extremes of moods and behaviour. In several ways, the inner life of a Libran is that of a fluctuating sensitivity, often torn between selfish and selfless attitudes, and the difficulties of decision making.

Libran children are usually attractive, having an aura of refinement and sensitivity around them, although this is more of an alert mental sensitivity than an emotional one. As one of the main personal tasks of Libra is to be a fusion point for both emotions and intellect – Water and Air – the internal bias and balance is already tipped towards favouring the mind; Libra has a problem in integrating emotions back into harmony, and often becomes emotionally selfish and immature as a consequence of such a failure. Yet there is a strong magnetic energy which appears to attract people towards them – as perhaps could be expected in social relationships – but this is not a consistent attraction. Often the energy fluctuates, and the relationship ties dissolve quickly, and your Libran child may have many friends and playmates, but few who remain constant over time. Because that inner Libra energy acts like an ever-adjusting pendulum, at times that attractive energy can become a repulsing one, and friendships can become temporary and superficial unless that inner balance is properly harmonized. Because of this, your child could feel confused as to the mutability of friendships at times, although it is likely that because of his sociable nature there will always be friends around him.

The social dimension of life is vitally important to Libra, who also wants to be socially admired and liked by others. As she can find her life confusing, with its mood changes, and phases of interest and apathy, she develops a tendency to rely upon others to provide her with a reflection of her own nature. Libra can be greatly influenced by others, and as she wants to maintain her relationships, she is likely to be swayed in her actions and choices by a dominant parent or friend. As there is that sense of personal insecurity, she tends to act in ways that will gain approval from others who are important to her, such as parents, so that most of her actions are determined by what she believes others want from her. Allied to the challenge of being decisive, this can create future problems in independent self-assertion.

He's unsure of his emotions, and probably attempts to deny and repress them in many instances, because he's uncomfortable with the feelings that are stimulated within. You should realize that young Libra needs considerable love and support, but because of this emotional inhibition is often unable to ask for it openly, and reach out to receive it from loving parents and family. Libra often seems unable to understand properly the process of giving and receiving love in a natural manner, and can become reticent about appearing even to need such human emotional needs, giving the impression that he is cold or indifferent. An acceptance and relaxation into the soothing and healing waters of love can help to balance him enormously; he needs this, but fails to accept it easily, owing to emotional confusion. As a parent, try to ensure that there is plenty of physical affection and obvious love displayed to the young child and, as he grows older and more independent, remember that this need is still present and needs to be satisfied in him. Libra often displays a possessive attitude, an attempt to dominate others as a way to ensure that the person remains there whilst Libran's emotional needs are tied into that person. It can seem to be one-way traffic as Libra absorbs from the other but fails to return any love; this is a sign of the Libran selfishness and emotional immaturity.

Libra can appear to be quite self-sufficient and independent, but with a sign that is founded upon relationships this is just an illusion; the opposite is true, and the ideal state for Libra to exist within is that of interdependence, which is a mature awareness of the reality of life. Unfortunately, Libra often becomes dependent on others. You should ensure that your Libra child does not spend excessive amounts of time alone, because this tends to destroy the natural Libran role in life, often creating changes in their personal temperament which forces them to become introspective. This is really the wrong direction for them to move towards, and will cut them off from the social vitality that they need, as Libra is more extro-vertedly inclined.

You'll soon learn that Libra has a problem with decision making when he's still a pre-school child. Giving him choices and asking him what he wants to do . . . and then waiting . . . and waiting . . . and waiting for an answer is a certain route towards frustration and a rising impatience. What you'll probably do is make all decisions for him yourself – as it seems to be the only way to ensure that anything gets done – and yet this can't really be the answer. He'll just rely on you then and his ability to choose will remain undeveloped and pose future problems for him. Whilst acknowledging that you should avoid a possible nervous breakdown waiting for his decisions, the best way is to help him to learn how to be decisive. It will certainly be of great value to him in adult life, and indeed could positively transform his future.

Libra tends to see life in terms of decision problems, all of equal importance, irrespective of many being relatively trivial, and she dislikes being forced to choose in a hurry. Underlying this is a deep fear of being wrong, of making a mistake which devalues her personal confidence in her judgement. As her mind likes to be active, it tends to indulge itself with the issue of choices, wrapping itself around the problem, evaluating and considering it from every angle, turning it over and over; until it reaches a point where the decision-making will seizes up, and the mind doesn't know which way to go. This can be a problem with the Air signs; too much analysis and consideration leads to a lack of natural spontaneity and decisiveness. Water signs decide by that intuitive 'gut reaction', Fire by an impulsive spontaneous leap, and Earth by being cautious and following the established path.

So, how can you help Libra overcome this problem? When the situation is determined by time constraints, take control and offer them no choices, so that they do as you want, such as in dressing for school in the morning. When it's a non-important situation for you, give them options, let them have both the time and responsibility to decide for themselves. If it's within their own playtime, it doesn't really affect you if they take an hour to decide what shoes they intend to wear; the only one who either benefits or loses from that process is them. Eventually, they'll learn how to make their own satisfactory decisions, more quickly and efficiently, and how to determine the relative importance of choices in either trivial or more important situations, thus gaining a sense of perspective too. A few lost hours caused by indecision can help to shape them up!

The environment surrounding your Libran child is extremely important and influential to his development, whether it is the family home, school or his social life, physical environment or 'subjective atmosphere'. He has an intrinsic aesthetic sensitivity, which includes visual and sound stimulation, a psychic awareness and sensitivity to material building structures and furnishings. If the environment is ugly, dirty and unpleasant, then part of his temperament will shrink away from involvement, inhibiting his natural style of expression, and throwing him out of balance, creating an unsettled inner state. Harmonious order is what he needs, a civilized, cultured, pleasant atmosphere surrounding him will encourage his development. Discordant sound and strong primary colours have a negative impact, whilst a more tastefully designed decor of pastel shades and visually harmonious design suits his sensitivity. Libra tends to reflect the environment that he is spending time in; if he starts to become agitated and disruptive and acts out of character, then it could perhaps be the influence of a school classroom that is affecting him, with its undercurrent of noise and tension.

School violence or aggressive behaviour can also upset him, as he naturally hates violence, loving peace and a cultured lifestyle.

Your own relationship as a parents will also have a profound influence upon her. She'll register those intangible undercurrents of the state of your relationship too, as well as observe the outer display of your mutual behaviour. If there's friction and tension between you, then expect Libra to show some signs of being disturbed, perhaps through withdrawing from her relationship with you, because it becomes too painful for her.

She'll also need to create a private environment for herself within her bedroom, where she takes responsibility for 'designing' the decor if possible, and for organizing the furniture – that is, if you can stand the strain of waiting for her decisions to be made, but let's hope that you've helped to sort her out on that when she was younger! Perhaps try to cooperate with her and help her develop personal ideas for her room, making suggestions and guiding her towards making appropriate decisions with which she'll be content.

This sensitivity often develops towards an artistic appreciation and inclination, where that innate love of beauty and harmony can be developed and cultivated by the caring parent. Guidance by you can enhance the child's future prospects once they begin to display this artistic or musical ability, and it is likely that any future work containing some artistic element or personal expression should be the direction that the child is encouraged to look towards.

Concentrated and conscientious perseverance can be lacking in Libra, as their minds act like butterflies, moving rapidly from one interest to another without staying with anything for very long. Superficial knowledge and being a 'jack of all trades and master of none' can occur due to a lack of sustained disciplined effort. One way to help him develop a longer attention span, and achieve higher levels of knowledge and skill, is to become a co-partner with him on home projects, so that both of you work together to achieve an agreed objective. He'll enjoy that; both your focused company and support will help him to unfold his latent abilities.

By adolescence, you'll see that Libran nature quite clearly, as several of its major characteristics can be hard to discern in the younger child unless you know how to perceive them. For instance, Libra can be accused of stubborn resistance, but their lack of response is just that failure of decision-making, or some could see them as rebels, when all they are doing is trying to consider or present another point of view. Misunderstanding children's attempts at communication is common, both by parents and teachers, and one of the purposes of this book is to offer guidelines in understanding children's personalities and styles of individual expression through the perspective of astrological types.

The Libran adolescence will be socially orientated, mixing with a large variety of friends, being preoccupied with all the relationship issues that arise at this stage. She's liable to be more moody, as that inner balance swings more widely and regularly under the impact of her personal changes and those of her friends. Young Libra will serve as a magnet and mediator between her friends and their early romantic experiences. Relationship threads will intertwine around her, and she'll become a confidante to several friends. Sometimes, she can act to restore harmony between friends, as her effective charm and persuasion can build bridges between hurt feelings and mutual misunderstandings. She hates conflict, any conflict, and tries to smooth it all away.

The pleasure-loving side will emerge stronger in him now, and his attraction towards teenage romances will begin to absorb more of his time and attention. That pendulum can swing so much that it seems in danger of breaking away from the fulcrum! The likelihood is that young relationships will not last long, both because of his own inconsistency and need for new stimulation, and because of his often vacillating decision-making confusing the situation. He'll get hurt, but probably not as deeply as you may assume; superficially yes, but you may be wrong if you assume that his emotional response goes deep; at this stage in his life his involvement will not be too deep or intense. He is just beginning to test the depths of real human relationships where emotions are shaken and stirred.

There's a Libran trait which displays that rebalancing process. Sometimes after a phase of socializing and perhaps a teenage romance, she'll suddenly seem to want to withdraw, to almost hide away from her friends, swinging from an extroverted temperament to one which resembles introversion. It is this pattern of periodic activity and then inactivity that recharges her batteries and stops her becoming too unbalanced.

He will seem to be fairly responsible and mature for his age. Because of the degree of consideration that he brings to decisions, his cautious nature can become a positive quality, in that conscious thought has been made prior to action. This should prevent him from becoming involved in reckless, dangerous and foolhardy teenage actions, which can cause worry to many a parent. It would be a rare Libra that would get involved in aggression or violence, or even anti-social actions, unless his environment or negative influences around him had twisted his natural temperament, and his inner balance was so distorted that he had to work out this pent-up frustration and confusion in that way.

As an attempt to buttress their personalities, some male Librans try to be argumentative with close family members, trying to 'score points' by demonstrating their greater intellectual knowledge. It can be most irritating for adults if the child is trying to assert himself in this way, but it is mainly an attempt to inflate their own uneasy self-confidence and, after all, who is the safest to try this with? You are . . . He will not respond easily to direct conflict, usually retreating when he's sure of your opposition to anything he has just said or proposed; open confrontation is not his style, and he can appear to be quite pliable and easy to influence. But Libra can only be really influenced by someone when it agrees with his own personal decision; he'll often seek another's opinion for support, and the real problem he faces is making that clear decision in the first place.

In family disagreements, Libra responds well to reasoned explanations; provided they understand your reasons, they will usually conform to your authority. Appealing to fairness and their sense of social obligation and responsibility should work, or if they genuinely feel that their point of view is being totally ignored, some degree of discussion to reach a compromise should be productive for mutual harmony. Whilst the male Libran will try to be reasonable, the Libra female is more inclined to use her femininity to gain her way. She will be absorbed in becoming the young woman, preoccupied with her looks and clothes and in being attractive. She can appear to be more superficial than the boy, and is often quite frivolous and flirtatious, taking full advantage of the 'allowable change-ability' granted to women, which is just a mask for that traditional Libran problem of choice! Libra wants to be self-assertive but has difficulty in recognizing which way to choose. The mirror becomes important in the female Libran's home, as does the bathroom; beauty and harmony must rule.

The Libra challenge is to unite their emotions into that cooler mental perspective on life; otherwise lurking under that ordered and controlled appearance lie those repressed wilder emotions and feelings that have been denied. All relationships, social and intimate are constantly evaluated by that mind, until sometimes the vitalizing emotional content becomes lost. Head and heart need to coexist; this is the nature of the Libran scales where moderation and equilibrium are essential to discover, both in the individual and society.

THE LIBRA CHILD AND EDUCATION

Libran children are usually quite intelligent and mentally alert, reflecting the fact that Libra is an Air sign, but throughout their school life there can be a question mark over their application and full use of their many and varied personal talents. This can eventually result in becoming what has been termed in academic circles an 'under-achiever', although that is a concept related to projected expectations by teachers and parents, and does not necessarily have any relevance to the actual quality of the Libra child.

Yet this does indicate one of the facets of educating the Libran child, in that both teachers and parents have a responsibility to help Libra unfold and apply her many talents and personal potential. Wise guidance is necessary to encourage her to realize that she is much more capable than she believes or has achieved so far. Libra can have a sense of insecurity based on their problem of indecision, and in that struggle to choose and decide, the energy to actually do anything can fizzle away. Additionally, most Librans lack any natural motivation to fully express their real potential, withdrawing from the effort that may be required to be successful. If the child is not consistently encouraged and motivated by a parent, or lacks a powerful wilful Ascendant (like Scorpio) that can come through in later years, then that effort is unlikely to be made. Libra is not really an ambitious spirit, and is more naturally attuned to perform a balancing role in society and between people; if a Libran displays an aggressively ambitious attitude, then it is likely to have been absorbed from a dominant parent.

At school, the child will be sociable and friendly, acquiring a wide group of friends and playmates. Libra loves communicating, and is often very talkative as a major method of self-expression. The environment will be important to their well-being, and to draw the best out of them, they'll need to be settled in a reasonably pleasing and civilized school, where the general level of behaviour is good. Otherwise, they'll only become distracted, and the surrounding discord and conflict will slowly have an increasingly negative effect upon their ability at school. Order is important to Libra, and with that more intellectually biased mind, organization and structure is appealing too, and they will often try to create an ordered pattern in their own life attempting to discover that inner balance.

What can become noticeable with Libra is her tendency to enthusiastically embrace a new idea which happens to stimulate her mind into activity, almost seeming to create a temporary 'obsession' as the idea opens up all sorts of new possibilities for her, yet which can suddenly disappear as interest wanes, and that 'spark' is then struck by a new, fascinating idea. Her problem can be lack of consistency and perseverance; not just in attractions to ideas and interests, but in most areas of her developing life. The adult Libran can have problems with all kinds of long-term commitments, as a natural tendency is to follow those passing temporary fascinations, and most lifestyles are too fixed (through marriage, children, work) to easily allow the sort of flexibility that Libra may prefer.

As the Libra child will need a variety of interests to occupy him at school and home, his education progress is likely to be erratic if he fails to be genuinely interested in his studies. He can appear to be quite apathetic and lazy at times, but that is just the outer display of a loss of interest; he'll soon come alive again as soon as a new idea catches his mind. As the child grows older, a solid foundation of more longer-lasting interests will probably accumulate, and potential directions for the adult life may begin to appear.

The problem of completing school work is one that the young Libran can face, especially once the first flush of enthusiasm has worn away; as many education techniques require continuous assessment and extensive project work, this can work against Libra receiving high grades if the child lapses into this tendency of losing interest. Some support and supervision may be valuably given by a concerned parent so that they establish a consistent pattern of studying along regular and methodically organized times, whilst simultaneously ensuring that they have sufficient time too for relaxation and to pursue any personal interests.

Libra has an enquiring mind; curiosity is a great driving force for her, and will create an underlying motivation for many of her choices and actions in life. Even though a main strand of that mental temperament is towards intellectual concerns, there is a parallel and balancing interest towards the artist and dramatic flamboyant dimension of life, as noted in the possible ideal Libran careers. This artistic sensitivity is perhaps more intellectually inclined than one arising from the emotions and feelings, in that it is the ideas mediated through art and music that appeal and interest rather than a sensually felt creative experience. As Libra is so people orientated, the child could move towards drama at school, or some kind of performance art for a possible audience, perhaps music. Great encouragement should be given to the child if they display such interests, guiding them towards exploring and unfolding their talents in a naturally compatible direction.

Despite the traditional Libran love of interpersonal harmony, once he's capable of reading and learning for himself, he can become argumentative regarding facts, so be prepared. In many parent–child conversations with him, you'll start to notice that he wants both sides of any topic, and that he intuitively recognizes that there is a least one point of view on a topic that you are not referring to or considering. This will be clear when it involves a family matter, and he wants to know what someone else thinks too. This is the Libran love of balance, justice and fair play shining through. He hates a distorted bias, and can easily join the other side just to reassert equality again. Sometimes he'll act in a contradictory manner because of this inner impulse and, because he's keen on that type of antagonistic debate, can take the position of devil's advocate, joining the 'underdogs' in his view. It could be valuable for a teacher or parent to understand this Libran tendency, so that the child is not misunderstood. Receiving the full picture is what Libra demands, and a partial statement or piece of information leaves him inwardly unsatisfied and feeling incomplete, hence his additional requests for further information or other points of view. It can be a positive request really, as it can open an adult's often fixed personal way of perceiving events to include a much broader inclusive panorama, often creating new insights in the process. Teachers can often get stuck in a rut of presenting material the same way, year after year, without ever gaining a new perspective on it; a questioning Libra can create a new angle with which to look at the familiar. In a similar way, children often serve to make parents look again at aspects of life that have grown boring through familiarity, or to perceive the ordinary world through the child's eyes, restoring that quality of mystery and fascination again.

This can seem quite frustrating to you at times, especially if it becomes an habitual pattern of response. The likely time for this is during adolescence, when she's more capable of successfully holding her ground against an adult, and is more interested in testing her mettle in confrontatory situations. Yet this is often not done through a genuine sense of agreement with another side; it is purely an intellectual game that Libra is playing, balancing the scales, and one where awareness can be lacking as to the impact such expression can have on parents, teachers and friends. The real Libra influence is harmony, and she is rarely a rebel, unless she genuinely feels a need to love and act in such a way as to oppose someone or a dominating social attitude; then she will strive to restore balance in her own way.

Libra usually responds well to school discipline and rules, and is not a mischievous or troublesome type, unless he becomes involved with a group of awkward children. Then a tendency to depend and lean on others could make him behave in an untypical manner, as he tries to act in a way that such a peer group expects of him; he can be influenced by others, especially as his indecision erodes his personal will-power.

LIBRA CAREERS

The two main aspects of ideal Libran career are those which involve either expressing that artistic temperament, or working with people. Libra can become a creative fluent dancer, a musician or singer, or an actor where the more flamboyant, extroverted, socialite dimension of the sign can emerge in a dramatic guise. Part of that appeal is to impress others, as well as the inner motivation to express personal talents. More solitary creative pursuits can suit the other aspect of the Libran personality, such as becoming a writer or painter, where the gift of communication and facility with words can be applied, and that gift of visual harmony and appreciation can flow through colours. Most Libran art would be intrinsically harmonious and balanced, often in good taste and stylish in essence, and would rarely express discordant clashing colours or content. A Libran writing style would have an elegance, a sensitive delicacy and wit, although could suffer from a surfeit of style and superficiality and lack real depth.

These talents can also find a place in architecture, interior design or anything to do with the consumer market where beauty, design and visual attractiveness are important in creating a congenial, satisfying, and suitable environment. Currently much effort is being made to build pleasing environments, in offices and public places as well as in homes. Personal beauty is another sphere where Libran talents could be useful, such as beauty specialists, hairstylists, and in perfume and cosmetics. Libra is ruled by Venus, so all aspects of the modern woman and the attractive stylish man who is fashion conscious can benefit from the style and taste of Libra.

The intensity and competitiveness of the commercial business world is perhaps too immoral and unsubtle for Libra, whose ability to be decisive and take the initiative could be lacking. But Libra could find a suitable role in the marketing and public relations or personnel side of an enterprise, or through offering administrative services to executives, such as conference facilities. Some Librans prefer to aim higher, to have careers in a more cultured sphere of life, where international diplomacy may offer a satisfying lifestyle of travel and sophisticated communication; or in spheres of the international art and antiques market, becoming a connoisseur and dealer, mixing with wealthy clientele.

That need for relationships, and the emphasis on the personal factor, can lead towards social and welfare work, especially if the Libran heart has been touched, or the early environment has sowed the seeds of a sense of social responsibility. Community work appeals greatly to some Librans, who consider it an expression of re-establishing balance and harmony within society, trying to restore concepts of equality and fair play for all, irrespective of colour, nationality or creed. If Libra moves into this direction, then it is likely to become a personal crusade to reclaim order from perceived chaos, expressing that ideal of social duty and the 'impossible dream of a perfect world'.

SCORPIO
(OCTOBER 23 TO NOVEMBER 21)

Planetary Ruler: Pluto, Mars

Element type	Water
Type	Negative/Feminine
Triplicity	Fixed
Symbol	♏
Image	The Scorpion, The Eagle
Part of Body	Genitals, bladder, rectum
Theme of Self	I Desire
Key Qualities	Will, resourcefulness, secrecy, transformation
House Affinity	8th House

Famous Scorpio Personalities: Prince Charles, Jawaharlal Nehru, Indira Gandhi, Charles de Gaulle, Robert Kennedy, Billy Graham, Richard Burton, Grace Kelly, Pablo Picasso, John Cleese, Kim Wilde, Kenneth Baker MP.

THE PRE-SCHOOL SCORPIO CHILD

Births which involve either a Scorpio Sun sign or Ascendant, and sometimes Pluto placed near the Ascendant in the 1st House, can be associated with 'life and death dramas'. What this tends to imply is that the birth may be traumatic in some respect, or where the birth is the culmination of a period of concern, perhaps to do with the well-being of the child, or a concern regarding the health of the mother. As examples, one case involved the trauma of a forceps birth, another needed a Caesarean section performed, a third had worries about the mother's past health, or it could be a personal drama related to

136

a long period of attempting conception, or a pregnancy after a previous miscarriage or stillbirth. Be assured that such drama is not inevitable and many Scorpio births are quite normal.

Often it appears that the new Scorpio child is not very happy with her emergence into this world. She may tend to cry quite a lot during those early months, perhaps as a reaction to the comfort and immersion of the womb phase, which would fulfil the watery affinity of Scorpio. In fact, the child will like to deeply withdraw from the world, and takes great offence at being woken from any deep sleep, so it may be best to allow the natural rhythms of the child to operate without disturbance. Whenever she wants feeding, changing, comforting, you'll be informed; it will be hard not to hear her demands! And she can be very demanding and persistent in her attempts to gain her own way. Before long, she'll be paying distinct attention to her surrounding environment, and you'll start to sense that her bright, alert mind and senses are busily absorbing and processing her new experiences. She may be a little resistant to adapting to new changes in her 'lifestyle', and tends to prefer the comforting familiarity of regular routines and schedules. She tends to approach anything new with a degree of caution, checking it out before allowing herself to enter the experience. You'll probably observe that after she can focus her eyes and have some control over their movement, that she can tend to fix her vision on something and stare at it intently, almost entering a quiet semi-trance-like state of concentration and focus. Through this, she's trying to sense beyond the appearance of the object, and in the process contact her own depths. It's the early signs of the infamous Scorpio penetrating stare! By the end of the first year, she'll be thoroughly enjoying the delights of water and bathtime.

Between the ages of one and two, young Scorpio is a great enjoyer of his physical senses and sensual appreciation of the world. Physical exertion and rough-and-tumble seem to be great fun, and there can be a early enjoyment of playing with balls, kicking or holding and trying to run with them. A later

Scorpio trait is shown in the early demonstration of perseverance when the child is faced with learning new skills, it is a 'I will not be beat' attitude that can impress you when watching his efforts in walking, talking or doing simple things. If he has become too tired to be successful though, then signs of anger and frustration can also be displayed at his own temporary failure. But come tomorrow . . . Unlike Gemini children, for instance, who flit quickly from one toy to another, young Scorpio tends to favour a few special toys, and you'll notice that most of his time spent playing with toys tends to involve these favourite few. Toilet training may be a little erratic, and his progress can be a little slow, but developing a regular routine should help to improve the situation if the problem of training persists. When he's in company, he can seem shy and quiet, but this is because he's intent on trying to work out the nature of the stranger before he decides to have anything to do with him. This is much like the adult Scorpio who always checks out people before beginning to open himself to them. 'Friend or foe' is the unspoken challenge!

By the age of three, the child is showing signs of self-sufficiency, in that she is capable of keeping herself occupied, playing alone and enjoying it. She still needs a fairly fixed routine structure around her – which offers security – and can be very sensitive to parental attitudes and treatment. Any kind of rejection is felt very deeply and painfully, so be aware of any signs of excessive impatience or anger that you may show in some situations. She may go to a playschool now, or mix with other children more, and it can seem that she is a self-confident child in such an environment, often being a 'leader' and a dominating figure in play. She is more aware now of family life, and this is an important security for her and gives her a sense of belonging. She may question you about the 'family', and seem intrigued by the concepts of uncles, aunts, cousins, grandparents, and all, and this serves to build a foundation of tradition and roots for her. Usually she can be quite loving, although the ways that she expresses this may be subtle and sophisticated at times, and she doesn't often display exuberant physical demonstration of love for parents; she tries to express it as a natural part of her daily relationship with you and the family. What may seem more apparent sometimes are those times of family upsets with her, when her revenging spirit is unleashed and she can make all sorts of nasty threats at whoever has upset her.

This dual side to their nature becomes more apparent by the age of four. Sometimes it shows itself through unsettling dreams, and over-active imaginative nightmares and fears of the dark when things go bump and ghostly presences cluster around their bed, whilst they cower in fright under the bed-clothes. Leaving some lights on and regular reassurance can help them to pass through this phase successfully. There is, however, a part of them that enjoys such fears, as they help to inspire intensity, and all Scorpios look for that in later life. You'll wonder just what type of child your Scorpio is, as they display both good and bad aspects to their nature – will they be a 'saint or sinner' is a Scorpio-type dilemma! Their nature can seem very erratic and contradictory now, and their behaviour can be likewise. They are reasonably competent in daily life and tend to complete any tasks that they have started.

As she approaches the age of five, she may become a little withdrawn, sometimes more negative and moody, and at playschool can tend to become an observer rather than joining in; part of this is a reaction towards those changes and contradictory pulls that are occurring deep within her, making her less self-confident at this time. By five years old, this phase is still active, and she is expressing a more cautious spirit, being less dominant, more self-conscious and keeping her own company. She tends to enjoy her times of privacy more, and occupies herself well, although she does value adult company and may sit quietly in the room listening to adult conversation. She's starting to want to grow up now, to participate in the adult world, the one that appears to be so fascinating to her, so full of excitement and wonder, and she's beginning to prepare for her grand entrance. You may feel that somewhere you've lost touch with her, that an intimate communication has started to break down. Part of this is the more adult-orientated mask that she is building around herself; the inscrutable Scorpio mask, which reveals only what Scorpio wants it to reveal. You'll wonder just what is going on in there . . . especially when she's upset, and she just glares back at you, refusing to say anything, and withdraws into a brooding silence. More than likely she's repressing those volatile and passionate feelings, afraid of allowing them to escape into the outer world, and this of course can pose problems later on in life.

THE SCORPIO CHILD PERSONALITY

Having a Scorpio child is a challenge. At times you may have a glimpse of 'something other' coexisting with your child's personality, perhaps in the way they suddenly look at you, penetrating through all of your defences, touching your secret inner self, and then disconcertingly smile knowingly. Scorpio is the most mysterious of the twelve signs, and probably the most difficult to comprehend, because essentially it concerns the mysteries of duality; light–dark, good–evil, angels–devils, life–death, profound issues that puzzle many an inquiring adult. It's hard enough to understand your own nature, let alone your child's who sits at the doorway to such mysteries!

Unless you are also a Water sign (Cancer or Pisces), you will probably fail to sense the sheer depth and power of the passionate, emotional, feeling nature of the Scorpio child. Scorpio is like an ocean compared to rivers or streams, but an ocean that is well aware of its powers to support life and to take it. The energy of Scorpio is one which poses great problems for many in natal charts, especially when it is in Ascendant or has several major planets placed in its sign, or a strong Pluto emphasis. Natural Sun sign Scorpios can learn how to live with its power, but other astrological signs can have great difficulty.

Being a parent of a Scorpio is more like a guardianship,

because all you can really do is to try to ensure that the powerful influence of your child is directed towards positive and constructive social ends, so that as an adult he is walking the right path. Most Scorpios are very independent at an early age, quite self-sufficient and determined to go their own way. As a Scorpio parent you know what this means! From an early age that intense will shines through, and you'll have many a battle with young Scorpio if he sets his mind against you. If you stand your ground, and don't capitulate in battle, firmly saying 'No', then eventually he'll begin to respect your strength and will grudgingly and perhaps temporarily acquiesce to your will in admiring acknowledgement of your current superiority. But it's only a short-term defeat, the war isn't lost yet! When he's older and stronger . . . Yet conflict is not inevitable with young Scorpios. Most are quite well behaved, rarely showing their real hidden nature, except when it is very important to him or has some personal meaning.

Scorpio can be misleading. A quiet temperament can disguise that inner strength, conserve its power through allowing it to build in secret, never wasting it on superficial pursuits. Even when she is playing games with other children, young Scorpio wants to win and is testing her ability to dominate. She may have no intention of abusing that position once achieved; knowing that she 'has the power' is often quite sufficient. Scorpio has considerable self-confidence in her abundant capabilities, but she can fail to really apply herself to reach her true potential. Challenging her rarely fails; if you even suggest that something is beyond her, then she's likely to strive to prove that it isn't, by achieving that target. As she grows older, it will be her own privately created challenges that will motivate her into sustained action. She has little regard for the opinions of others, and can become indifferent to them, providing she is attaining her own private ambitions. She goes her own way through life.

Scorpios respond to the world through their feelings, with a natural psychic intuitive sensitivity. Their emotions tend

141

towards being extremist; lukewarm feelings do not stir them, only intensity and passion awakens the Scorpio nature. This is the hidden source of the Scorpio mystery and power; that beneath an often cool, controlled temperament lies a raging emotional volcano which can – under great pressure – erupt. It's an inner pressure that they control with great natural skill, releasing it as if there was a controlling valve in situations where the energy is required. Hidden within a calm and relaxed personality, is a volatile inner self, which at some point will burst out into the open, probably during adolescence or a little later.

The younger child may display this through periodic mood changes and phases of withdrawal; it's as if relative isolation and quietness enables her to contain and control her emotional reservoir. Some Scorpios may suddenly erupt into surprising anger and aggression. Either style of energy discharge should be carefully handled and accepted, although excessive aggression should be diverted towards healthier channels such as releasing it through physical exertion and sports. The competitive aspect of sport should not be overemphasized, as Scorpio already intends to win or be first, and overheating that aggressive and assertive spirit through competitiveness can draw out several of the more socially negative Scorpio characteristics. Another effective outlet is the use of imagination in play, where the energy is diverted into fuelling a powerful imagination. In the Scorpio male, war games are fought out between toy soldiers, and the realm of imagination becomes the battleground quite safely. Care too should be taken in monitoring that the young Scorpio is not sinking into moods of emotionally resentful brooding, excessive secrecy or jealousy, because if such a habit pattern becomes established, then these festering poisons can seriously warp the unfolding personality. Scorpio has that darker side close to the surface.

Mentioning the 'darker side' recalls the traditional Scorpio 'sting' in the tail. Often the source of this is the emotional extremism and intensity of Scorpio, and a need to exact a suitable revenge against anyone who has the temerity to hurt them in any way. Like the 'elephant's memory', Scorpio never forgets either, and many a relationship is soured by this tendency, which even operates when the conscious mind is forgiving. Somewhere, sometime, that sting suddenly hits someone who has crossed swords with a Scorpio; the saying 'Hell hath no fury like woman scorned' was directed towards the female Scorpio. In younger children, the sting is toned down a little, but still quite effective, and taking action to 'get their own back' will be made, quite deliberately too, as the means of revenge has been carefully considered. Most may dislike the concept of revenge, yet, to a Scorpio mind, it is merely the means to restore balance: to punish someone who has caused pain. It is akin to the Judaic 'an eye for an eye' approach, although in Scorpio's case, two eyes would probably be taken just to drill the message home. . . . In order to make their mark on the adversary, Scorpio is willing to endure more pain to do so; revenge is sweet – to that temperament – and satisfying. It's hard to imagine your child being like that, but scratch any Scorpio and watch out for the return blow, when you least expect it.

For parents, it can be a difficult balance to achieve in raising the Scorpio child, one that might easily fail through a lack of understanding of the complex nature of this personality type. To draw the best out of your child requires sensitivity and a faith in her that 'something inside knows what is best for her', so that as she grows older, you are not constantly clashing will to will over provocative issues. Scorpio is a very independent sign, and hates authority over her or being ordered to do things, the attitude being 'I will if I want to'. The child will certainly need clearly defined parameters of behaviour and discipline, but, provided that there is mutual respect between parents and child, this should pose no insuperable problems, and Scorpio will probably conform sufficiently to them. Acknowledging the child's ability to make decisions is a major step, and trying to accommodate that will into daily living is very beneficial, giving Scorpio choices and allowing him to experience the resulting consequences; imposing your will on him will only stimulate opposition and conflict. Treating the child in a serious, responsible manner through discussion and reason will evoke a correspondingly mature response from Scorpio. Sometimes it may seem that young Scorpio is more mature and intellectually superior than you are, based on the attitudes they express. The parent–child relationship is not just a one-way learning exchange; parents can learn a lot about themselves when their behaviour is mirrored back by a child.

Because of Scorpio's empathic intuition related to people's emotions and environments, there is often a natural grasp of psychological complexities, which whilst they cannot perhaps be clearly expressed by the child, are still deeply felt. The home is of vital importance to the child, and should ideally be full of all the more positive enhancing emotions that a family love and life can provide. Unfortunately, this is not always the case, especially in the modern world with the increase in divorce and separation. Scorpio will soak up all the emotional home atmosphere, and this will have a powerful impact on their psychological development and the patterns of attitudes that will influence later adult choices. The child will much prefer parents to be direct and honest, because she'll sense deception anyway, and growing up with a deep impression that adults do not tell the truth is not healthy, adding more social suspicion and doubt into her relationships. Scorpio usually strongly supports home life and family values, viewing it with a traditional sense of respect and acknowledging its importance.

You'll probably find that the core of your relationship with Scorpio lies deep under the surface, more of a subjective meeting place than a close objective contact, a non-verbal emotionally intuitive bond that is mutually recognized, yet is rarely spoken about, because really there is no need. It is private, a sense of mutual knowing, strong, sensitive and unchanging. You've been welcomed into the world of Scorpio, the ocean beneath the tangible earth. All that you can do is to help socialize Scorpio sufficiently to adequately fit into the world, encouraging those qualities that help adaptation to the world as it is.

Scorpio will see this world through serious eyes, and an open heart. Despite that tendency of 'balancing revenge', there is a real sensitivity to suffering in the world, and a desire to alleviate some of that suffering. Real problems and issues can begin to attract Scorpio's attention, and the child begins to display less interest in time-wasting games of no significance or intrinsic value. The focus begins to shift to interests that imply an underlying meaning with some real point to them, that really affect the world or people; superficial pursuits – for entertainment value only – are progressively dispensed with by the maturing Scorpio.

The Scorpio child tends to dream great dreams, seeing a future bright with achievement or the attainment of a secret destiny that time has unfolded. Encourage these dreams, because it is through the focus of a distinct challenge that the real strengths of a Scorpio emerges. That perceptive, discerning, probing mind and powerful will need a personal mountian to climb. When there is no accepted challenge, there is no motivation or incentive, and young Scorpio conserves their inner power into an intense concentration of energy. Your role is to guide Scorpio towards challenging and beneficial paths. Once that will is fixed to that personal aim, the self-discipline and perseverance of the child will be focused. This is what Scorpio needs, because the natural capacity for endurance and application is very impressive, and the objective will be strived for with a wholehearted spirit. This also invokes that obsessive tendency of Scorpio, where 'tunnel vision' occurs, and the total personal focus is turned towards the destined direction; this ability also conveys the method Scorpio uses to achieve aims, through will and natural talent. Scorpio and obsession walk side by side, generating the fuel of intensity and achievement, which is compatible with their inner nature. This is why it is so important to ensure that the child is travelling a constructive and productive path.

Scorpio is not usually an extrovert as a child, although she will be friendly and sociable enough. Until she gets to know someone better, she can be wary of establishing friendships, always keeping something of herself back and only slowly revealing selected aspects of her nature to carefully selected friends. Close relationships are few, and with such friends Scorpio offers considerable personal affection and loyalty; emotional bonds are formed in Scorpio which persist for a long time, even when the winds of life blow people in different directions. Loyalty is a key quality in such friendships, and the young Scorpio can expect the same from others, and be very disappointed and upset when such expectations are shattered. Emotional blows are experienced very deeply, and if rejected the emotional scars take a long time to heal, and even then their memory retains the personal anguish.

This can be especially evident by the teenage years, when Scorpio is swept by the transformation into adulthood. Many Scorpio children tend to withdraw into their own inner life at this time, and do not display many outward signs of the changes that they are passing through. It is like a private initiation process that they enter deep within, with privacy warnings established around them, carrying messages saying 'Danger, Keep Out'. Young Scorpio is rapidly moving away from parental bonds now, almost regenerating and being reborn into the new path of the adult life. The tendency is to become more taciturn and reserved; a strong silence is common, and many parents lose touch with their Scorpio children during this phase. They have become preoccupied with their own inner psychology and emotional well-being, and they sense that what is occurring to them at this time is too important and fragile to be exposed to others who are less sensitive.

With a private period of mourning, but also with a mounting excitement at the promise of the future, Scorpio is shedding off the skin of childhood. The imagination is very rich in the teenage years, and looks for stimulation in imaginative fiction or films, such as fantasy, science fiction, comics, myths, adventures, monsters and horror. It is to these more fanciful productions of the human mind that Scorpio looks for fascination and entertainment, interests which often spill over into adult tastes; anything that is considered to be taboo or forbidden tends to fascinate the Scorpio mind, which is associated with the eighth natal house and the themes of rebirth, the occult and hidden secrets. Where any mystery is to be found, Scorpio arrives, waiting to probe and investigate. Other themes which have a great attraction are the mysteries of sex, death, drugs and the physical elements of fire and water. This is the Scorpio attraction towards the darker side of life, and the irresistible intensity of those socially taboo themes.

Yet it may need stating that an acknowledgement and acceptance of their existence in the human personality is much more psychologically healthy than denial, rejection or repression, which can then erupt into uncontrollable, aggressive violent outbursts against others. Confronting private fears and phobias is ultimately liberating and health enhancing.

You may also begin to observe a more clearly formulated personal philosophy emerging from your child, which reveals the depth, power and passion of their idealistic conviction and self-assertion. Scorpios have looked at the world, and have made their minds up, creating a directional foundation for themselves to follow in their exploration of the adult world. This will be intellectually framed, but will also contain an inspirational emotional charge as its essence. Your Scorpio child has reached the point where they can declare 'I am what I am', and be prepared to follow their star towards that destiny that they feel is beckoning to them.

THE SCORPIO CHILD AND EDUCATION

Passing through the school system, the young Scorpio can become a mystery to many of her teachers, posing the question 'What makes her tick?' Different teachers seem to perceive and experience her in distinctly different ways, and even the parent can fail to know the answer to that question.

Scorpio is complex to most outsiders, ruled by that mysterious planet Pluto, God of the Underworld, and even if you ask young Scorpio to offer some insight into her nature, she's likely to either answer in a way that only adds fuel to the mystery, or just smile enigmatically and ignore the question. She's giving nothing away. That Scorpio mystery is one of the deepest and most profound that you can contact. In essence, it's the mystery of life and death, of rebirth and resurrection, of the passionate mythological Phoenix rising. No wonder few people understand it!

There's an aura of brooding intensity surrounding most Scorpios, as their contemplative introspection deepens; in many cases it is the struggle to keep the lid on extremely powerful and volatile emotions, trying to cap the volcano and stop it from exploding. It may not be obvious that this is being done, due to the apparent ice-cold control being applied so effectively, but those few puffs of sulphurous smoke give the game away to perceptive observers. Few teachers really notice it, unless they have given offence to a young Scorpio, and then they may feel that glaring presence sitting there like a trainee Mephistopheles. Parents may intuit that their child is sitting on a 'secret', which like a time bomb is ticking away, waiting for that moment to be revealed.

Scorpio does not really fit in at school and often fails to fit in to most forms of society, but this is an inner alienation rather than one which is openly displayed, and reflects that perpetual outsider image that is deeply etched into the personality. Even when Scorpio is at his most extroverted and social, there is still a distance established between him and others. It isn't that Scorpio is anti-social – in fact Scorpio has a strong social sense – but distance is maintained for everyone's good. The intangible energies that can be communicated by Scorpio are those of transformation and rebirth, for individuals and society, and are thus not to everyone's taste or comfort.

They'll have particularly keen and perceptive minds, capable of seeing right into the heart of any matter. What attracts the Scorpio intelligence is the source or essence of any topic, and that mind will bore through as though diamond tipped. It can be disconcerting to be creating a verbal façade or smokescreen around something, only to find Scorpio ignoring all those diversionary efforts and summarizing the content without those tactful and diplomatic evasions. 'Oh yes, Mummy, what you really mean is that Uncle Joe is nasty to Auntie!' As Scorpio grows older, one of their favourite games is called 'Deflation'; it might not be guaranteed to win friends and influence people, but Scorpio is very turned on by the intensity of truth, and finds the social evasion of it a source of entertainment, loving to prick those ego bubbles.

Scorpio is very self-confident; there's a natural strength of character and maturity that is hard to oppose, at whatever age conflict may occur. If a teacher chooses to clash head on with a Scorpio, there's no winners; at best a stalemate occurs. If Scorpio is determined to oppose someone, then that will is fixed and in the Scorpio mind, the battle never ends, even if the teacher has forgotten about last month's disagreement. Even retreating is against the Scorpio philosophy, and if he has to, it is only for a tactical regrouping of forces, waiting for the next opportunity to strike hard. When strategy is necessary, and Scorpio knows that an outright confrontation is unwinnable, then the tactics are usually those of ongoing subversion, stirring dissent in the classroom, A slow erosion of teacher's authority is likely, as is the creation of a group of classroom dissidents!

A wiser route to ensure that any prospective Scorpio subversions are not made is to give young Scorpio some class responsibility to perform, or a position of leadership in sports for instance. They'll discharge this new commitment seriously and diligently, as it corresponds with their own inner image of being a leader; and if they are responsible for the well-being of an established system, there's no incentive to erode it. Pushing a Scorpio toward the edge is asking for problems, and it is much safer to try to pull them towards the social centre and to integrate them there.

Scorpio at school offers the potential and promise of likely achievement, yet she often fails to realise her own capabilities or attain the higher ranges of that innate potential. Often she becomes an under-achiever because she follows her own 'star' wherever it leads, and can become independent at an early age. What fuels the Scorpio interest is an emotional accord with subjects; if there is no sense of intense feeling with a subject, then Scorpio lacks all motivation to actually pay attention or study. It would be a rare Scorpio who achieved success in all subjects. Most tend to gravitate towards a particular sphere of study, which they enjoy and feel a real connection with. Scorpio's grades tend to reflect this, with poor marks and reports from certain teachers, and praise and encouragement from others who teach her those favoured subjects. If the interest is lacking, Scorpio cannot fake it. It's all or nothing, extremist tendencies, where passionate involvement is red hot or there is nothing there. Scorpio and pretence do not coexist. Yet this can be the key to future Scorpio success, when specialization is available rather than a broadly based education. The child is suited towards a wholehearted participation in a subject that absorbs her intense concentration, and if she can manage to reach the higher stages of education and gain a place on a course for a subject that she is genuinely interested in, then there are few who can match Scorpio's commitment and ability.

Scorpio's ability to persevere, impose self-discipline and determination are rarely matched by any other sign, and if Scorpio decides to be the best at anything then they are sure to make at least a success out of it. Helping to channel their natural gifts in a positive direction has to be the aim of the caring teacher and parent, whilst incorporating ideals of helping in a broader social context. These should ensure that the Scorpio energy flows into constructive channels for the benefit of all in later years, rather than just being involved with self-advancement and greed.

If schoolwork becomes too easy and boring, then Scorpio can act in a lazy fashion, failing even to apply himself in favourite subjects. That vitality can turn inwards, creating emotional disruption and increased moodiness, especially during adolescent years, when Scorpio is feeling quite mature and ready for the adult world. School life then can seem almost wrong to him, and as this is often the time of important examinations, Scorpio can fail unexpectedly due to the diversion of his interests. Under the influence of emotional changes and puberty at this time, the Scorpio male can become aggressive and more combative, as his new masculinity triggers off unfamiliar feelings of power and sexuality, and some Scorpios can become troublesome at school if they come from a background where physical assertion is acceptable.

Scorpio reacts against most forms of imposed authority, preferring to oppose it by a fierce independent spirit, so authoritarian behaviour by either parents or teachers will usually create the opposite response to the one intended. Scorpio likes intense confrontation, and can sometimes manipulate situations that way, perhaps just as an excuse to release that stored emotional energy, so try not to get manoeuvred into a corner. Scorpio plays to win. Always. Compromise is not a natural quality.

Imagination plays a vital role in the inner life of Scorpio, and a perceptive teacher or parent would be wise to encourage their child's exploration of this human gift. An early training to read will help, so creating a love of story books that can last a lifetime, and provide a regular source of mental interest for the inquiring, penetrative, Scorpio mind. Tales of mystery or exotic locations will appeal, offering the young Scorpio images and costumes to wear in her imagination. Even Scorpio girls have a strongly masculine personality, and will rarely appear ultra-feminine. They can be very attractive, but possess a powerful inner strength that is rare in both men and women. Using their imagination is one talent that most Scorpios possess, and writing or drawing imaginatively is a way to draw this out. Using language in an accessible direct style is also a talent that the Scorpio child can exhibit.

SCORPIO CAREERS

It may seem obvious to suggest that the ideal Scorpio career is one which attracts a genuine interest, but this is very important with a Scorpio; if there is little or no interest there, then application and motivation will be lacking, as with certain school lessons. Yet suitable Scorpio careers are quite dynamic and interesting, often founded upon those qualities of penetrating perception, analysis, intuition, conviction, emotion and love of mysteries. As a parent, unless you really understand what makes Scorpio 'tick', then it is best not to force your idea of an ideal career onto them, because such an imposition is likely to be rejected, as the young adult is determined to follow their own way. Observe the direction that they wish to travel in, and then help them to walk their own chosen path.

Physical and psychological health is one sphere that attracts, both because of the challenges which that career involves, but also out of a genuine desire to improve life for people. This includes being a surgeon or doctor, dentist or psychologist, where a personal curiosity can, through training, become a talent that helps to heal others, or reveal their own psychological mysteries to them. Some Scorpios tend to combine this healing talent with a religious approach, becoming spiritually orientated healers and therapists, especially today with the field of alternative health rapidly growing.

That spirit of investigative enquiry can be most useful, finding satisfaction in areas of research, science, detection and law, or where analytical skills are required. That probing persistence is always looking for the truth, and this tendency can be very positive if applied through appropriate channels where determination and will can become the keys to eventual success.

The realms of the subjective and intangible provide an inexhaustible supply of mysteries for the Scorpio mind to explore. Occult investigations and expositions are attractive, as are the parallel associations with mainstream religions and psychology. Magic and the emphasis on the magician's will can cast a spell over many a Scorpio.

That need to reveal the real is one which can dominate any artistic expression of Scorpio. Through writing or art, their imagination can roam widely, but always returns to that need to explore those socially taboo areas, holding them up to the light, exposing their secrets. Many Scorpios can express themselves with artistic fluency and power, uniting both their emotional and intellectual sensitivities, and having a broad range of content which embodies the complexity and ambiguity of Scorpio, where opposites coexist in mutual harmony (at least for most of the time!).

SAGITTARIUS
(NOVEMBER 22 to DECEMBER 21)

Planetary Ruler: Jupiter

Element type	Fire
Type	Positive/Masculine
Triplicity	Mutable
Symbol	♐
Image	The Centaur, with bow and arrows
Part of Body	Hips, thighs
Theme of Self	I See
Key Qualities	Explorative, aspirational, freedom-seeking, idealistic
House Affinity	9th House

Famous Sagittarius Personalities: Winston Churchill, Beethoven, Edith Cavell, Walt Disney, Maria Callas, Frank Sinatra, Steven Spielberg, Laurens Van der Post, Uri Geller, Jane Fonda, Chris Evert.

THE PRE-SCHOOL SAGITTARIUS CHILD

A typical Sagittarian birth is one where the baby comes with an eager and enthusiastic rush, often before people are properly ready. Some can be premature, or born in transit to the hospital, but the tendency is to emerge as quickly as possible. This intrinsic rush is a tendency that can remain with the Sagittarian child into adulthood. During that first year, the child tends to be quite physically active, enjoying pumping his arms and kicking his legs as if he's consciously preparing for the future independent mobility by 'revving his engine'. This eagerness to become mobile can be displayed in the Sagittarian tendency of attempting to walk early, often before the age of one. Even though such attempts can end in failure and falling over, the child seems to recognize the joy that can be experienced by such physical action, and he bounces up all smiles and grins as he prepares to try again until he succeeds. Sagittarian children tend to transmit a sense of good humour, and having such exuberant and pleasant children around can be very pleasurable for a parent.

Usually, Sagittarius will respond well to new experiences in life, and seems to adjust quickly to progressive changes made in routines and lifestyle. Between the ages of one and three, early signs emerge of that childlike love of performing. These performances often involve demonstrating his newly acquired physical skills, and he will insist that you pay sufficient attention to his antics, and will expect an appreciative round of applause! He gives a gracious bow in response, and once he can speak is liable to murmur 'Thank you, thank you' as a pleased grin spreads across his face. He's also apt to pull funny faces as a way of extracting a response from you, or to encourage you to forget your annoyance if he has been misbehaving. Sometimes his whirl of activity in the house can become a little wearing, and often you find yourself half wishing that he'd never learnt to walk as he takes advantage of this skill in explorations of accessible rooms. But Sagittarius often gives his intentions away; because his presence is usually unmissable by his noise and activity, when you realize that a sudden silence has descended you may suspect that he is up to mischief somewhere . . . There's a tendency to be sneaky and crafty in Sagittarian children, whose curiosity can often lead them into poking their nose into forbidden territory. Cupboards and drawers are favourite places to explore, and they will enjoy hiding too, so sometimes you'll lose sight of them; best places to look are behind the curtains, under tables or chairs, or in any large baskets.

As Sagittarius expends so much energy in physical activity, there's less left for other areas of her development; whilst some can learn to talk early, the majority tend to take longer to really develop a wide vocabulary and proficency. The child is quite capable of talking, and often understanding is soon prevalent, but actually speaking takes a little longer. Once the child realizes that it is also physically enjoyable to talk and activate that tongue and mouth around those strange sounding adult words, then progress will suddenly quicken.

Between two and three years old, mind development intensifies, and the child will begin to display increased interest in simple forms of learning and show more signs of attention to their environment, rather than just being a forum to run, scamper and somersault around. An interest in books starts to develop; stories and colourful picture books begin to be enjoyed, and the child is more capable of sitting quietly with you when you are telling the story. Sagittarius is fun to be with, and soon develops a sense of humour and fun, and especially enjoys playing silly games and chasing. Their behaviour is generally quite good, and they tend to be obedient at this age, although periodic temper tantrums can start as they approach the age of three.

As they are exploring more aspects of life now, their energy is diverted into several channels throughout the day; this creates a situation where they can suddenly grow tired at times, and may still require a midday sleep to replenish their batteries. Toilet training can be a little fraught, as they are not the type to easily fall into regular and predictable patterns of behaviour, and their natural motions may be irregular. Mishaps are to be expected, especially as they often fail to register their body sensations quickly enough in those earlier training attempts. Trying to impose fixed toilet times is unsuitable for Sagittarius; the most appropriate way is to encourage them to give you sufficient warning of their needs, and to become aware of their body sensations in time to reach a potty. They'll usually soon learn the lesson, and then it'll be fine, apart from those occasional times when preoccupation with play makes them ignore those body feelings for too long.

Between the ages of three and four, there is probably a renewal of that physical exuberance again, where rough-and-tumble and exerting physical prowess and energy will be one of his favourite games. He can be a little too rough for some children though, and if he gets angry can deliberately hurt another child. Play fighting with brothers or sisters is common. You'll also observe him climbing around at home; on the furniture, standing on tables, swinging on the curtains, climbing up wall units. He'll love doing all this, and has absolutely no respect at all for furniture apart from its potential play value. However, as he stands on the back of the settee preparing to launch himself at the chandelier, you will probably have something to say to him!

She's a friendly child, and quite sociable with other adults and strangers. Unfortunately in today's world, this is often not really encouraged in children because of child abuse and abductions. So you may need to keep a wary eye on her, due to her trusting and naive nature. There can be some difficulties with her sleeping patterns at this phase, as she can tend to wake regularly in the middle of the night calling out for attention, which can be very disturbing for parents too.

Between the ages of four and five, he becomes more self-assertive and can be resistant to parental authority, attempting to ignore your instructions and commands especially when he is enjoying himself. Life is seen as a round of play and fun, and enjoyment is his main preoccupation and purpose. His interest in the world begins to increase, and he will start to ask more incisive and curious questions about everything. His fascination is with the world in which he lives, less as a local physical exploration, but as a questioning, mental approach. Reason and rules are now making some sense to him, and he may demand that you properly explain all those commands and instructions to him. He'll attempt to evaluate these, and is likely to object to some that may not appear to be sensible to him, especially those which prohibit him from doing something that he wants to do. He may be more verbally cheeky with you, standing his own ground in a disagreement, and asserting his attitudes and points of view on contentious issues. He's showing signs of an independence of mind and a willingness to assert his own will. If you try to teach him some simple lessons at home, of picture–word association, numbers, the alphabet, etc., he's likely to respond more enthusiastically now, and you can help to prepare him for school.

THE SAGITTARIUS CHILD PERSONALITY

Overflowing with natural vitality and exuberance, the young Sagittarius rushes through the house with more enthusiasm than grace; he can be awkward, bumping into furniture, carelessly knocking things onto the floor, falling over, bruising himself and rising up again with a smile ready to carry on. Like a jetplane he speeds around, trailing cast-off energy in his wake, which you frantically try to grasp for yourself so that you can keep up with his activity. Like the Sagittarian symbol of the centaur, he's like a horse let loose and running free. Sometimes he'll stop, perhaps stand in front of you, ready to perform; now he's a whirling dervish, slowly turning with arms outstretched, until he becomes dizzy and starts to stagger around the room.

Sagittarius is a congenial child, cheerful and fun to be with; a big grin spreads across his face through sheer enjoyment and fun as he loves to play. They are the sort of children that will wander off, family dog at their heels, cheerfully intending to explore the woods and nearby fields. They're not particularly serious; their basic attitude is that life is to be enjoyed and that they can't see any reason to worry. The sun's shining, they feel good, so why spoil it? They're alive, there's plenty to discover and enjoy, and they intend to taste life as deeply as possible, which is why they have to rush around trying to fit everything in!

She's an optimistic little soul, friendly, good-humoured, trusting and a positive thinker, tending to assume that everyone else has a similar nature. It is quite possible for Sagittarius to grow up into adulthood maintaining these qualities and, indeed, their faith and trust in the essential goodness of humanity can be very refreshing to more cynical minds. The problem may be that these qualities will often be abused by others during the child's development. But a belief in that essential goodness of humanity is like a light that everyone should keep lit, because in the struggle to prove that belief and faith is true can lie the seeds of progress and continuity for the human race.

Sagittarius is not an overly extroverted type in an egotistical manner, but is very fond of socializing. The outgoing energy is always exploratory, attempting to gain a clear understanding of the world, which is a theme that becomes more relevant to Sagittarius as they grow older, and that earlier phase of physical exploration is transformed towards a mental curiosity. Life is the real teacher of Sagittarius, who tends to learn the appropriate lessons from making mistakes, which displays their natural intelligence as distinct from many who fail to learn and repeat mistakes again and again. The constraints of schoolwork and their need for playful exploration can sometimes clash.

Sagittarius needs to feel free; it's almost as essential as breathing is to him. Freedom means continual expansion and creativity, being the wellspring from which his abundant vitality flows. The challenge for the parent is to acknowledge and understand this fundamental tendency in the child, and to allow it space to be expressed, yet also be capable of disciplining and directing the Sagittarius energy. Trying to dampen down their exhilarating enthusiasms and joy is probably the worst thing a parent could do in the name of control. What needs careful erecting around Sagittarius is a structure or framework that focuses their attention and energy into specific channels, yet which does not excessively inhibit their nature and talents. Helping the child to focus is the key to constructive use of his qualities, otherwise the expansionary tendency of Jupiter and Sagittarius is to go too far, losing focus and control; impulsive behaviour takes the place of caution and careful thought, as the urge to be free becomes obsessively dominating. A flexible framework which slowly begins to encourage responsibility, self-control and concentration in order to gain the best experiences out of life and study is the ideal to work toward with the child. This can develop an inner balance or regulator in Sagittarius, so that a more mature and responsible freedom can eventually be attained.

As the base from which exploration can proceed, the home and family life is vitally important. If Sagittarius had her own way, she would have a collection of different pets and she would have a very loving attitude towards them, although her ability to regularly look after them might be variable. If she has pets, then this can be a good training ground to establish a sense of responsibility and discipline within her. Making her responsible for their well-being, food and cleaning can help her to become less self-centred. Family security is important, and she's likely to always retain powerful emotional family ties, as she sees that as the cohesive force that binds people together in society, although her concepts of this will expand as she grows older. Sometimes her emotions can be a weak spot for her, and sentimentality can replace deeper emotions, especially as she matures and a more mental focus develops. Yet in younger years, she spends considerable time trying to gain parental attention and approval for her clownish antics, as she needs to be genuinely loved and to feel that warm glow of the loving heart surround her. Even so, she does not want to feel that the family is smothering her freedom and need for self-expression, and will react strongly against any threats of restricting her to a repetitive and confined home life.

Sagittarius has a direct, honest style of communication, which can often lack diplomacy and tact, and which some can find too blunt and lacking in consideration of other's sensitivities. He is a natural opponent of hypocrisy and deceit, and expects others to be as honest and trustworthy as he believes himself to be; otherwise he becomes offended and his trust in them becomes diminished. Unfortunately, it's the clash between his idealistic innocence and the stark reality of the world that can become a regular experience. When he's younger, you may be asked by him, 'Why are people like that . . . ?' It's a hard question to answer, so perhaps start to practise your reply now; but remember that the knack is to answer in an honest way which does not shatter his optimistic view of life, by being positive and encouraging him to retain his confidence in humanity. He'll often understand better than you think, and grasp certain complexities reasonably easily, because Sagittarius can turn into quite a philosopher in later years! And he's training for it now . . . .

They may make you shape up too, become more honest and genuine in your response to them, because they won't allow you to hide behind any evasive veils either. Your authority is likely to be challenged by them and they'll need clearly defined reasons for any decisions or commands that you make; especially if they impose on their treasured freedom, or threaten to inhibit it. They'll often oppose your decisions if they think you are not right, or are derived from personal parental wishes rather than for their own good. Expecting wholehearted obedience from Sagittarius is unlikely to be fulfilled. It isn't that they are naturally antagonistic or dis-obedient, but they are likely to make you take a second look at some decisions or commands that they've just challenged. Sagittarius is not naturally anti-authoritarian either, but they'll only conform to an authority if there is genuine respect and an acceptance of the validity of a command. Explaining it to them with logic and reason tends to persuade them better; if it's an 'emotional knee-jerk reaction' then they are likely to oppose it. Fairness and justice are Sagittarian themes too. They need to be able to respect their parents, both in being able to rely on their judgement, honesty, and concern for them, and also to expect a trust and faith in them too, where the child's intrinsic value is recognized and his dreams supported. Sagittarius can show you – or remind you – of a simple, innocent way of enjoying and looking at life; perhaps they can reconnect you to a way that you lost a long time ago due to the influence of life experiences.

Sagittarius usually responds best to parents who treat him more as a friend than a child, and he'll respond much better to that friendly treatment than any attempts at parental dictator-ship. He'll listen better to advice and instruction, and you will be more successful in guiding him through life. As has been mentioned, the main area to influence him in is inspiring a responsible attitude, and in learning how to focus and direct that inner impulse to throw caution to the winds in search of the intangible dream of ultimate freedom. Once he realizes that self-control need not negatively inhibit his freedom, but can make his life more enjoyable, then he'll begin to reap the benefits of his own nature more effectively.

During childhood, most Sagittarians are quite athletic and sports-orientated, both as a means to use some of that excess physical vitality and also because they really enjoy playing games. Their legs are especially strong, and their running ability may be better than most. Whilst through clumsiness they may suffer many bruises and cuts, their general health is quite good, and that vitality helps them to spring back quickly from any phases of lowered vitality during those common childhood illnesses. Sometimes their play with others becomes a little too physical, and the first time that they realize this is when someone starts crying or objects to playing with them because they are too rough.

He'll attract a variety of playmates through his enthusiastic, playful nature, creating all sorts of adventurous games and fun by his constant quest of exploration. He may need some warnings though about being too inquisitive and entering potentially dangerous places, especially once he's old enough to play out of your sight. He'll be a little inspirational leader for many children, transmitting his high spirits to them, and can be a perfect friend for many an adventurous boy or girl. Hopefully, the development of common sense and a clear warning from you will ensure that any recklessness will be rare.

There'll be times when you'll wonder just when your Sagittarius is going to grow up; that perpetually playful child seems ever present, and yet by adolescence a new dimension begins to emerge as her mind wakes up. There can be emotional friction though, as she becomes more changeable and unpredictable in her reactions, and her self-assertion of personal freedom may seem quite demanding in her direct manner of expression. That inner clashing of her abundant physical, emotional and mental energies can make her more challenging and confrontational, and she'll seem to be very resentful towards anyone who attempts to restrain her choice of actions, which invariably means parents can become her opponents.

This possible challenging of authority, parents or teachers is partly self-assertion but also another aspect of his inquisitive nature, where his mind is demanding answers to questions, perhaps challenging parental or social habit patterns of behaviour and attitude. Sagittarius dislikes general social rules being applied to him; he feels their imposition too strongly, and would rather tear away those imprisoning shackles. Unless he is informed of the valid reasons why he must conform to some assumed social standard, or why he should behave in certain acceptable ways, he will adopt a position of doing whatever he wishes to do. His 'Why?' is less a stance of opposition as an inquiry, giving you an opportunity to inform and educate him, to persuade him of the rightness of your position; if it makes sense to him, then he'll willingly obey the rules. Sagittarius is an independent free-thinker, building his own outlook and opinions on life, usually from a more idealistic perspective. He isn't naturally a revolutionary or social adversary, or a traditional upholder of established social values and unquestioned beliefs.

They may be tempted to oppose convention, as they struggle to make their teenage statements of their unique identity, perhaps through fashionable clothes, hair, attitudes, interests; and in some cases may choose to act in direct contradiction to social laws as an assertion of personal rights and freedoms. The assumptions of dogma, belief and social attitudes begin to interest them now, and political, religious and social conditioning are areas which they will choose to question. As the tendency of Sagittarius is to discover truth, they are likely to pass through a variety of such beliefs and ideas in their exploration, as they slowly form their own adult perceptions, and you may be aware that they appear to change their minds quite frequently during this phase. This is potentially valuable, because at least they have an open mind rather than a closed, narrow, and fixed one, and this can be beneficial to them all their life. Some Sagittarians begin to be more serious now, especially once they are aware of the real nature of the world, with its inequalities, injustice and unnecessary suffering for many, and may take on a crusading mantle. Sagittarius often needs a cause to focus around and to pour those energies into, and if they come into contact with altruistic and humanitarian social groups at this time, then their influence can stay with them as a personal philosophy. They will then look for opportunities to apply their idealism, either through groups working for social betterment, justice and equality, or through more service-orientated groups like the British Voluntary Service Overseas, or the American Peace Corps, or international charity organizations. After all, these directions are logical consequences of the Sagittarian spirit and that inner light that has been lit of trust and faith in humanity.

He can be touchy about any emotional adolescent relationships, and is often surprisingly vulnerable to the impact when they dissolve, even if the relationship has only lasted a couple of weeks. Sagittarian girls have a tendency to play with relationships, exploring the nature of their own budding womanhood, rather then ever being really serious. They can be superficial in their teenage emotions, as they realign themselves from acting like tomboys into becoming young ladies.

Sagittarius starts to distance himself from the family now, and that powerful impulse for freedom begins to motivate and direct his choices. He enjoys considerable social variety, meeting new people, travelling to new places, and intends to 'do his own thing', so there is much less time spent at home or in parental company. Some parents can feel this change in the relationship quite acutely and, as the Sagittarian assertion grows, can feel quite hurt by his apparent ignoring of the family, especially if he manages to leave home early. But letting go is an essential part of the parent–child process, and is necessary for all concerned. Teenage friction and conflict is an integral component of this distancing, where family emotions can run high as the relationship begins to be re-defined.

He may need some economic guidance, because Sagittarius tends to spend quite easily, often without due thought for tomorrow's bills, and can create considerable problems for himself if he allows his use of money to be unwise. In today's world, with credit so easily available, prudent financial sense and careful budgeting is a valuable skill. Also, he may need some feedback about his actual capabilities and talents, because with that expansionist spirit he can exaggerate them in relationship to the actual social reality. Being capable of creating unrealistic dreams is not a valuable commodity, unless one is in the fiction business! When it comes to working, Sagittarius tends to be quite ambitious. The main difficulty can be that through impatience and restlessness he moves from job to job, partly because he is not willing to wait years for the prospects of promotion. Finding the right sort of career is important to him, and can help to stabilize his life.

THE SAGITTARIAN CHILD AND EDUCATION

Sagittarius is ruled by Jupiter, and it is the expansionary nature of Jupiter that presents both great opportunities and challenges for your child. As young Sagittarius becomes more aware of the world, what makes the deepest impact on her is the sense of immense potential, so much to explore, so much to know; and by the time that reading is discovered, a totally new world opens up for her, the world of human knowledge and culture. This poses too many options and choices for the free-ranging Sagittarian spirit, who basically wants to explore everything, and this expansionary awareness underlies the Sagittarian dilemma when confronted with the learning process.

Sagittarius is a very energetic type, often displaying signs of restlessness, and much preferring to be constantly active. The image of the astrological sign is the centaur (half man, half horse), and reflects an affinity with both physical and mental levels of the human being. Your child will be like this too, enjoying both the physicality of life and the pleasures of the senses and, as he grows older, the intellectual dimension of life. The issue can be how he succeeds in balancing these two tendencies in his nature.

The child is naturally exuberant, openly showing a genuine enjoyment of life, looking for all chances to have fun, and taking delight in rushing around. How Sagittarius adapts to formal schooling is variable, because their impulse for freedom suddenly confronts the structure and order of school. For all of their education, they will probably be straining at a leash to be free, and reacting against that imposition of order upon them. Being forced to restrict their outgoing energy can be uncomfortable for them, unless they can redirect it into expanding their capacity to learn; this is an early task for Sagittarian children to achieve, or else they can become disruptive in a classroom.

The natural intelligence is there, and the child will be mentally alert and eager, although actual application can be lacking, and consistency is not her strongest virtue. There are two stages in the basic Sagittarian approach to learning; the first is an enjoyment and appreciation of everyday life, and becoming absorbed with that takes most of the energy available for mental learning. It is a simple education from living that provides a deep, lasting foundation for the child. The second stage is when the fruits of our knowledge make a real impact on the child, and her mind wakes up to realize that an intellectual dimension to life makes it even more interesting and enjoyable.

Taking the step of becoming proficient at reading is often

the trigger for this second stage and, through his natural curiosity, the process of learning is transformed into a game, one that can prove fascinating to him for the rest of his life. Many Sagittarians become scholars with specialist knowledge of particular subjects, especially ones which have succeeded in tapping a personal ideal, and which offer some degree of personal freedom. It is at this point in the child's development that the role of teachers and parents can be crucial in determining possible future success.

Discovering and enjoying the world of thought and ideas is a vital step to be made in balancing the Sagittarius nature. She's a restless type, and has a variable attention span, so her teachers need to be able to grasp her interest and keep it long enough to communicate their lesson. If her early school experience emphasizes fixed order, routines and discipline over the children, then it will not suit her. If the lessons are transmitted with a lack of enthusiasm and are boringly presented, then she'll switch off. If the teacher is too dominant and authoritarian, quelling natural childhood exuberance, then she and the others will not benefit from such an approach. What young Sagittarius needs is a teacher who will fan her inner fire until it catches light, and she realizes that learning is really fun; a teacher that ignites her imaginative curiosity, so that she really wants to know.

Once Sagittarius is hooked on the joy of education, he'll still need support and guidance in making the most of his talents. That expansionary tendency leads him towards rushing things, so that he can reach the next stage as soon as possible. He often needs to be reined back from rushing forward before he's learnt the current lesson properly and can often make careless mistakes in that attempt. The teacher needs to ensure that each step is understood before allowing him to move onwards, although equally ensuring that the Sagittarian enthusiasm is not quashed. Sagittarius is often planning the next move before he has successfully made his current one, and this forward-looking tendency requires some deliberate control. The child needs to be carefully encouraged to complete one piece of work correctly at a time, before accepting the thrill and novelty of the next challenge. Sometimes Sagittarius leaps to conclusions before knowing all the relevant facts, and makes embarrassing mistakes.

It is this support with focus, organization and structure around the innate Sagittarian temperament that is essential for the later success of the child. Otherwise, the child will 'under-achieve', failing to live up to his capabilities. Helping him to develop a more concentrated approach on the work in front of him, becoming self-disciplined and beginning to create a framework of application can serve him well in future life. It is essentially an earthing process, so that the impulsive and spontaneous fiery temperament can become productive. Establishing certain boundaries around him – as in emphasiz-ing successful completion of work before allowing him to move on – helps to focus his attention, whilst hopefully not inhibiting his interest either. Enthusiasm can temporarily carry him away into impractical spheres, so guidance is needed to help him gain a more realistic perspective on what is possible and how to achieve it.

It is necessary to harness that energy of enthusiasm that Sagittarius will have in abundance, so that she learns the lesson of self-restraint and that time is well spent in careful and thoughtful preparation before commitment to a project. All of her dreams can succeed if she takes it slowly step by step, until tangible signs of success begin to appear. Directing her energy into constructive and productive channels is the key for her inventive and often inspirational ideas to bear fruit. Wisely handled, Sagittarius has great potential which requires careful development, reining in that free spirit enough to achieve her goals, but not by too much to imprison her.

SAGITTARIUS CAREERS

The ideal direction for Sagittarius to follow will depend upon which aspect of their varied natural talents and interest has become dominant during their teenage years. These include intellectual and scholarly pursuits, sports, or working with people in some capacity. The more suitable careers should include some variety and personal freedom, so that restless impulse does not create too much inner agitation, but has some potential for advancement or expansion.

Sagittarius can develop strong moral, social principles and beliefs and, with a tendency to explore our cultural and intellectual knowledge, can move towards that type of environment. Ideals can attract, and religion can serve as a focus for such a search. For some, joining a church can combine several of these threads. Others are attracted towards a free style of philosophy and cultural exploration. The intellectually demanding world of law can involve variety and social involvement, or aiming to be politically active can embody their higher aspirations and ideals. The world of bureaucracy does not appeal at its lower level of routine and form-filling, but certain aspects of its higher managerial and administrative levels can attract, such as civil servants engaged in researching ministerial options, social administration and local government decisions. Becoming an educator and teacher can satisfy several Sagittarian tendencies, especially in the communication of more advanced studies for the adolescent and university students. Their self-expressive and enthusiastic presentations of subjects can stimulate a corresponding interest in their pupils. The act of interpretation can be a Sagittarian talent too, both in translating foreign languages or through the processing of knowledge and information into a more accessible form that people are able to grasp.

If these intellectually vigorous careers are not so suitable or possible for the child (for a variety of reasons), then they may be attracted towards sport and working with animals. Sport and physical endeavour can be appealing, especially in today's context of increasing leisure time and physical recreation centres. Coaching others, or even promoting sporting and leisure events can be possible options to explore. Some

Sagittarians prefer to devote their time to travelling and exploration in various ways, nationally and internationally, another path that can become a career through film, television and books. Working with animals can lead to veterinary training, or association with zoos, or animal care and kennels.

If Sagittarius is especially devoted to ensuring his personal freedom, then he may decide to create his own business, become self-employed and in full control of his own decisions. In such a case, his choice of a business could be extremely broad, although he may need close financial advice regarding his financing and business projects. His enthusiasm and expansionary impulse may make him a little too impulsive otherwise.

CAPRICORN
(DECEMBER 22 to JANUARY 19)

Planetary Ruler: Saturn

Element type	Earth
Type	Negative/Feminine
Triplicity	Cardinal
Symbol	♑
Image	The Goat
Part of Body	Knees
Theme of Self	I Use
Key Qualities	Conservative, organised, conscientious, ambitious
House Affinity	10th House

Famous Capricorn Personalities: Martin Luther King, Mao Tse Tung, Richard Nixon, Isaac Newton, Louis Pasteur, J. Edgar Hoover, Howard Hughes, Cary Grant, Humphrey Bogart, Edgar Allen Poe, David Bowie, Sade, Rowan Atkinson, Michael Aspel, Carlos Casteneda, Gurdjieff.

THE PRE-SCHOOL CAPRICORN CHILD

As may be appropriate for a sign that signals the ending of one year and the birth of the new, the newly born Capricorn tends to look somewhat old and quite wrinkly, rather worn even at a few days of age. It may be that serious frowning look on her face, a sense of disapproval, and something that reminds you of a traditional grandmother, but you still can't shift that feeling that this child seems older than she obviously is . . . Capricorns have a tendency to look more mature and older during their childhood, and then reverse their appearance to seem young in old age. Birth tends to be traditional in nature, and usually straightforward, although Capricorn does not rush into this world, and she may resist being born, giving a few false starts before she bows to the inevitable.

You'll notice that early serious attention that he has towards everything; he seems to be very concentrated in his attempts to absorb all those new sensory experiences through his eyes, ears, tastes, smells and touch. He's weighing up this peculiar world, warily and cautiously experiencing life, before he decides that he will explore a little more, practise those simple skills, and slowly he'll decide to participate as his natural confidence and enjoyment grows.

Learning how to walk is an important step in development for them, and this tends to be between a year and fifteen months. Standing upright inspires them to feel the same as their parents, and now they have access to a wider world, and can see it from a different perspective. Looking around encourages her curiosity to flourish, and she starts to explore her environment. She is sensitive to your admonishments and warnings when she approaches certain items in the room, and whilst she may acquiesce to your finger wagging, another time will see her slowly moving towards those same forbidden areas, watching to see if you've noticed; but she has a sense of what is right and wrong, and whilst she may not be able to resist the temptation, inwardly she feels a sense of guilt, which may emerge by mutterings of self-admonitions such as 'No, no' recognising that she is about to do something previously prohibited.

Between the ages of one to two, he is likely to imitate you, following you around, walking in your footsteps. This is partly to give him a sense of security, but also because Capricorn wants to be grown up as quickly as possible. When you watch him moving around the room, you will probably get the impression that he has decided exactly where he intends going to, and the path that he will take before he actually moves – even when he was crawling this was his approach. Random movement and activity is not really favoured by the young Capricorn. He adapts easily and naturally to family schedules and routines, preferring a structured, regular lifestyle, and such phases as toilet training usually pose few problems with Capricorn who needs fixed, repetitive order in their lives. He will value your appreciation of his functional abilities though! If and when mishaps occur, try not to tell him off severely, because he will respond better to a disappointed look on your face, and an encouraging acknowledgement that he can do better, he will do better next time. He isn't the most exuberant of children, and sometimes you may wish that he was more childish and played silly games and had more fun; but he's quite content in his own way. There may be an early attraction towards music, singing and rhymes, as well as simple numbers and counting as he nears the age of three. It may be rudimentary, but it is a sign that his mind is waking to the thinking skills. At this time too, his temperament may be a little erratic. He isn't normally a child who throws tantrums, but his attitude may be a little grouchy and touchy, and he may be less cooperative.

This tends to spill over into her early days at playschool after the age of three, where she can feel a little unsettled about being in the company of other children, and she can tend to withdraw. She still prefers the company of adults, and may try to spend more time with the adult leaders of the playschool rather than the other children. Yet eventually she will feel more confident, begin to loosen up and enjoy herself. Some Capricorns tend to display a self-critical tendency around the age of four, when a deliberate 'inner monitoring' comes into force which is really a form of defence against failure or being made fun of by others. This can manifest itself as a slowing down of speech, even speech mannerisms that imitate adults, or by refusing to become too involved with others in case it results in not being highly regarded. This tendency is looked at more closely in the Capricorn personality.

Between four and five, this isolationist tendency can still be present and active in some Capricorns, and cooperative behaviour can still be lacking as a natural spontaneous behaviour pattern from the child. They now put considerable attention and effort into whatever they are doing, becoming much more absorbed and probably less self-conscious. They still display great care and order in playing, and can chastise any playmate for not behaving according to their standards. The toys that are preferred and most regularly played with are those which imitate realistic adult possessions, such as vacuum cleaners, irons and ironing boards and nursing sets, mini-tool sets and plastic hammers and the like, so that they can play at being Mummy or Daddy. Generally it is toys or interests that have an obvious practical value in daily life that appeal. In this year before commencing school, you may begin to wonder how she'll get on when she's on her own at school. Sometimes she seems to have some difficulty in understanding certain ideas, and she appears to resist accepting some realities of life, although she is usually quite adept at basic practical duties. She can be very sensitive to any critical words from you, but equally responsive to words of encouragement and praise, and you see her wither or glow with pride depending on the nature of the communication between both of you; although this makes you wonder how she'll respond to a teacher who may be critical. She may need some additional preparation to help her settle into school; she seems mature, but you know how vulnerable she really is, and how uneasy or insecure she can feel. So helping her to spend more time on her own away from you can help, as can playing with other children; whilst ensuring that when you are together you are consciously and deliberately helping to build up her own self-confidence, and dismissing any failures as not worth getting upset about, provided she tries again and eventually succeeds. In so doing, you help to evoke the Capricornian strengths and character.

THE CAPRICORN CHILD PERSONALITY

Living with a Capricorn child can sometimes be disconcerting. From time to time you'll sense another personality coexisting within the child. With that thoughtful serious demeanour, you'll often wonder about the unusual maturity that reveals itself, especially when you have perhaps been relating with them on a childlike level, and they respond in a surprisingly adult manner. Capricorn tends to reverse the roles, so that you'll feel childish and frivolous in the face of that serious maturity! You'll get the feeling that there's an adult trapped in that small body.

Generally, most Capricornians act older than their years, and, because of this, parents may begin to expect better behaviour and achievement from the child than she is actually able to maintain. The impression of Capricorn is that the child seems to carry the weight of an adult burden on her shoulders, she has a tendency to willingly accept responsibilities, such as helping in the home, and she tends to enjoy the feeling of importance when trust is placed in her to successfully perform those duties.

As Capricorn is naturally biased towards a more serious, sombre temperament, it may be wiser for parents not to transfer the concerns of adult life too quickly onto their shoulders. The child will tend to absorb parental worries too easily, without really comprehending the nature of the adult problems. Parents often forget how much children hear or register about family difficulties, such as the family budget, and whilst in several ways this is all part of the child's ongoing education, it may be wiser to discuss such matters when the Capricorn child is not present.

It may be more beneficial to Capricorn to encourage him in normal childhood pursuits, to let him stay in touch with his actual child nature for as long as possible, and not to over-emphasize the process of gradual maturation. Helping him to enjoy play and fun may be of more long-term value to him, and treating life with a cheerful spirit can help to transmit a positive approach to enthusiastically enjoying and embracing life. Displaying to Capricorn that sense of perspective and humour can help to balance out an overly serious tendency.

Often, Capricorn has a deep feeling of fear and insecurity

toward life, which appears as a lack of real self-confidence, and is often masked by the ability to appear grown up. The parent should acknowledge this, and try to increase their confidence by demonstrating their love for them, and by offering encouraging praise for their efforts and development. There is often a deep underlying dissatisfaction with their own nature, which in later life is often transferred to a driving ambition to achieve in some particular sphere of life. The child is especially vulnerable to direct criticism, as it serves only to reinforce their own low self-esteem, and a more subtle approach is required in order to help them build and unfold their own unique identity. Ideally, the child should be aided by an approach first of praise for what they can do, followed by a constructive piece of advice guiding them to do what they should be doing, and correct them in that way. All teaching should be expressed with a belief that the child is quite capable of understanding 'the lesson', and that, with an encouraging optimistic attitude and supportive participation, Capricorn will soon learn quite effectively.

It may be that in the full natal chart of your child, that there is a natural balancing of the essential Capricornian nature by the positioning of planets in lighter and more extroverted signs, so that the serious characteristics are not so evident in the child's behaviour.

Even so, the child is likely to be self-conscious, possibly too deliberate, polite and mannered to appear real and spontaneous, almost as if she is continually monitoring herself to ensure that she is doing and saying the right thing. Capricorn finds a sense of security when she is living within defined and restricted limits of behaviour, as this reduces the possible options that can confront her. As caution is a Capricorn quality, she prefers the least amount of choices that have to be made, so that action is not excessively inhibited.

It is in this 'inner monitoring' that difficulties can lie, and it is the source of much of the personally repressive Capricornian tendencies. The creation of an 'image' of how he should be, act, think and feel can lead him to be inwardly unforgiving when he fails to match this perfect image of himself. Capricorn builds high social ideals and, when the inevitable failure occurs, can be condemnatory and judgemental on himself, which reinforces that lack of inner confidence, yet more importantly splits the personality under the conscious domination of the 'high image' of how he should behave, repressing his possibly equally natural ways of child-like spontaneous reactions. This situation is often expressed by adult Capricorns, where a degree of intolerance is often expressed, both towards themselves and to others. Parental criticism can amplify this tendency if it is applied in an unsuitable manner, which is why helping the young Capricorn to develop a sense of humour and perspective on life can be so valuable.

It is often the child's emotions that fail to match this ideal, and Capricorn can tend to keep a sense of distance from fully experiencing her emotions. Such emotions can remain pent-up and unexpressed, although a sensitive adult may perceive the undercurrents rippling beneath the cool and calm appeerence. Controlling these can create those occasional phases of moodiness and quiet brooding that Capricorn can display.

Capricorns tend to prefer spending time at home, and are not the outdoors type that Taurus or Sagittarian children often are. Part of this is that need for security that dominates choices especially as Capricorn grows older. Because of this degree of childhood reticence, the young child rarely attracts a large number of close playmates, and is not overly attracted towards those aimless or frivolous childish games that are so commonly enjoyed. Playing at being grown up is more a Capricornian game.

The type of toys and games that suit them best are those which are related to real life, miniatures of everyday items, so that they can pretend to be mimicking Mummy and Daddy. Capricorn children probably prefer toys that are practical and serve a purpose. Having a 'purpose' becomes a driving theme in the Capricornian's life, something of importance which can become a centre to their life, providing a cohesive stability and focus. This need emerges early in the child's development where there is a natural aversion to excessive frivolous time-wasting. Even if Capricorn is given considerable freedom from responsibilities, before long she will be filling the time with 'things that have to be done', and can only rest when these tasks have been completed. Searching for freedom may be a Sagittarian impulse, but it is not one of Capricorn's needs.

As a parent, you should find that raising a Capricorn child is relatively easy, because the child will be cooperating with you in the process! He can display a strong will, and likes and dislikes will be quite clear, but he isn't the type to descend into temper tantrums when his will has been denied; oh no, such behaviour is too childish for him to contemplate. Well, normally . . . he might have a few lapses. The Capricorn strategy is often to get his own way through sheer dogged persistence, wearing the opponent down over time. Her relationship with her parents tends to be very influential, as the child often uses them as her role models of what an adult should be, and will absorb parental attitudes and styles of expression which then act as a foundation for her own in later years. Having awareness of this, you should ensure that you are providing a suitable image for her, and that you can help to lighten that taciturn temperament from becoming prevalent. Certainly look at your own tendencies in the section on parent's signs, and evaluate your natural perception of the world through the lens of the elements too; and then see how they are liable to relate with your earthy Capricorn child.

If there are younger brothers or sisters in the family, the Capricorn can be relied upon to help take good care of them, because it is both a genuine action from them and also because it is the right thing to do, although, as with their relationships with friends, Capricorn can seem to be a little bossy sometimes in their attempts at organizing them. They'll be equally solicitous of your well-being when they have grown up and you're older, out of love, duty and respect.

Entering worlds of fantasy is not a favourite Capricorn pastime, and he'll be less attracted to exotic lands and dreamscapes than the majority of children are; he rarely spends much time lost in daydreaming. His nature is too practical and grounded, preferring to be active in the real world where he senses that his destiny and achievements wait for his arrival – that's why he's in such a rush to become an adult.

It is in the teenage years and during adolescence that Capricorn begins to come closer to their innate temperament, and where the main assets of that sign start to be clearly displayed. It is the impulse to achieve and gain social respect or influence that begins to condition choices. In a quiet manner, Capricorn intends to fulfil those ambitions that they have been secretly developing. They'll rarely announce them out loud, but through patience, self-discipline and perseverance move step by step towards achievement. Sometimes they may surprise many who suddenly become aware of their presence passing them on the 'winning line'; Capricorn can be a dark horse or more, accurately perhaps, a dark goat.

The foundation for later success is based firmly on a realistic appraisal of the situation and his assets; keeping those feet planted on the ground gives great stability and strength whilst he begins to cautiously reach for the skies. Capricorn knows that unless you do that, then at some stage the balance will be lost and the only result will be a toppling over. The Capricornian knack is to aim for what is imminently possible, reach that, and then aim towards the next step, and in so doing gradually climb the stairs to the top. Many people tend to overreach their real potential by wanting to jump up all the stairs in one leap, perhaps through being overly eager and exaggerating of their actual abilities. This is a lesson that Capricorn demonstrates to other less cautious and less sure-footed types, that there is a safe way up that mountainside, but being prepared to spend time finding the right path can be crucial. Capricorn has the ability to realistically evaluate personal potential and resources, and then apply these in the most effective manner possible. These are part of those organizational and managerial skills that adult Capricornians often display, and for which they do like to be respected. You may have noticed the early stages of this in your child's tidy room, where his life became organized into the security of fixed routines, and where even his toys became objects to sort out and place tidily away or posed in attractive display positions on shelves. Sometimes it may have seemed that young Capricorn gained more enjoyment from these activities than actually playing with toys!

Eventually gaining some sort of authority position is a Capricorn goal; it fits their temperament, and fulfils that natural sense of reponsibility that has always been present. Capricorn is a 'social climber', but this is more to satisfy personal needs rather than to egotistically assert a superiority over others.

During the adolescent phase, there may be some tension with the child related to her struggles with emotional upheavals and, whilst she may be interested in relationships, that self-consciousness may tend to inhibit her, and she may become painfully shy and embarrassed if you invade her privacy. Her willpower may sometimes clash more openly and directly with yours, as she begins to focus her aims and objectives more clearly, as well as asserting her growing independence. Her future life is viewed with often grave seriousness, and she will create feasible and practical dreams to aim towards in that step-by-step process that has been mentioned. She will take examinations quite seriously, and you may need to convince her that any failures are not the end of her dreams, that she should not get so tense in such situations, and having a sense of relaxed perspective over them is likely to increase her chances of success. Capricorn may tend to withdraw into solitude during these teenage changes, and can often be attracted towards painting, drawing and music as a means of creative self-expression, and a coming to terms with the dawning of her real adult self.

THE CAPRICORN CHILD AND EDUCATION

Most Capricorn children adapt easily to school life and studies, and feel comfortable in a well-regulated, structured environment. Like the other Earth signs Taurus and Virgo, Capricorn has an intrinsic need to feel secure and stable, and any well-organized school should be able to satisfy this need. The child tends to prefer receiving clear instructions regarding what to do, rather than being given a free choice in subjects. Less structured progressive styles of education would not suit the young Capricorn so well.

Capricorn is not the quickest of children in development or learning, but has the advantage of being able to eventually establish a real understanding of the basics of a lesson, building a foundation of knowledge that is secure and correct, and upon which future steps can be taken to increase that knowledge. Thoroughness and care are Capricornian qualities, and that methodical approach can become increasingly beneficial to the child's advancement. Whilst an attentive teacher will gradually observe the way in which she slowly grasps her lessons, and find nothing wrong with the child's attitude to school, some teachers could begin to express some impatience with Capricorn's early struggles to understand the fundamentals of the lesson. If she was with a group of primarily Air element children, then she could appear slow in relation to their bright, alert, comprehending minds, yet in her own way she is quite capable of having a successful education.

Over a period of time, the assets and qualities of the Capricornian nature will unfold themselves. That ability of personal application and perseverance is very valuable towards eventual achievement of goals, as are self-discipline and concentration. These are qualities that many people lack and, whilst they may not appear to be flashy and dynamic, are the keystones of future success.

In the classroom, Capricorn is usually well behaved, basically obedient, attentive and relatively quiet compared to other children. This is a result of the Capricornian nature, which has an inner impulse to conform to socially disciplined behaviour. Most Capricorns uphold traditional and established social behaviour patterns, preferring to maintain the status quo and the familiar rather than reacting against such personal impositions. Unlike Sagittarius, individual freedom is not a motivating impulse, nor do they have the urge to be uniquely individual and independent that Aquarius often displays, Capricorn feels safer when acting in a 'majority way'. It is order that is looked for and a predictable, defined lifestyle, even at a risk that this may become stultifying and inhibitive. In that willing acceptance of routines and rules, Capricorn can often appear to be almost middle-aged in attitude, unwilling to 'rock the boat'. This is a necessary function in society, where personal and social cohesiveness is required in order for successful functioning, but should not be taken to the point where it becomes deadening and repressive. A flexible balance needs to emerge for natural change and vitality to flow.

The teacher will realize that Capricorn is one of the more reliable and conscientious members of the class, and can take advantage of his willingness to take responsibility and his desire to please. He may take over certain minor class duties in the school, and certainly will do his best. He will plan his schoolwork and homework projects carefully, treating them with seriousness and responsibility, unlike many children to whom it is an onerous burden, and something to be finished as quickly as possible – if it's started at all. Capricorn is not a dreaming type, and pays sufficient attention to actually remember what the lesson was about. It's very rare for him to sit staring into space, lost in a private dream world and oblivious to whatever is going on around him, or to be chattering away or planning mischievous pranks in an attempt to distract attention from the lesson. Capricorn is a serious personality and is not attracted to excessive frivolity; time for relaxation is only allowed when 'duty' has been successfully completed. Honouring obligations is an essential part of the Capricorn nature, and is rarely transgressed, even at a younger age.

Capricorn usually is quite competent at schoolwork, and this becomes more apparent as their education continues. If only through application, success will eventually come. They may have a more natural bias towards an education that involves a practical dimension and result, where seeing a tangible consequence of their efforts satisfies them. Again, this is similar to the other Earth signs, and education which incorporates more abstract intellectual thinking may not be their favourite themes. Life is viewed mainly from a practical perspective, and the uses of education are preferably immediately relevant to everyday living. Thus arithmetic is considered to be useful, but algebra has a less immediate appeal. Capricorn becomes more inspired when they receive approval for their achievements, and openly acknowledging these can help to give them additional confidence in their abilities and self-worth, especially if progress is made in those subjects where they may feel less confident.

Sometimes young Capricornians can be inhibited in company, such as in the classroom, and are rarely the most voluble children there. Part of this arises from self-consciousness, and she may not wish to draw too much direct attention to her during class question and answer times, or within discussions. Yet she often knows the answers and has valuable comments to offer in such class participations, but personal inhibition is often more powerful, and she'll sit there quietly unless directly asked by the teacher. Drawing her out from this reluctance can be done by a skilful teacher, who recognizes her self-consciousness and can sense this, asking her directly for her answer. However, the only danger here for her confidence is in choosing the right time when the teacher believes that she does know the answer; failure can inhibit her more, although being put right by the teacher is to her own benefit.

School is a valuable environment for helping Capricorn overcome this basic shyness and personal insecurity. Some

Capricorns tend to favour their own company, uneasy about making approaches to other children to play or be friends, but this arises from the fears of rejection. He will want to have friends, yet can seem unable to relax that serious temperament enough in order to play without inhibition. Friends will help to erode those self-created barriers, and help to make him more outward-going, instead of reverting into solitary pursuits and self-sufficiency. It's unlikely that he'll make firm friends with those who are natural extroverts, unless it's as a tag-along follower; it is more likely that he'll want to spend time with either other Earth or Water signs, who will appear less threatening to his basic nature.

Capricorn often turns to private reading and studying as she grows older, and can enjoy personal hobbies considerably. She needs to be doing something, and isn't physically or mentally passive, so these hobbies can become quite time-consuming and educative for her. Sometimes these can include the accumulation of detailed data about a subject, where the child becomes 'expert' in a narrow field, and being able to catalogue and sort this into appropriate sections is a Capricornian skill. Boys can be attracted towards the sciences, with their rational, logical and experimental practical dimension. Chemistry sets or engineering construction kits can be greatly enjoyed. Applying reason and deduction are two other Capricorn qualities that can be enjoyably expressed, especially as the child enters the teenage years, and is more capable of following his inquiries through different but associated avenues of investigation.

CAPRICORN CAREERS

Ideal Capricorn careers include those where there is a strong element of efficient practicality required, where patience, persistence and responsibility are necessary attributes for the successful completion of duties and tasks. They are often attracted towards gaining positions of authority and responsibility, especially those which also have a more direct involvement with the local community, as this can offer social status as an additional benefit.

Most Capricorn career choices are associated with 'social foundations', reflecting the established or traditional social functions that are performed by certain careers. These can include teaching, especially roles performed at senior level such as head teacher. This plays a dual role in satisfying the administrative ability of Capricorns as well as in the education of the future generation, with the forming of social values and attitudes and in the choices of information and knowledge that is communicated to them. Local or national politics is another sphere that can interest, as Capricorn believes that they have something of value to offer that can benefit the community, and they would probably treat such a responsibility seriously and with integrity. Police work can similarly appeal, both in its structured discipline (like military service) and in its function of upholding social order.

The practical nature of Capricorn as an Earth sign is demonstrated in their attraction towards farming and building, where the emphasis is placed on essentials for life, food and shelter. Hard work, competence and efficiency are qualities that are displayed here as in the business world, where Capricorn will strive to become a manager at least. In business, the resourcefulness of this sign can pay great dividends, and any business run by a Capricorn will usually be economically proficient, although the personnel management may leave a little to be desired. Administration is one of their strongest talents, and giving Capricorn such a job will ensure that the office and business will work smoothly and effectively. The supportive structures of the Civil Service and local government can appeal, as they also embody the firm foundations of civilized society, as well as being able to exploit the natural Capricorn talents.

If the child has maintained an interest in science and associated subjects, then following that as a career could be suitable. The areas that would be favoured are those where the practical application of science is of prime importance, perhaps science as applied to engineering problems. The more hypothetical research functions would not interest Capricorn so much, or make the best use of their ability.

AQUARIUS
(JANUARY 20 to FEBRUARY 18)

Planetary Ruler: Uranus, Saturn

Element type	Air
Type	Positive/Masculine
Triplicity	Fixed
Symbol	♒
Image	The Water Carrier
Part of Body	Calves, ankles
Theme of Self	I Know
Key Qualities	Humanitarian, independence, thoughtful
House Affinity	11th House

Famous Aquarius Personalities: Abraham Lincoln, Charles Darwin, Charles Dickens, Galileo, Thomas Edison, Lewis Carroll, Charles Lindbergh, Clark Gable, Placido Domingo, Germaine Greer, Barry Humphries, Dan Quayle, John McEnroe.

THE PRE-SCHOOL AQUARIUS CHILD

There is usually an element of upredictability about an Aquarius birth, and such children can come early or late, depending upon whether Saturn or Uranus is dominating the outcome. If it is Saturn, then the birth could be prolonged and after the expected date, but if it is Uranus, then the birth could be premature and a surprise to all concerned and quickly over.

Similarly during the first year of life, the young Aquarius has an erratic pattern response to attempted routines and schedules of feeding and sleeping. Even at this early age, passive conformity to expected ways of behaviour is rejected by Aquarius in favour of following their own innate rhythms. The child tends to be mentally alert and pays full attention to their environment, bright eyes flashing around, quietly absorbing all information. Despite that resistance to routines, the child is well adjusted to life and seems to be quite happy and contented. Attempts to force definite schedules upon them can be matched by a less obliging baby, who becomes tearful and fractious.

By the ages of one to two, this essential personality pattern is becoming more obvious. The child seems determined to assert his own unique identity, and intends to attempt doing everything in his own way, even when he is incapable of success. 'Doing it my way' is the theme of the young Aquarius who is willing to fail even when asserting his own approach. Some are fussy with their choice of food, and often enjoy a particular meal one day whilst totally rejecting the same meal the next time it is served. After a while you tend to become immune to the Aquarius unpredictability. Curiosity comes to the forefront of the child's life now, and he is an insistent explorer of his enviroment. Most of his mobility is designed to take him to that point where some bright object has attracted his interest; what he wants to do is to hold it, examine it thoroughly and probably play with it. If it's a vase or exotic plant, you will probably want to dissuade him from such action. Then, as he waves his prize around with you frantically trying to encourage him to put it down, you realize that he doesn't always listen to your commands now . . . .

At two years, you're wondering how she'll respond to the trauma of toilet training. Knowing her independent spirit, you are not overly optimistic. Yes, she still wants to do it all by herself, resisting your efforts to help her undress quickly, and she certainly isn't as quick as your skilled hands. Mistakes happen; she can resist your attempts at establishing a routine. Yet just when you are ready to throw your hands up in surrender, the miracle happens; all your efforts at training her suddenly click, and Aquarius is reasonably well potty-trained. You breathe a deep sigh of relief, pleased that you've crossed that hurdle. But wait; just coming up are those 'terrible two's tantrums', and with your Aquarian's contradictory temperament could you expect her not to perform in a like spirit? Well, she may surprise you and pass through her second year without such tantrums, but, before you get out the flags, wait and see if she's not saving them up for when she is three. Remember, her timings can be unpredictable!

Three years old and there he goes, trotting off happily to playschool. A few hours' rest from him is much appreciated, even though he is a lovely child. He responds well to playschool and the company of other children, and is quite open and friendly, enjoying his early experiences of social participation. He especially enjoys adult company though, and can seem advanced in his little conversations and questions that he has with the playschool supervisors and parents. Underlying this is an urge to be more grown up, and he may be inclined to mimic parents or older children in the family. His resistance to fixed routines is still present, and by now he has devised several techniques for avoidance, and there may be power struggles ahead as you persuade him to follow your instructions, or else!

By four, she feels more confident in her grown-up state, ready and able to take you on. She's realized that all you are is just a larger version of herself and, full of four-year-old vitality, she's starting to flex her assertiveness. Her behaviour can be troublesome at this stage, as she intends to act in the way that she chooses, irrespective of parental wishes or acceptable social behaviour. She can tend to act in ways that are designed to create a reaction in others, purely as a way of personal assertion and to attract attention to herself especially when she feels she is being ignored. You may have to discipline her more at this time, just to shake her out of such reactionary anti-social behaviour that she can lapse into; although being willing to allow her more freedom in the hope that as she develops will moderate any behavioural problems could be attempted by some persevering parents. Certainly a careful watch needs to be kept on her at this time, so that she doesn't move too far out of line; explaining why she should behave in certain ways within the family may help to improve the situation.

His playing tends to be quite inventive now, and he loves building things with Lego or bricks, possibly simple engineering-type toys. He is curious about how things work, and will often ask questions concerning his need for knowledge and information. This is the start of his mental quest that becomes more developed as he grows older. 'How' and 'Why' are two of his favourite opening words.

By five, these tendencies are firmly established. Their behaviour has settled down more now, and whilst it wasn't too bad before, it was more a question of attitude and resistance to authoritarian imposition of commands. They'll still question your instructions though, and certainly don't see you as an infallible authority. Whilst that can irritate some parents, it is a really healthy attitude to have, and is the source of future personal exploration and free thinking. Giving personal power to so-called authorities is the quickest way to lose all power over your own life and to become a slave to the choices of those to whom you have surrendered. The emphasis in the child becomes more serious now, and their practical interests are dominant, especially those which they can enjoy first as ideas and then translate into practical existence. These interests include a curiosity about how things work, and this will probably remain with them into adult life; exploring simple mechanisms like clocks or watches can intrigue them, or watching their father attempting to mend the family car can provide them with a source of probing questions at a time when father is struggling to keep his temper when faced by an intransigent nut. It may be safer to keep them away from Father at such a time, because whilst it may be safe enough and fascinating for them to watch, they may also absorb a few words that are too adult for them to repeat!

THE AQUARIUS CHILD PERSONALITY

As most people are aware, astrologically we are experiencing the early stages of the birth of the Age of Aquarius, passing through the transitional labour pains of a new birth into a new social vision of life and planetary existence. It is a confusing and traumatic time, when the old patterns of social life and attitudes are clashing with the new ideas which embody apparently disturbing changes. Aquarius is ruled by Uranus and Saturn, and the incredible scientific and technological changes that have happened in the world since the discovery of Uranus in 1781 are symptomatic of this Aquarius influence, as are a growing world social conscience and international interdependence.

So what has that got to do with your Aquarian child? Well, over the time of your child's development to adulthood, you're likely to observe and experience these tendencies coming from them in your own home; an expression of world issues and struggles reflected in the personality of a child.

Aquarius is usually an intelligent child. His focus will be found in a mental involvement and experiences of life. He's a 'sparky' child, electrically charged like a live wire, and often highly strung. His mind tends to be restless, perpetually seeking some interest or action, moving like quicksilver from one subject to another. As something new catches his attention and interest, you'll see his eyes gleam brightly, his mind clicks into gear, 'focus on' and he'll be happily preoccupied for a while – until his need for exploration begins to diminish that interest, and he starts to look around for the next fascinating topic. With that Uranian need for variety and newness, he'll seem to be very changeable, and can lack persistence and commitment to complete whatever he has started. At times, you'll believe that you saw him with mental antennae waving around in the air, acting like a human radio receiver, picking up invisible communications and transmissions from out of the air; he's very sensitive to subtle, intangible vibrations. Part of his problem can be tuning into the right channels!

Aquarius tends to be two steps ahead of most people in her thinking processes, and generally one step ahead of herself too . . . Her mind tends to live more in the future and less in the present; and in her preoccupation with her next step forward, her ability to function in the present can be impaired, and through that mental absorption she can often be absent-minded. She's still there, but not easily accessible or conscious of what's going on around her sometimes. Yet if she's in a daydreaming phase, she's often applying her mind seriously to work out some puzzle or curiosity that has intrigued her; she isn't a vacuous or fantasy dreamer. It's just that whatever she's absorbed in is probably nothing at all to do with her present reality. Knocking on the door and asking if there's anyone home will bring her down to earth with a shock, and she's likely to peer around a little dazedly wondering what is going on!

With that active mind dominating him, he can also be surprisingly observant and perceptive, and his acuity can be expressed with tactless directness too, which may create several embarrassing moments for you. Excess activity of his mental antennae can lead to problems in properly processing information, and he can seem scatterbrained to some who fail to realize the hundred and one separate puzzles that he is simultaneously working on are causing a slight mind malfunction. This tendency can of course create real problems in adult life, where excess nervous tension and mental activity are not recommended. Learning to relax is a lesson that Aquarius needs to absorb.

One of the main difficulties of this hyper-active mind is that related to the speed of his logic processes. Aquarius can appear to be able to access the intuitive faculties of the mind, where sudden Uranian-lighting flashes of illumination and realization strike, solving a particular puzzle like the famous cry of 'Eureka!' by Archimedes in his bath tub. Yet more often than not, this is the result of a prolonged Aquarian contemplation of a problem, and a rapid progression of logical steps to arrive at the answer. It is logic jumps that Aquarius makes, and asking them to fully explain how they arrived at a conclusion is often very difficult for them, because of these jumps in the logic progression. That's why having Aquarius explain logic to anyone tends to confuse rather than illuminate!

Whilst most Capricorns are born middle-aged, Aquarius is normally one of those precocious children whose minds develop quickly. It's as though he's in a rush to explore this curious and fascinating world that he has just discovered, and there's so much to discover that he has to fill his mind to bursting point immediately. And then try to sort it all out; in that effort he can make some unusual and unlikely connections at times, yet, looking at it positively, this 'talent' is often the source for new inventions and realizations – or so many concerned parents repeatedly tell themselves when his attempt at communication gets too garbled to make any sense. But he'll grow out of this; in later life he's often got his intellectual act together, and then he can baffle his listeners in an impressive manner!

Aquarius is not a natural extrovert and, concerned mainly with her own interests, can seem to be a little withdrawn at times. She tends to have less interest than many children with childish pursuits and games, preferring either adult company or time spent in exploring her own peculiar fascinations. Her need for her parents may not be obvious, as a degree of independence seems more distinct, but she does have a private need for inner reliance upon you for a long time, with parents and home serving as a focal point of security for her.

They'll have genuine feelings and affection for parents and family, but are not so demonstrative of their love and emotions. Usually Aquarius is more impersonal in such expressions and, whilst they are kind and sensitive enough, will rarely declare their love or smother anyone with it. Their style is more like adult friends, genuine connections but not excessively clinging or overly sentimental. Up to their teenage years, they'll be basically obedient and well behaved, provided that they can respect their parents and accept the logics of their home disciplines and guidance of them. If, however, they have parents who fail to explain their decisions and actions concerning them, or who emotionally react against their behaviour, then they can begin to assert their independent spirit more and enter into greater conflict with their parents. What they prefer is for their parents to be more like big friends, companions in exploring life, so that a deeper personal and friendly relationship can develop. This approach has both pros and cons, and much depends upon how both child and parent can handle such a relationship, and keep the correct balance of parental authority against the developing child's assertiveness.

By his early teens and dawning adolescence, the main Aquarius characteristics should be emerging into clearer view; both positive and negative tendencies. Underlying everything is that uniquely individual spirit of Aquarius. The tendencies toward being unpredictable and contradictory can be more evident, and his whole approach can rapidly become quite unconventional in attitude and expression. He may choose to display this through his selection of clothes and hairstyles, as well as through a more confrontational disagreement with parental attitudes or beliefs. For a sign with such high social awareness, this is probably the time when Aquarius is at his most anti-social and negative.

There is always a tendency with Aquarius to prefer the lures of the new in a direct choice with those of the old and familiar. Part of this is to be different from others, but also because they are more thrilled by the potential of the new, excited by the new horizons that it promises to open and because of that heady whiff of the future that bewitches them so much. New designs, new music and fashion trends, new advanced social attitudes and ideas are sparks to enflame the Aquarian's Uranus urge for change and novelty. Aquarius may initiate such ideas themselves, 'or at least ensure that they travel closely in the slipstream. This attraction towards the unusual can turn them towards social eccentricity, but usually it is only because what they are recognizing now is what will become the future norm in society. Given a free choice, they would always prefer a revolution in favour of the new; the old order is perpetually passé, even though that is the only reality that the majority know and enjoy. Being capable of thinking for themselves, they are quite likely to make as many mistakes as successes; but asserting their free spirit is worth any such consequences.

Opposition from a parental 'No' is not welcomed at this time. They will believe in their own freedom and rights to act how they see fit; they are expressing their own declaration of human rights, 'I've got my rights, you know', can be a regular stance of objection, whenever parents assert their rights to be the authority in their own homes. Yet if such disagreements can be suitably explained, and the differences between Aquarius and parents understood, then quite often Aquarius goes away, considers your point of view, and assuming that they are reasonable can return willing to accept them. But, they are equally liable to try to argue with you, trying to wear you down by a persistent stubborn logic – or pseudo-logic – and, as they may not pick the most appropriate times for such exchange, can become irritating or annoying, leading to a direct imposition of parental authority and domination!

Aquarius can often experience problems with his relationships with authority and fixed social structures. At heart he's a nonconformist and anti-authoritarian, and can find himself in an adversarial role almost without thinking sometimes, as rejecting the consensus orthodoxy is such a natural position for him to take. Playing the devil's advocate is another favourite role, and with his intellect he can often perform a few persuasive tricks against less adept minds, putting them on the spot and enjoying watching them thrash around trying to respond to his cleverly crafted questions. You've probably experienced this, just as have several of his teachers by now. Personal power can be gained in some situations by asking awkward questions, irrespective of personally knowing the answers. As a psychological powerplay, it is one that

Aquarius instinctively recognizes. The art of questioning is as important as the art of answering.

She has a strong need to have plenty of friends, acquaintances and a social life. Communication is one of her deepest needs, and that is linked with a need for social variety too which can stimulate and refresh her mind by different ideas and interests. She can be quite voluble, having a tendency to enjoy talking. That verbal and mental energy can overflow, and keeping her quiet can be challenging at times. Yet many can value her ways of looking at things, those new insights and ideas can stimulate the minds of listeners, and her real enthusiasm can be easily transmitted to vitalize others into activity. The role of Aquarius is to open society up to the influence of the new visions that sit like dreams at the threshold of consciousness waiting to be recognized and become real. In so doing, she may tend to tread on the corns of social conventions, and is indifferent to established ways of behaviour, attitude, belief and thought. What she wants to do is to think of new ways, new thoughts, create new beliefs and, if she has to challenge the world for the right to do so, then so be it! The problem is that this can make parents worry, because most of the traditional parental impulse is to guide their children to fit into established society and to perpetuate the acceptable ways of behaviour. However, you've had the privilege of raising an Aquarian child, so it may be wiser to change your expectations now – or ideally, change them before she's born. Aquarians walk their own way.

But try to listen to him when he's on his soapbox talking about his ideas about the future world. He has a genuine insight into the nature of society that will eventually come, and has a real conscience too about our treatment of other people and the planet. Aquarius wants social betterment for all, irrespective of race, colour, creed or ideology. He's essentially tolerant and understanding of people's differences, even though he might argue and maintain his own views, and knows that greater tolerance and contacting different points of view on life and culture can serve to make life much more

196

rewarding and interesting, and should not act as divisive barriers between people. For such a strong individual, he also has probably the most developed social group consciousness of all, and in this embodies a next step in the Aquarian Age. This is the development of each individual towards greater personal freedom but with an equally enhanced social awareness and sense of planetary responsibility, so that others do not suffer at the expense of the advancement of a few powerful individuals.

She'll have good relations with others, and be friendly and sociable. She is fun to be with, and tends to encourage the more positive characteristics to emerge from her friends, as she supports their efforts and talents, rarely aiding them in more childish displays of thoughtless behaviour or pranks. By temperament, she's a sharer, and is relatively unpossessive about most things except those which truly have a deeper meaning and personal importance for her. Provided that she can fill her mind with interesting ideas and fascinations, she will remain quite indifferent towards materialistic advancement and possessions. It is the currency of thought and ideas that genuinely attracts her rather than the currency of money. She can be like a social magpie, moving around her circle of friends, getting up to date on all the latest goings-on and the variety of interests and experiences that they can share with her. Her spirit of goodwill can be contagious, and her efforts at restoring or creating social harmony can be very healing, and show the way that society can resolve some of its differences.

The Aquarian impulse is to be of use to others, and some form of community involvement can attract them. These can become more distinct humanitarian ideals later, possibly leading to an association with political philosophies and ideas, although the Aquarian interest tends to be on a larger social scale than just individuals alone.

One of the Aquarian problems can be that of personal motivation and commitment. He can find it difficult to generate a persistent effort just for his own interests, and is too easily sidetracked down other appealing routes to have a single concentrated approach. Sometimes this can be misconstrued as laziness, but generally Aquarius is too active to be that, although his activity can move down a variety of avenues simultaneously. It's just that he has short-term dreams, which lead him to explore his interest for limited periods of time. His effort is more easily compressed into short bursts than steadily over a long time, such is the Capricorn ability. Unless he's at a point between consuming interests, you can't easily tear him away from his current preoccupations, and his response can be an uninterested 'I can't do that' if you try.

She can become evasive and uncertain in respect of her emotions and feelings. These are not her most integrated aspect of her nature, and she has a tendency to try to ignore or turn them off in certain situations so that her mind can retain its dominance and rational logic. She can be uneasy when her fluctuating emotions seem powerful, and may deny their influence on her. An emotional clash caused by beginning to feel for a person can cause her to respond by reasserting her ideal of freedom. Often Aquarians need some support in accepting their emotions and needs, and a major step requires some acknowledgement of this and a realization that having emotions does not necessarily inhibit freedom, and that it does in fact enrich life. Many Aquarian teenagers are not overly interested in relationships until the later teen years, but when they do start then they can be turned almost upside down by the rush of emotions that can be stimulated.

The home life of the Aquarius child can be very influential in their development, and they can be susceptible to their 'psychic atmosphere' of the home and family relationships. If there is tension in the air, then their nervously active, sensitive antennae will certainly register its presence, even if nothing appears obvious on the surface. Parents should ideally try to build an atmosphere of openness and relative peace so that undue stress isn't created to inhibit the Aquarian character; although the teenage Aquarius can create enough stress themselves. Because of their nature, offering advice to

Aquarius is not the best way to influence them, and they can be very contrary in rejecting it, even if it is sensible guidance that has been offered. Remember, they prefer to choose their own way, even if it is wrong.

How the Aquarian tendencies will manifest themselves can be variable. He has natural talents which are often multifaceted too, and the problems in using them fully lie in the difficulties of choice and application. Also, he may forge his way strongly along unconventional routes, pioneering progress and explorations into new horizons. Through the phases of his development, try to be aware of his main interests and talents, so that he can be encouraged to pursue his particular gifts. Considering the ideal Aquarian careers shows how varied these can be.

THE AQUARIUS CHILD AND EDUCATION

Aquarius has a natural alert intelligence, but they can become erratic in their progress through the school system, mainly as a consequence of their uneven ability to concentrate, and because of their mental insistence on pursuing their own thoughts and interests, especially when they fail to coincide with the subject that they are supposed to be studying.

It isn't that she sees no value in education, or has no interest in knowledge and studying at school, but that she only wants to spend time exploring whatever is interesting her, and to follow her own individual path towards knowledge. It is another attempt to assert her love of freedom. With this underlying attitude, she finds it difficult to easily settle into the formal structures and teaching which is found in most schools, conforming to fixed scheduled lessons and time-tables, which probably include several subjects in which she has no interest.

His ability to concentrate or focus on a specific topic fluctuates according to his degree of interest. It can be a total concentration or a minimal one, his mind looking around for a more fascinating diversion. His school reports should show these tendencies occurring, and over time you'll be able to discern those subjects that continue to evoke his interest, and those which repeatedly fail to do so. These reports are erratic and often contradictory; in his less favourite subjects his intelligence and commitment is regularly questioned, whilst in others he is praised highly for his ability and grasp of the subject, with comments like 'should go far' and 'exceptional student' indicating future directions.

During those earlier years at school especially, Aquarius tends not to be the best pupil in his class. Adjusting to the demands of school life may be an initial struggle for him, as his mind begins to wake up as he grows older. He may require some parental help and encouragement to ensure that he stays on a par with his classmates. Part of his difficulty lies in an erratic and unreliable memory (a tendency that can remain with him all his life), and in the fact that he has little love for formal education, where concentration and application in all subjects is necessary, and the routine of learning to read and write and study books can seem too tedious for him.

These earlier tendencies are modified with age and experience, and his abilities at studying his favourite topics expands considerably, offering a great potential for achievement through higher education.

Aquarius will often test those limits and boundaries that are placed around them by teachers and parents, testing these as an assertion of their demands for personal freedom and as a dislike of routine. They can be challenging at times, demanding why it is that they can't do this or that, and expecting a sensible, logical and rational explanation of why they have been prohibited from what they want to do, or else they'll see no valid reason why they have been prevented. If they receive a satisfactory answer, then they will normally conform. If they receive stark commands, then they may feel opposed to the teacher or parent. To Aquarius, the fact that someone is in a position of authority does not actually make them a real authority; that is achieved by real talent or knowledge, and is not necessarily present in all people in such positions. So they are always likely to challenge, to see the nature of the person who has authority over them. Respect is not automatic.

This is seen in the Aquarian resistance to attempts at imposing points of view or information upon them by an 'authority'. If that authority is not acknowledged by the young Aquarius, then his independent and free-thinking mind tends to reject the teaching, or at least to re-evaluate it again himself. He's willing to disagree, argue points, and suggest alternative ways of doing something. In several ways, this can be very positive and may contribute to understanding or expanding concepts beyond imposed restricted limits. But in a classroom it can be interpreted by some teachers as an erosion of their authority, or a diversion to what is being taught, and the child can be viewed in a more negative light. Most education is passive in nature, with children receiving the knowledge from a teacher and then applying it in formalized and acceptable ways. It is only in later years that allowing children to express more of their own opinions becomes more common, and is less penalized.

The young Aquarius can pass through phases when she becomes absorbed in relative inertia and a lack of concentration, almost as if her mind is paying attention to 'elsewhere' rather than to the here and now. She may need to be convinced of the personal enjoyment and development that she can gain from school and education and, once she accepts the value of learning, then her application should become more persistent and regular. She tends to be attracted towards more open-minded subjects, where she knows that if she takes this next step, then there is another equally interesting step to follow it; tuning into the future through the present is an Aquarian need, and in a strange way tends to justify her making efforts now.

Mentally, Aquarius is not really an information dilettante – such as Gemini perhaps – and much prefers to be focused down certain channels; if they can find the right routes for their attention, then they can exhibit specialist knowledge. Fragments of indiscriminate information fail to really interest them. Their preference is to be self-taught, to follow their own path and fascinations to a satisfactory conclusion, and so can often develop their own personal parallel path of self-education to that of the school curriculum, especially as they enter their teenage years.

He often has the gift of being multi-talented, quite capable of being proficient in several directions, and possessing a natural inventive imagination which can be turned towards either practical results or in developing alternate, intellectually biased theories and concepts. The problem can lie in making full and proper use of these intrinsic gifts and spread of potential interests. Aquarius can want to move in several directions simultaneously, and being able to cultivate and guide these into positive results can be difficult, as his interests are diverse, and he may not have a focused attention. Generating the momentum to actually work to his real capacity is hard, because he often fails to vitalize his own individual drive.

The nature of his mental processes has been mentioned in the Aquarian personality, but, with those speedy logic jumps and 'intuitive flashes', his school work can reflect these tendencies, especially where he can omit stages in a logical presentation of ideas, or fail to properly communicate an understandable explanation to others. Yet he can still offer much of value in the classroom through his mental perceptivity and his acute probing questions which apply sound logic to the validity of the teacher's statements. He may need to learn how to apply his thought into a suitably organized and logical format, especially when he intends to communicate them to others. He may know what he means, but a failure in explanation means that others do not.

Aquarius can be very helpful in generating a spirit of teamwork and cooperation at school; whether in working in small project groups in the classroom or in sports teams, she can make an important contribution to eventual success. In teams, she is usually a generous and unselfish 'team-person' who values the team more than any individual success. With her social attitudes, she prefers working and participating closely with others rather than following a solitary path, although she still has to insist on her own individual and independent style in doing so. It is the degree to which this style is individual that determines her success in working with others, and Aquarians tend to display both extremes; some are amongst the best to collaborate with, and others are too determined to express a divisive individuality, and become virtually unworkable with colleagues.

He will respond well to any positions of responsibility and trust at school, discharging his obligations in a competent and mature manner. It is his social conscience and humanitarian instincts that will become more prominent with time, and often one of the main things that really will motivate him is some form of community work, where his social awareness can be expressed and developed.

AQUARIUS CAREERS

In most Aquarians, an underlying motivation includes a need to aid in the development of humanity, to improve the quality of life in some way, to add to the storehouse of human knowledge. Because of a natural versatility and fertile mind, Aquarius can enter a variety of careers which can suit their inner requirements. Working with a small group of people is a situation that Aquarius enjoys and, providing that their inspirational social spirit is to the forefront and not their more eccentric individualistic opinionated self, they can be very effective in such a role.

Science and technology can be two broad fields of human endeavour which attracts Aquarius. He has the ability to grasp the concepts which are involved, and the innate skill to apply them. Research work can appeal to his forward-looking nature, especially all forms which are exploring avenues which could offer great benefits for society if they are successful. He likes to forge new paths, using his intellect and intuition to reveal new directions to travel. Medicine or medical research can be suitable, or psychology, where the mysteries of the mind and psyche can be investigated. Aquarius likes mysteries, and always feels potentially competent enough to solve them. The mystery of the human mind is one that can still tax many an Aquarian inquirer. Engineering or associated technical trades such as electronics and modern computers can fascinate, as can computer programming and system analysis. Acting as an inventor can become a consuming preoccupation, connecting both mind and physical skills.

Work which is more directly involved with individuals in a social context is another sphere that many Aquarians move towards. Social reforms and improvement can satisfy the Aquarius spirit, who likes to believe that what she is doing is for the good of others. Welfare and social work projects in a community context can display many of the assets of Aquarius. Law as an expression of mental acuity and skills can become another social platform for some, although there may be a bias towards creating a legal platform to build social change. Virtually any type of employment that has a humanitarian focus will attract Aquarius.

A certain degree of independence and freedom is needed, and the various forms of media have many Aquarians working there. Radio and television can embody the vitality and changes that are enjoyed, as well as a sense of social involvement and influence. Being a writer or creative individual also shares that perception of the world with others, as can more visual arts like modern styles of photography. Involvement in publishing houses can also appeal.

Work that involves serious enquiry and research can also tap that Aquarius curiosity, although even there they would welcome a regular diversity of theme. And perhaps last, but not least, many Aquarians are attracted towards intangible mysteries, the occult (especially from a pseudo-scientific angle) and, of course, astrology, in their efforts to understand the mysteries of life.

PISCES
(FEBRUARY 19 to MARCH 20)

Planetary Ruler: Neptune, Jupiter

Element type	Water
Type	Negative/Feminine
Triplicity	Mutable
Symbol	♓
Image	The Fishes
Part of Body	Feet
Theme of Self	I Believe
Key Qualities	Compassion, sacrifice, universality
House Affinity	12th House

Famous Pisces Personalities: **Albert Einstein, George Washington, Frédéric Chopin, George Frideric Handel, Nureyev, Elizabeth Browning, Elizabeth Taylor, Michael Caine, Rik Mayall, Paddy Ashdown, Mikhail Gorbachev.**

THE PRE-SCHOOL PISCES CHILD

Birth comes as a real shock to the Pisces child, as she is suddenly expelled from the soothing, watery bliss and security of the mother's womb. The initial response to this shattering of comfort, peace and dependence is tears and noisy cries. Some Pisces need encouragement to enter this world, and she may be reluctant to be born, dimly sensing that the forthcoming experience of life may not exactly suit her. Certainly the noise, bustle and lighting of the delivery room, and the tense, expectant surrounding atmosphere, are not conducive to feeling safe and secure. As soon as possible, the new mother should hold the child, trying to settle her down and starting the bonding process. Over those first twelve months especially, Pisces needs considerable love and affection as she gradually adjusts to life. She can be a highly sensitive baby, her nervous system is extremely responsive to her environment and to her mother and father. She can be very dependent upon the presence of her mother, and can hate being left alone at all.

This reliance on parents still persists through those first two years of age, and often Pisces will be 'holding onto Mother's apron strings' afraid to let go. Tears and upset behaviour can be common, both for genuine reasons of physical discomfort, food, nappies, sleep, but also as a demand for the mother's attention and love. As Pisces tends towards insecurity, such comfort is necessary for his own sense of security.

Entering the new perspective of independent walking can surprise many Pisceans, who can find that new view of the room to be initially more disturbing than exciting. He then decides to progress at a cautious rate, sometimes reverting back to previous stages of mobility, such as crawling around, although this will be a short-lived phase. He isn't the bravest child around for exploring the new, and even then tends to do so only when you're close at hand, protecting him. Resistance to some of his 'demands' can trigger off emotional dramatics, as his will is thwarted, although most of the time he seems generally passive and no trouble at all.

Between the ages of two and three is usually toilet-training time, which is a major step for most children and parents! For children it is a point of growing physical control and independence, and for the parents it signals a time when less work will be demanded from them. However, Pisces is not usually one of the more obliging signs; in fact, their response to the training is often erratic. Two tendencies account for this: an inbuilt reaction against the imposition of routines and patterns of behaviour (as you've probably noticed with sleeping and feeding at times), and an inner absorption which means she may fail to pay attention to her body sensations. She may tell you, but only when it is too late, and it can be hard to predict her timings! Don't overdo any criticism; she knows that you're disappointed in her and, if she feels more upset and confused, this can make her worse. Just sort her out, console her, and encourage her to tell you earlier. And be patient; it'll pass. Approaching the age of three, she may be liable to throw those emotional tantrums, and at least the positive side of this is that she is expelling excess energy and learning that the world does not revolve around her desires. She may become susceptible to the influence of music, 'soothing those tortured brows', and what could be beneficial to her and to yourself are those kinds of 'New Age' music that are designed to promote relaxation, peace, tranquillity and harmony.

Having to deal with making choices is another area of development that can pose a few difficulties for Pisces. Decisions can be hard to make, and generally they will prefer you to decide for them, as in any case your influence will be dominant over them. The best approach for the present is to try to agree together on choices of clothes, play activities, food, and yet to begin to encourage them to make personal decisions without your guidance on less complex decisions, or where time is not an important factor.

Between three and four, as his language and comprehension faculties increase greatly, you should become aware of his imagination, which tends to spill out into daily life. Discerning between his imagination and reality can be difficult for Pisces, and he is certain to embellish his daily life with all sorts of creatures and happenings. Monsters, invisible friends and living toys all inhabit the world with your Pisces child. Sometimes he can conjure up things that seem to scare him, so you may need to become adept at waving your magic wand and banishing away all such scary beings! The wide range of highly evocative children's cartoons available today are certain to fascinate him and, like most children, he will probably play-act at being his own favourite characters.

As she begins to mix more with other children, such as through playschool, you might sense that she seems to reflect other personalities at you, sometimes in ways that do not really feel right coming from her. What is occurring is that she is absorbing the traits of other children and, as Pisces is like a sponge absorbing everything that makes an impact upon her, she is unconsciously imitating these influences upon her. If she starts to be awkward and shows signs of bad behaviour, then you may need to check out just who is currently influencing her and, if need be, change the situation. In her open way and with her trust in people, Pisces can be vulnerable to all influences, so a wary eye should be kept at all times. Whenever she confronts difficult or unpleasant situations, Pisces often reacts by withdrawal, either at the time or shortly afterwards. She may often retreat into quiet periods, when she may appear to look vacant, but at these times she is wandering in her own private world.

In the year preceding school, you become aware that they tend to progress in erratic leaps of development, almost overnight in some cases. They can still be very attached to the parental bonds, and may not be overly confident when left on their own or with other people. You may sense that they are growing further away from you now, and that you find it harder to take a step into their world to see what is affecting their moods. The defensive barriers are becoming more entrenched and protective. There may be a need for you to help them participate more in this world, and to grasp their attention by displaying to them how interesting and fascinating this world is too, perhaps through letting them investigate the natural world or the world of artistic creations. In this way, suitable pathways are established for them to venture on, and along which they may demonstrate future talents.

THE PISCES CHILD PERSONALITY

Of all the twelve Zodiac signs, Pisces is the most unworldly. Ruled by Neptune, it can be a peculiarly evasive and elusive sign, refusing to be defined in simplistic terms. True to its watery nature, trying to grasp and contain the Pisces spirit is like holding water in your hands; it soon begins to overflow and escape. In several ways, Pisces stands with one foot in this world, and one foot in another world, not totally at home and comfortable in either, yet needing this dual awareness to maintain some semblance of balance. The symbol of Pisces is like two fishes which are joined together, but which are each pulling against the other in opposite directions. This sums up the essential Pisces dilemma and nature of the individual character.

Most Pisces children have a natural intelligence, which, whilst not always academically inclined, can be quite perceptive, intuitive and imaginative. One famous example of a Piscean child who was considered to be below average intelligence at school was Albert Einstein, who obviously managed to fool his teachers as well as he now baffles the majority of 'intelligent adults'! But at least it shows that teachers' reports on children's ability are not infallible.

Pisces is the greatest idealistic dreamer of all the signs, and her essential way of looking at life reflects this other-worldly dimension. This involves an intrinsic belief that everyone and everything in the world is good. In the West, it has been the teachings of Christ that have expressed this spiritual philosophy of compassion, universal love, service to others and a self-renouncing attitude. In fact, Christ is often considered to be the embodiment of the World Teacher for the Piscean Age (which is now passing away to be replaced by the Aquarian Age).

Unfortunately, not everyone can live to such high standards, and this Pisces faith in people can appear to be overoptimistic, naive and even simplistic when confronted with the stark harshness of man's inhumanity and lack of universal compassion. Most Pisces children have to encounter a progression of disillusionments as they walk through life, where their inner ideal clashes with reality. Much of their future adult attitudes will depend upon how they handle such experiences; whether it is one which offers a positive and constructive inner growth, or one which leads towards a sense of bitterness and betrayal by people and life, where trust has been shattered. As a parent, you will not be able to protect her from such facts of life, although there may be times when you are able to guide her through troubled waters, and perhaps carefully prepare her to deal with such confusing situations better.

Underlying this though is an extremely fluid and mutable emotional and feeling nature, which is unstable and unsettled, and bears the full brunt of the encounter with life. Whenever his experience of life becomes too confusing or painful to his sensitivities, you'll see the young Pisces cutting himself off, almost like pulling the shutters down over his participation. The causes of this vary; he could be upset because he has not got his own way, he could have been told off for bad behaviour, or he may just be in a situation that he doesn't like for some unknown reason. Pisces escapes through that inner door into the other world. It is an intensely private, dream-like world where he feels safe and secure, able to shelter and evade those unpleasant realities that seem to oppose him in our reality. Each Pisces child has their own key to this secret inner world; it is their most important possession, and the source of their imaginative vitality. Like the other highly sensitive Water signs, Pisces needs an escape route; Cancer retreats into a shell, and Scorpio enter's Pluto's Underworld, hiding behind an inscrutable mask.

Any observant parent should recognize when this process is occurring in your child; she's likely to be very quiet, and has perhaps gone alone to her room, sitting or lying around staring trance like into space, oblivious to the rest of the household, lost in deep contemplative thought. With some Pisces it is as though a switch has been turned on or off – here one minute, gone the next! As this is a natural process for Pisces which is related closely to her ability to deal with life, a wise parent should not attempt to interfere or disrupt the inward turning of the child. However, excessive time spent in this half and half reality is not to be encouraged either, as it can create additional difficulties in later adult life. The best way is to draw Pisces out into a loving and supportive home environment, so that she can begin to gain extra personal strength and confidence in coping with the stresses and changes of the childhood experience.

Like the fluidity of their emotions, the personal identity of the Pisces child tends to flicker and waver according to the dominant influences of the time. Pisces is rarely a 'solid' character whose attitudes and way of behaviour is fixed and predictable; Pisces is more like a changeling, exhibiting a variety of personalities over a period of time. What links these are the conditioning influences that mould and contain that watery nature into temporarily fixed forms. Don't be surprised if your child displays some mediumistic or psychic tendencies. The focus of the Pisces personality is at the connecting point between the conscious and the unconscious levels of mind, hence standing in two worlds, and in practice this implies that your child could receive information from these other levels of mind, as well as sensing atmospheres surrounding people, houses or objects through her extreme sensitivity. Pisces can be like a psychic sponge, absorbing everything from her immediate environment without discrimination. They can be highly receptive and empathic with people, and know secret things about them, which could be disconcerting at times.

The problems that such sensitivity can create for an impressionable child are many. If your child displays such abilities, then even your personal attitude to them is of vital importance. Some parents would automatically deny its existence, because the existence of other dimensions to life does not exist in their personal philosophy and attitudes, and to think of such things is too personally challenging to their own fixed mind structures. Other parents could be frightened. Some may acknowledge the child's sensitivity, accept her connection to intangible realms of life, but wisely choose not to make a great deal of it or to unduly encourage the child to explore more.

Pisces seems unable to build successful defensive barriers around that vulnerable personality; so the only form of escape is to hide inside himself. This is where he renews himself, recharges his own batteries, ready to face the world again. This is the Pisces way; some adults do it by gardening or walking in the hills surrounded by nature.

As life is perceived through their emotions and the impact that daily experience has upon them, Pisces can become negatively affected and depressed from their participation at times. They are always open to emotional hurt, and very susceptible to reactions from people, especially from their parents and brothers and sisters. The simple image of Pisces is an opened heart, often bleeding from the harshness of others.

Usually the child is quite self-conscious, shy, perhaps timid even, finding it difficult to be very self-assertive; she likes to maintain a degree of privacy and personal secrecy, because she is so aware of those shifting inner waters that definition becomes impossible. This is often reflected in difficulties in making decisions, and in the challenge of applying a consistent will in perseverance, apart from the likelihood of changing her mind under the impression of another influence. The polar opposite sign of Virgo tends to introduce elements of idealism, perfectionism and self-criticism into the Pisces personality, and this can pose problems for a personality that already lacks a strong confidence in her own abilities and temperament. What can occur is that through insecurity, the child can become too critical of her own efforts and endeavours, feeling that whatever they do or create fails to match a high, idealized standard. This leads to a sense of failure, which often drains away the energy from them which is needed to create anything else. The danger is that the child can decide that she is wasting her time, refuses to make any more effort, and chooses apathy instead of the possible pride or pain of future successes or failures. She chooses to do nothing, and may just retreat from a challenging situation. A wise parent should support the child in ways that offer regular encouragement and praise, where the effort to achieve is highly valued as well as her own personal creation in writing, drawing, modelling or whatever. Providing that falsely excessive praise is not expressed – thus adding to illusions – the child will learn to recognize that there is a real value in her endeavours, and that, even though it could always be improved, her efforts will lead her closer to creating her ideal, and that she should continue to progress. You may find that she needs some prompting to be creative – if she has experienced disillusionment at her previous attempts – as excessive self-criticism can be damaging to the playful creative spirit, and often results only in uncompleted efforts.

Like all children, Pisces desperately wants to be noticed and given lots of love, affection and encouragement. Children offer many adults a taste of a joyous innocence and love that rarely exists in the purely adult world, and they should all be greatly appreciated just for that alone.

In acknowledging that your Pisces child may sometimes bend low under the weight of the world's sorrows, you may want to help them shoulder this burden. Offering a bridge of love to them has to be the main help that you can give, and the child will always respond to that. However, sometimes helping them to release some of that emotional pressure that builds up over time is another viable way. This can erupt during childhood in sudden emotional and traumatic explosions of temper, or phases of tearful sensitiveness and touchiness; but it is healthier to have it released than struggle to keep the inner lid on the boiling water; the longer that is attempted, the greater the explosion when the pressure becomes too much.

Working with the artistic temperament of Pisces is one approach to releasing emotional energy. Words, art and drama are three specific techniques that are often suitable. The value of using words, perhaps through the medium of creative writing, either about dreamlike fantasies or about personal attitudes and feelings can create a sense of detached distance from their personal emotional intensity, enabling them to be more defined, considered and understood both by the child and yourself. As with art, this channels the energy outwards into a tangible form, releasing it through creative expression. Painting images, real or symbolic, can provide keys to understand their own inner nature and preoccupations, and this is also greatly therapeutic for many. Drama, theatre and play-acting or dance are all techniques to express that inner self and allow the energy to flow freely, or through learning to play a musical instrument. All of these help to use that ability to live in an alternate imaginative world, whilst maintaining that essential contact to functioning effectively in this world, and can be used throughout the Piscean childhood.

The younger Pisces in particular can enjoy dressing up and pretending to be fanciful or powerful figures, and you may be surprised at the transformation that sweeps over her when disguised in costume, almost as if someone else has just possessed her who is full of exaggerated gestures, confidence and swagger. In fact Pisces can make a good actress or actor, like for example Elizabeth Taylor, but the child's most expert performances are often in attempting to hide her true emotions from others, and privately she is easily hurt, very vulnerable and open, so from a caring parental perspective it is essential to deal with her carefully to avoid creating unnecessary emotional damage.

As Pisces prefers to 'flow gracefully with the moment', fixed schedules and routines in daily life are not often to his taste; he would prefer much greater freedom than is often allowed in life, with schedules determined by the clock and convenience factors. Routines are usually favoured by parents too, to facilitate the household organization, so there may be periodic struggles when young Pisces attempts to break free of such a disciplined approach to living, and would prefer to eat, sleep, play as and when he wants. It isn't that he is necessarily wrong to want to be free from such social constrictions; it is just that one person living like that in a home can become an inconvenience and disruptive for everyone else; the result invariably is that Pisces too has to conform to the family pattern, like it or not.

This nonconformist attitude can become much stronger

during puberty and adolescence. As Pisces can have rather nebulous personal attitudes anyway, and is liable to be strongly influenced by others, or even relies excessively on others for decisions, adolescence can be a very changeable, confusing and disorienting time for the maturing child. Some may respond by attempting to retreat deeper into the security of that inner world, as they struggle with those changes affecting their body and pysche. Others may imitate dominating friends, mimic the latest teen fashions and accompanying attitudes, so that they feel as if they really do belong. Some may bury their heads in reading imaginatively evocative books or fantasy comics, or spend hours listening to music.

Whilst Pisces prefers more adult company, there is still a tendency to avoid real responsibility and maturing enough to face the real world. Dreams and illusions are still the Pisces stock in trade, and sometimes a real adult maturity of clear perception can be many years away from arriving. She'll tend to avoid any direct challenges to the parental authority, because she knows that she is unlikely to succeed in such face-to-face encounters over a difference of opinion. The tactics and strategy that Pisces often employs are related to confusion, diversion, evasion and weaving a web of bewitchment around parents, in the hope that she'll confuse them enough to enable her to get her own way! Be prepared . . . she'll have you searching your memory to try to remember what instruction you really gave her, instead of the Pisces version! Having said that, Pisces probably doesn't really know either, because more often than not she fails to listen properly to others anyway. In adolescence, the teenage mind is a great distorter of parental instructions and guidance; and Pisces would rather listen to her inner voices too. She wants to be free to follow her own rules, even if she does not know what they are or what she wants to do; she might not know where she is going or why, but she reserves the right to do it her way . . . Never expect a Pisces to walk a straight path; there are too many distracting influences on the way.

His head is usually hidden by low-lying clouds; Pisces is not very well grounded or anchored in the earth, and few become really practical adults. The summons of the dream world, and the siren call of the sea nymphs is too potent to ignore for long.

Teenage romances can be hard on her emotions. Passing infatuations will take their toll, as will romantic disappointments and the inevitable rejections and insensitive treatment. She'll probably withdraw to 'lick her wounds' before venturing out again. Basically Pisces is a sentimental romantic, dreaming of that perfect idealistic love affair, 'the prince in shining armour riding the white stallion' group of images. Unfortunately, there's not a lot of those about nowadays. Or the beautiful bewitching maiden, like Sleeping Beauty who can be awakened with a kiss, for our male Pisceans.

Friendships tend to become strangely idealized emotional attachments where there are other aspects of the unconscious psyche involved too, and where Pisces may become attached to stronger and more dominating influences, in an effort to help define her own identity more distinctly to herself. Such psychological dependency is not usually recommended, and she may need to become much more independent and reliant on her own power.

Parents tend to have a powerful formative influence on Pisces. Parental attitudes and individual difficulties or marriage problems can be easily received by the Pisces sensitivity. They may reflect and imitate your attitudes, both those which you have openly expressed and also those more private or secret ones. Always try to have a genuine positive set of attitudes that they can draw strength from whenever necessary.

Pisces is very loving, modest, often softly spoken and non-assertive, perhaps too passive and too self-sacrificing in fact. It is unusual to find a Pisces who is extremely competitive (if so it may be the influence of an assertive Ascendant), as this offends her sensitive nature and demands a type of spirit that she does not possess. She would much prefer to see everyone succeed, unlike a truly competitive spirit which prefers to be the one that succeeds when others fail.

Pisces enters life bearing very fragile gifts for the world; these are a breath of another world, sometimes gossamer thin yet innately powerful. The gifts are ideals, a belief in the essential goodness of humanity and life, compassion and sympathy for the suffering of all life. This belief in life is a vision that would be good for everyone if it could ever be made real, and this should be protected as much as possible, and through a Pisces child a sense of idealistic harmony can be born in the world, and any attempt that the child makes to express this in daily life is something well worth encouraging.

THE PISCES CHILD AND EDUCATION

Your Pisces child and the normal schooling systems may not really mix too well, and much will depend upon the nature of the child's early teachers, and to what degree teachers can subsequently grasp the Pisces type of personality, and perhaps adjust their standard teaching approaches to accommodate them. Otherwise, their real potential may not be properly realized at school, or steps taken to help them to unfold their innate talents.

Pisces can be very sensitive and vulnerable at school, both to other children and the teacher's reactions. She is often highly self-conscious, acutely aware of her personal insecurity and lack of confidence in her abilities. From day one at school, she needs all the encouragement and praise that a teacher can give, as she may have a tendency to shrink away from full participation in the class, and may hide away, attempting to be invisible to the teacher.

His ability to concentrate can be poor, especially if he is trying to escape into that Piscean dream world, and the teacher may have to prompt this dreamer *par excellence* regularly back into this world, which doesn't help a teacher's strained patience. In addition, he may not respond well to those school schedules and necessary routines, limitations which he finds too imposing and would rather ignore. Having

217

to do something when he does not feel like doing it creates a growing antagonism in him and, although this may not be expressed in a direct rejection of the instruction, attempts at evasion are common and reflect the Pisces style of resistance. Attempts to impose a natural conformism on Pisces usually fail.

Her lack of personal confidence is often displayed in self-critical rejections of her own work, as not being of a sufficently high standard. This is the Pisces perfectionist stance, and she can become extremely annoyed and frustrated at not producing the masterpiece that she has envisaged in her imagination. The Pisces imagination is always more vivid, rich and complete than virtually anything that she can actually produce in this world. This does not imply that her work is of a low quality, but her own attitude probably requires adjusting. She can become very afraid of failure and mistakes, and this could be amplified by any teacher who criticizes her in an insensitive manner, or by any mockery by her classmates. What can result is a real lack of effort, and attempts will be made to avoid every school situation that could result in failure. Certainly she would need careful handling in such a situation, so that she can adjust to the fact that mistakes can be corrected; that her misunderstandings can be rectified by a clearer explanation by the teacher (perhaps with a group of other children who probably failed to understand too); and that she should just relax and do what she can without excessive self-criticism either, because that only drains energy away and inhibits personal expression.

Pisces needs a greater understanding of perspective and proportion in relationship to the issue of 'failure'. Failure is always relative, and often quite trivial and inconsequential, but it can be hard to persuade a young child of this. Encouraging them to realize that apparent failure is only a step away from success may help them to persevere more. Pisces are certainly not failures, but can perceive themselves to be so.

If he has aware and sensitive teachers who can sense and accept the Piscean gifts, then they may help to protect him from certain of the harsher realities of growing up and school life. If he has insensitive teachers who fail to recognize his underlying nature, and who walk over his feelings with a lack of acknowledgement, then his eventual results at school are likely to be diminished. Sometimes that ability to don an actor's mask can mislead teachers, who may mistake the barrier of the mask as a cocky indifference to learning, when it can be just that fear of failing in another disguise.

What are these hidden Piscean gifts and innate talents? Well, Pisces has the 'artistic temperament' which manifests itself in literature, art, music and dance as a sensitivity to the inner life of people and the cultural fruits of society and civilization. Exerting their imaginative faculties is the joy of Pisces, and their essential capacity for creativity is greater than most. Their sensitivity to the environment can be communicated through the vivid colours of paint and crayon; their love of words and storytelling can be concentrated into evocative poetry; they can express emotional sensations through dance and rhythmic body movements in harmony with music; or they can reveal their impressionability, through dramatic action, assuming the persona of the fictional character. Acting is one way for Pisces to either help resolve that inner uncertainty regarding their own identity, or another way to evade the problem by donning the many faces of the roles. Yet through drama, many Pisces can grow in self-confidence as their vulnerability can be used to give a more complete performance, and they can also hide behind an assumed mask. Sometimes they can surprise by being a highly flamboyant type of character whose purpose is to bring a touch of glamour and colour into an otherwise routine world. These are the potential talents that Pisces can share with others and, if they show signs of interest or skill along these lines, then encourage the child as much as possible to exploit and develop them; these can create a lifeline for them to follow through their adulthood.

Expecting Pisces to compete vigorously is a waste of time; that spirit is not present in her, although expecting her to apply herself and to persevere can help her shake off that other-worldly lethargy that can periodically afflict her. She will be a difficult one for teachers to categorize, as understanding her will be beyond the insight or interest of many, and in a classroom of so many children personal attention is often lacking. In the end, Pisces learns in her own way, and becomes proficient in those subjects that actually evoke a good feeling from her; in the other subjects, where she has little motivational feeling, then she will inevitably do poorly. When a child wants to be free to follow her own direction, as Pisces does, yet is not personally assertive enough to actually do so, then certain conflicts in adjusting to the established conformity of school will occur.

There may be phases when the Piscean trait of an excessively active imagination run riot, and the distinctions between reality and fantasy become a little blurred at the edges. Childish lies can be common, and can be more predominant when they are moving through an unsettled and disturbed time.

Remember Einstein? School isn't everything, and many can be late developers, so if your Pisces doesn't achieve at school, then the child should never be 'written off'. Remember those Piscean gifts of gentleness, compassion, tolerance and artistic beauty? Well, maybe that is what she has to share with the world and, if so, then I believe that is much more important than being able to do algebra or geometry!

PISCES CAREERS

The ideal Piscean careers tend to be those which value the subtler qualities of the sign, such as imagination, intuition, artistic and creative abilities, and those like sensitivity, compassion and sympathy for others. Careers which require focused will and determination, dedication and analytical logical thought are not so suited to the Pisces temperament. This is not to imply that Pisces could not be reasonably effective in them but that they would not take full advantage of the Piscean talents, or be deeply satisfying.

Artistic and creative careers such as writing, painting, poetry, sculpting and music can all beckon Pisces, who usually has some latent potential that can be unfolded. Fantastic imaginative art or writing can be their strongest talent, weaving mysterious shape-shifting worlds into being, populated by alien or mythological creatures. Adding a colourful glamour to everyday life is a gift of such spinners of dreams and this is a very attractive media to enter, with a high public demand for such escapist fiction, art and ideas. The film world with the creation of celluloid worlds to entertain can be the peak of such endeavour, either as designers, scriptwriters, or as an actor/actress.

Work which deals directly with the suffering and support of less fortunate people is another area for Pisces. Some take on this burden directly, and even though it causes great personal emotional anguish is a part of that sacrificial spirit, especially when the impulse to do so is emanating from a high compassionate ideal. Pisces can be attracted towards the other-worldly dimension of religion and the priesthood, perhaps nursing and forms of healing, or service in more deprived areas of the world. Some perform as psychic healers or mediums, acting as a bridge between the two worlds. Social work can fulfil a need to help others, as well as offering social healing through attempting to change problem areas through community endeavours. Many Pisces gravitate towards the structures of hospitals and similar institutions, where their service is directed along firmly defined lines.

Some are attracted towards Neptune's realm, the seas and oceans, becoming sailors or assistants on ocean liners and cruise ships. A few may attempt to become politicians, vitalized by an impulse to change the world into the kind of world that they would like to see exist. Fortunately, the Pisces world would be a compassionate one, unlike the world of many politicians and world 'leaders'.

221

PART TWO

Parent's Sun Signs

Considering the main astrological influences on the personality of the child is the most important priority in this book, but it can also be revealing to look at the parent's Sun sign. This enables us to see their natural and spontaneous manner of raising their children, and the manner in which their own unique style of expression is effective in communicating to the child.

Using the focus of the elemental types, it can be observed that certain signs are more naturally in affinity with certain others, for instance, Fire signs have a preference for Air signs rather than Earth or Water signs. This preference or affinity translates into actual understanding and emotional empathy with personality elemental types. Whilst parents and children are genetically bonded into a family unit, it does not necessarily mean that all the family members actually like each other, or can even understand each other's points of view. In many families, communication between parents and children is really very poor and, just as being an adult does not necessarily mean that you understand your own nature and hidden motivations, neither does it mean that because he or she is your child that you actually understand them either. The priorities of an Air parent can be quite different from those of an Earth child, and a lack of mutual tolerance and understanding can easily occur over time through a lack of communication.

So, for each parent, consider your tendencies, your partners and your child's to see how in harmony they are, and how a better relationship could be created. It is quite possible to devote years of frustrated effort towards attempting to raise your Fire child in a manner that duplicates your own Earth temperament; the only results possible are eventual failure, and a likely warping of your child's natural vitality, personality and enthusiastic impulsiveness. Was that what you really wanted? As each parent ideally wants only the best for their children, the first step should be to establish the underlying nature of the child's personality, through his Sun sign characteristics. The following steps are then devoted to encourage-

225

ing the child to express his or her own nature, irrespective of your personal preferences as to what type the child should be. Allow the child to display his or her own strengths and weaknesses, to follow their own light and path through life.

It can be instructive to note the differences in your approach to children and those of your partner. These differences may be complementary or contradictory. Neither of you may have a natural elemental affinity with the child's Sun sign. If so, both of you may need to re-evaluate your relationship with the child, to see if through conscious changes in your attitudes you could create a more fulfilling relationship.

It is interesting to note that in the more psychologically orientated humanistic astrology, the positions of the Sun and the Moon in their respective signs and houses indicate the influence of Father and Mother on that child's natal chart, and by implication on the future adult. These can be very revealing as to their psychological impact on the child. So consider your influence carefully.

THE ARIES PARENT

Few feel as proud of their children as does the Aries parent, and they intend to do their best to help them develop; yet it would be a very rare Aries parent who would willingly disrupt their social life or personal interests for the sake of their children. With the exclusion of periods of childhood illness, Aries is determined to maintain that broad range of social friends and acquaintances, as well as enjoying personal hobbies and forms of leisure activity. Both Mother and Father believe that they still have a natural right to live their own lives, and that they are capable of doing so whilst raising a family.

Aries is usually energetic and outgoing, and the parent born under this sign will prefer to live in a busy way, filling time with a variety of activities, such a business pursuits, home improvements, socializing, travelling, sports or some type of physically based leisure entertainment. Children are expected to fit into this lifestyle.

In several ways, the parental attitudes towards child-rearing are influenced by an active lifestyle. Aries has a tendency to develop fixed ideas and beliefs, and this, linked with a strong will and organizational qualities, means that the child will be expected to conform to a certain way of life and development. Often these ideas of 'parenting' can be quite socially advanced and unconventional, where the emphasis is placed upon the early maturation of the child (at every stage) to become responsible and independent; obviously one aspect of such encouragement is the progressive freeing of the time and devotion required of the parents. The Aries parent is less emotionally dependent on their children, and are more than willing to see them grow and become independent. Each step towards this is encouraged by the parent. It is a particular thrill to Aries to see their child begin to walk, feed, dress and entertain themselves because it frees the parent more. Sometimes it can be hard to distinguish between a joy that the child is developing, and a joy that is busy considering how to use the liberated time!

The effectiveness of the Aries approach can vary depending on the nature of the child as indicated by their natal Sun position. Some, such as the more outgoing temperaments of the Fire element (Aries, Leo, Sagittarius), or the Air element (Gemini, Libra, Aquarius), can adapt more quickly and easily than those children whose Sun position is in Earth elements (Taurus, Virgo, Capricorn), or Water (Cancer, Scorpio, Pisces). Where initiative, independence and self-responsibility are taught by the parent, those Earth and Water signs can demonstrate some resistence, especially in the pre-school years.

This isn't inevitable, but children with strong Earth elements in their charts often need and prefer parents who create 'fixed containers' around them, clearly defining boundaries of behaviour and predictability, building a sense of support through limitation. With the essential conservatism of the Earth signs, parental encouragement to become independent can disturb their sense of security and stability. Those Earth sign children can develop slowly at times, disliking being pressurized, and can resist efforts to force them into directions that they intuitively feel are not right for them.

With Aries parents and the Water signs of Cancer, Scorpio and Pisces, the emphasis changes to that of the children's emotions. Despite having an often naive and idealistic perception of life – which some could accuse of being childish and simplistic – the Aries parent can fail to see life through children's eyes. There can be a lack of real sympathy and understanding of the child's position and experience of life. The Water sign children feel this as a lack of emotional empathy and contact, where they rarely receive the amount of emotional support that they need. Emotional security is vital for such children, as it helps to stabilize and build a centre for their own emotional and feeling tides to coalesce around, helping them to learn to deal successfully with their essentially feeling response to life. At early ages, and perhaps before they are ready, encouragements to independence can be felt by them as threatening, and fears of being cast away or losing their parent can rise. Reacting against such fears, the child can act even more possessive, demanding more attention and emotional 'feeding' than before; a situation that the Aries parent is not likely to deal with in a totally successful manner.

The Aries mother takes her role very seriously, and is often much more suited to being a parent than the Aries father. She will have a better expression of those heart values and energies that children need, more patience, and an efficient way of handling the daily routines of the domestic household. Sometimes she may become too free with her children, especially if she requires time to follow her own interests, and the abuse of freedom develops when children take advantage of the situation. This can become a problem at the adolescent stage, where the rebellious child, having been taught independence and initiative in earlier years, can become extremely difficult to control. All children need some form of discipline or structured parameters of acceptable behaviour; these provide the framework and guidelines for them to grow within. The problem can be to develop appropriate ones that suit both the parent's and children's natures, as indicated by their natal signs.

In the Aries household, there is likely to be an emphasis placed on practical needs and the ability to function effectively in the physical world. Sometimes, overly materialistic desires can begin to dominate, directing the lives of the adult Aries, especially the father, who sees his main function as providing all the material needs of the family. He can fail to be aware of other more subtle needs of his children, who, whilst enjoying a comfortable home and those toys he brings home, may sometimes miss his involved presence actually at home. The Aries male tends to be a busy man, perhaps work or career orientated, or who has a full social life, and whose time to relax and just be with the family can be lacking. Yet he can be extremely good with children, who enjoy his spontaneity and impulsive quest for activity; he can bring a burst of vital energy into the house which the children respond easily to, yet equally he can become impatient and irritable when the children are not behaving, or he is having to occupy himself in fulfilling their needs and demands. He'll love them, but certainly doesn't intend to have to sacrifice himself; but then, most men are similar, and fail to understand how a woman can spend so much time with the children. Often, it's because the woman has little choice, and the man is not available to share the role.

The Aries man is uncomfortable with his emotions; he prefers to ignore them by throwing himself into a whirlwind of activity. It follows then that he is not particularly good at dealing with childhood emotions and needs. He'll play with them (when it suits his schedule), he'll perhaps teach them practical skills (to make them more independent), but he'll display little emotional sensitivity towards the children. He will fail to realize that the children need him to be at home and available more in situations of everyday life, rather than just those times when he suddenly decides to take them out in the car to go somewhere new because that is what he wants to do . . .

There can be a tendency to let the children learn through experimentation, and there may be attitude of physical hardness with the Aries father. This is because of the belief that life and experience is the most effective teacher, and that if the children choose to follow their desires, then they have to be willing to face any possible consequences of their actions. He will definitely encourage the children's choices of physical activity, and is likely to instil attitudes of competitiveness and stimulate a need to win in them. He wants his children to succeed, because that validates his natural pride in his offspring; the problems can arise in his relationships with them if they are not naturally capable of fulfilling his desire for them or if his expectations are too high for them to achieve.

It is of more value to the children to experience their parents within routine life, to have the opportunity to relate to the father as much as possible and to feel a regular emotional contact with him. Otherwise, as time passes, the father remains essentially a stranger. The nature of the Aries male with that underlying competitive impulse can lead to a devotion to a career, with a cost to any family life, and increasing the pressure on the mother to raise the children.

THE TAURUS PARENT

Having a Taurus parent can enhance the sense of security and stability in a child, as both the Taurus father and mother place great emphasis on building a suitable home environment which is as pleasant, comfortable and peaceful a possible. For them, life revolves around home and family, and priority is given to 'domestic bliss'. For their own peace of mind, Taurus needs home security and stability and, within that haven of relative harmony, children can find it easy to grow and explore life safely.

A home is not complete without a family, so the Taurus parent is especially welcoming to any new additions, and will ensure that all material needs are satisfied and that the child is given the protection and love that they need. If necessary, the parent will be willing to make extra sacrifices for the benefit of the family, especially if money is lacking; many children of Taureans have grown up having their desires met, being ignorant of the hidden hardships that their parents have endured in order to satisfy their children.

Taurus is an Earth sign, and one which is mainly concerned with physical and material needs. Security involves a stable home base, which reflects a conventional and traditional lifestyle. There is little scope for impulsiveness and change in the Taurus household; life moves smoothly and easily along clearly established routines and organizational patterns. That need for stability arises from a predictable way of living, where the possible vagaries and sudden changes in life are hopefully kept at a distance. The practical dimension of life is paramount, and the children will receive an effective teaching related to physical functioning in society, and those demands that will be inevitably expected of them as they mature.

Yet the Taurus parent is not totally absorbed in the material world; there is a sometimes hidden sensitivity (especially in the man) which recognizes the emotional fragility of children, and is aware of the impression that family friction can make on the development of young personalities. Sometimes this is a reflection of the adult Taurus, who does not always know how to deal with their own emotions and feelings. Generally, Taurus is apparently placid in nature, yet, surprisingly, can erupt with great emotional power and outbursts, which can frighten not only themselves but others. In this characteristic, there is the recognition of considerable emotional power within themselves, which they know they do not really control. Patience is usually there with children, yet there are times when – for various reasons – it disappears, and the child suddenly receives the loud roar and violent activity of the enraged bull!

Unlike Aries, who is in a rush to stimulate their child to become independent, Taurus is more willing to let time bring development to the child's progression. There is little attempt made to 'force' the natural unfolding of the child's potential, nor is pressure placed on them to achieve parental expectations. The Taurus parent is a more accepting spirit, determined to nurture and support their children's efforts to mature as they naturally evolve. Where the main encouragement will come is towards competent physical funtioning and later, during teenage years, of preparing for adult life in a complex modern world.

Taurus believes in the virtues and values of traditional social life. Old-fashioned ways of child raising will dominate that household, and there will be little room for any new, modern-istic attitudes.

Contemporary schooling can be viewed with distrust, and perceived as less effective than older techniques of education. Similarly, the Taurus parent holds the ideal of the family life to be a foundation of society, and will put much effort into the family to ensure its cohesiveness and success.

Children of Taurean parents are likely to reflect their parents values and insistence on the virtues of family life. Certainly it will be a core image that they may attempt to duplicate in their late adult life, using their parents as role models of stability. Problems can occur during adolescence, when the teenager may perceive their parents as 'boring and stuck in a rut'. Friction will develop if both parents and child continue to maintain their polarized attitudes, and clashes will happen. The Taurus parent should not become emotionally involved in defending their position against a teenager who is looking to explore the world and find excitement; because both ways of experiencing life can be appropriate at the corresponding stages of adult and childhood development. Yet despite such almost inevitable conflicts, the children of Taurean parents often mature to create good stable marriages and families themselves, because they do recognize the value of such lifestyles.

Taurus will teach their children traditional manners and socially acceptable behaviour and sensible morality. The social dimension of life will always be to the forefront, and the quality of relationships will be emphasized with the 'right way' to live in harmony with others being highly developed over the years. Personal values of integrity, honesty and compassion will be encouraged, and childhood failings to live up to these are likely to be penalized, especially if they become a regular expression. Obviously, no child is perfect, and whilst some laxity will be allowed, the Taurean intent is to help that child to achieve full potential and to be a contributing member of society.

233

The hope is that by building on a firm stable foundation the child's personality can unfold in an healthy manner, and that, over time, expanding degrees of freedom and independence can be granted relative to the child's ability to handle them sensibly. Perhaps the word 'sensible' is the key to the Taurus' child's training.

An appreciation and respect for nature will be encouraged in children as the Taurus temperament prefers to enjoy the spirits of nature in the countryside, and the feel of the earth beneath the feet. Taurus would prefer to live in the country-side, as the stability and continuance of the natural world satisfies their own need for permanence, and the slow but persistent growth of the seasonal cycles mirrors their own inner psychological process. City life and a lack of nature and greenery is not their favourite environment; if possible, the family home would be at least in attractive suburbia, because Taurus knows the value of a suitable environment in the development of children. Nature walks and spending time in the garden will assume a high priority in the home.

In contrast to Aries, the children's natal elements of Water and Earth will more naturally respond to the family qualities of Taurus, where emotional support and lifestyle organization will develop those embryonic personalities. The element of Air (Gemini, Libra, Aquarius) and Fire (Aries, Leo, Sagittarius), may find it a little inhibiting, even though they too will definitely benefit from such a family unit.

Much depends on the development of the Taurus parent; some can become very staid and stolid, deeply immersed in mundane practical concerns, lacking time or interest in intellectual or imaginative dimensions; others can integrate enough of a broader perspective on life to offer their children an introduction to the variety of life's rich tapestry. If the Taurus parent has children of a dominant Fire, Air or Water sign, then they should never try to fully immerse them within the earthing aspects of life. Allow them space to be active, dreamy, contemplative and imaginative, or to be creative through art, music or writing, because it is towards such experiences and expressions of life that they will gravitate as they grow older. After all, nature provides a vast variety of flowers and plants in different colours, all of which can be enjoyed in their own unique nature. So it is with children; each child has their own potential, each is different and should never be moulded in an attempt to force them to become something that they will never be.

THE GEMINI PARENT

Being a parent is not the easiest of roles for Gemini to perform; their changeable and restless temperament is not totally suited to the demands of raising children. The restrictions that young children can have on a Gemini parent often feel too excessive; those demands of time and attention, discipline, organization and teaching can be inwardly reacted against by the Gemini who needs more personal freedom.

Gemini is an Air sign, and tends to experience and respond to life in a more restless, mentally excitable manner. There is a high charge of nervous energy, which can make for a some-times volatile temperament with frequent changes of mind and attitude. Consistency is not one of their basic character-istics, and this can be reflected in the way that the Gemini parent guides their children's development.

Most children need repetitive patterns of daily upbringing and a consistency in the relationship with their parents, so that they can feel secure and stable in an often confusing and bewildering world. Children need clearly defined ways of behaving and a regular structure, so that they can explore life and develop safely within a protected, structured environment. The Gemini temperament can tend to be erratic, and if this becomes a feature of the parent–child relationship, then the child can become confused and uncertain of how to behave or to relate to the parent.

As the Gemini tendency is to be quickly bored – looking around for something new to attract the attention and interest of the mind – there are parallels with the childlike mind. But such an adaptable and varied outlook on life does not serve to offer a suitable model for the child, who is attempting to build a sense of his own separate personality. Perhaps a more deliberate, conscious effort by the Gemini parent to act and be more consistent with their children could be worthwhile; this would ensure that a clear sense of parental guidance and personal security were felt by the child.

The Gemini mother is often very versatile and ingenious, and can be extremely energetic around the home. Sometimes the home interest wanes, as her activity varies with her moods. Gemini feels uncomfortable with emotions yet is deeply affected by their inner movement. This accounts for the occasional volatility, as pent-up emotions suddenly burst out through the restraints of the mind, because the control and repression cannot be permanently maintained, but have to erupt under pressure like a volcano. Some manage to release this inner pressure in smaller outbursts, and this leads then to frequent changes of mind, attitude and ways of dealing with children. This plus the fact that the Gemini mother is not necessarily a natural home-maker, and has a personal need for socializing and mind stimulation, creates a domestic life with pre-school children that does not really satisfy her.

Any husband of a Gemini mother should consider such tendencies, because if the mother feels under strain (and all mothers do), he may be able to help alleviate any problems; perhaps through helping more, or ensuring that his wife has regular breaks away from the domestic demands and time perhaps to pursue her own interests. This would defuse any possible build-up of family tensions, because if the mother feels under pressure, then that will also affect the adult marriage, and a vicious circle of perpetuating stress can develop.

Running the daily household seems limiting to the Gemini woman. She is quite capable of doing a good job of it, but it doesn't really satisfy her as it may the Taurus mother. Gemini will dislike untidiness, and can be quite fussy about the state of the home, but there can be a distinct fluctuation in her level of interest, involvement and activity. Housekeeping chores which need self-discipline are necessary but not particularly enjoyed. There are other interests with which she would prefer to occupy her time. Certainly she will try to continue an active social life, and she may also attempt to work as well, for her own sake and not just for the family's income. Gemini will believe that self-sacrifice is not the right approach to take in raising children, and that she has a right to live her own life too.

What will fascinate the Gemini parent is the nature of the child's mind. She will prefer the stages when the child becomes more mentally alert and starts to talk and communicate. Gemini will gain most of her enjoyment with children after they have started talking, and she is likely to put a lot of effort into helping her children to develop at this stage. Her own needs for social communication will then become an advantage for the child, as the relationship becomes fuller as Gemini invests more of her energy into exploring the childhood mind.

As the child grows older, the Gemini parent will encourage the development of mind, through teaching numeracy, literacy, and speech communication. As these are all aspects of the adult Gemini with an emphasis on the intellect, it is interesting to note that each parent will basically teach their children to reflect their own adult characteristics. With some children, there is an affinity with both their own and parent's natal signs, and such family education can be very effective; in other cases, where the natal sign characteristics are less in harmony, it can be a source of family friction, where the child is unable to correctly respond to the particular adult emphasis, and fails to fulfil parental expectations.

Gemini helps to encourage their child to become independent, capable of free thinking and free speech; all movement in this direction helps to free the parent more. The child's adolescence can be a testing time, as they begin to assert their freedom from parental domination and clashes are inevitable. With the Gemini parent, their relationships with children are more mind-orientated than emotionally based; after the early years when love and support are demanded by the young child, the emphasis of the relationship will change as individuality and independence flourish. The sensitivity of the child is not always fully understood or appreciated by Gemini, and the tendency is to reason with the child rather than relying on any empathic feeling. If taken to extremes, this can develop into a lack of emotional contact as the child grows older.

At adolescence, children's development of the reasoning faculty is overlaid by a bewildering emotional and physical turmoil, as hormonal changes at puberty stimulate the necessary changes. A clash between the adult Gemini and the teenager would be a conflict between 'reason' and 'emotion', and that mental freedom of communication previously encouraged by Gemini can be difficult to deal with. Adults often find that assertion by children is difficult to handle wisely.

The Gemini father prefers to socialize and involve himself with his own interests, rather than become too absorbed with domestic requirements. Routine life bores him anyway, and he will try to avoid it as much as possible. He enjoys children and home, yet it is only a part of his life, and not one that he elevates into a dominant position. His involvement with the children can vary. He is more effective in short bursts of activity, where his nervous energy stimulates the children through sudden play or visiting somewhere; but he cannot keep his interest and commitment for prolonged periods of time. If he is a typical Gemini male with that focus on intellect, then children can often seem to be quite alien to him; he is not sure how to relate to them, and can feel insecure and inadequate in his ability to successfully 'lower himself' to the level of childish play. He prefers to keep a sense of distance, where he plays a more authoritarian role of strictness as a form of protection. He is not naturally authoritarian like Scorpio and Capricorn, but adopts that as a mask for his own lack of confidence.

A Gemini parent will find that children born under the Air (Gemini, Libra and Aquarius) and Fire elements (Aries, Leo Sagittarius) are probably more suited to the natural way that Gemini will raise children. They will be capable of stimulating the mental curiosity and question of the Air signs, helping to develop their intellects, and can allow the active and imaginative qualities of Fire to be expressed. The Earth (Taurus, Virgo, Capricorn) and Water elements (Cancer, Scorpio and Pisces) can find that they are being expected to act out of character. The Earth children will require physical grounding and stability, with an emphasis on practical development, and may be a little slower with the communication and mental skills beloved by the Gemini parent. The Water children may lack that deep sense of love and emotional empathy that they need to feel protected and secure. Gemini may not appreciate their sensitivity and feeling response to life, and through emphasizing a different outlook can cause these children to withdraw more into an emotional shell (like Cancer the Crab, or into a private, secret and dreamy world like Scorpio and Pisces). With the Fire children (Aries, Leo, Sagittarius), Gemini can enjoy their vitality, exuberance and enthusiastic response to ideas, and can help them to learn to think and plan more carefully before springing into impulsive action.

THE CANCER PARENT

Cancer is one of the signs that finds it easy to be very devoted to their home environment and family life, and children born to a Cancer parent will certainly receive their share of love and affection. Yet because of the depth and quantity of feeling that the parent can feel for their children, aspects of possess-iveness and dependency can occur, linked with a quality of love that is effusive and sentimental in nature.

Due to the strong Cancer emotions, the parent pours loving energy into their children, making the relationship one which is based on emotional intimacy. There is such a powerful need in Cancer to nourish and protect that their influence over the developing child can become too dominant, as the closeness creates an absorption of the growing personality within the parental embrace. Problems can be created through excessive love as well as too little. Cancer can manipulate through emotional 'blackmail', and guide the child to become too dependent upon the parent as a necessary response to the parental need to depend on the child for security, meaning and purpose in life.

The Cancer characteristics can be more effectively expressed by the mother rather than a Cancer father. This is because they are more naturally in harmony with the mothering role and the female temperament. Most Cancer males have consider-able difficulty in living at ease with their fluctuating emotional sensitivity, especially as such a heart response to life is not often encouraged in a masculine-dominated society.

For the Cancer parent, home life is a safe retreat from the world and its demands. That sensitivity can be more easily protected and safely expressed in the loving atmosphere of the family. For the smaller pre-school child, this can be a very secure environment to grow within, but as the child grows older and more independent, friction may increase as attempts to become free of the parental absorption are felt to be necessary. Conflicts will then occur on emotional levels, with the possibility of emotional manipulation by the parent, and accusations of a failure to love the parent may be made. Cancer can be easily hurt, and proceeds to retreat back into its shell as its natural defence mechanism, there to sit and brood on real or imagined emotions.

Cancer wants to give their children everything they desire; time, attention and money will be freely given. Partly because it is a natural action for them, partly to gain the child's love and dependence, and also because it helps family harmony. Children with Cancer parents will receive an interpretation of life that is feeling based, where heart values are given the prominant position, and colder logic and reason are definitely secondary in importance.

For both the Cancer mother and father, one main area of personal difficulty lies in the volatile, changeable nature of their emotions. Cancer is a Water sign, and has its own inner tidal patterns of ebb and flow; these have a very powerful influence on the adult personality, and can transform the inner state from exaltation to depression, swinging like a pendulum between extremes. It is a nervous energy that operates mainly through the emotions, and so can be intangible and hard to understand.

The Cancer father is especially susceptible to this, and is often moody, hiding emotions and sentimentality within a disguise of being in control and the head of the family. Underneath that crust he is very soft and insecure. Yet because he has to be so aware of his emotions – in order for him to repress and control them – he often fails to demonstrate a real responsive awareness of the emotions of others. Often he 'demands' that the family takes careful consideration of his feelings, yet fails to realize that, in doing so, others may have to deny their own feelings and emotions about things. So that he can buttress his own feelings of insecurity, the Cancer father can resort to expecting respect from his children irrespective of how he actually treats them as a result of his moods. There can be a hidden tendency that expects as much in return as has

241

been given and, when it is not forthcoming, to enter a brooding state of complaint. Emotional immaturity is not restricted to lack of years alone.

But the Cancer father will willingly sacrifice much for the happiness of his children; the only question at issue is what the unspoken 'rate of exchange' is, and when and how the 'bill' will be presented? It is likely that first signs of this will emerge during adolescence, when in fact the child will be least able to properly respond, as she is occupied with her own growth and development through puberty and early adulthood. When this situation emerges into the relationship, there will be friction and, in varying degrees, the intimacy between father and child will begin to break down. The same process can occur with the Cancer mother too, but is probably diminished by her greater contact with the children over time, and by having more opportunities for intimacy to be released in their daily relationship. Because of that repression of emotions, the father can store this tendency, until through inner pressure it begins to overflow and affect relationships.

Cancer parents will take a great pride in their home, and children will be expected to value, appreciate and care for it too. This will include clearly defined ways of behaviour at home, which for more active and explorative childish spirits may tend to be restrictive and inhibiting, perhaps making them more cautious and less spontaneous. Bad behaviour can be responded to in two contradictory ways; if the Cancer parent is having a withdrawn phase of sensitivity, then it may be virtually ignored, because the friction is too much to deal with at that time; or, if the child stimulates an emotional reaction from the parent, then severe punishment can occur, 'retribution for bad behaviour'. Irritation can cause sudden mood alteration, and as the power of emotions seeps through the Cancer parent, children can often be confused and shocked by the dramatic outburst that can follow, as the parent struggles to release the inner pressure and tension that has built up. It can seem such a change from the loving and affectionate parent of recent memory; yet children are very adroit at increasing tension in parents and, because of the emotional link between family members, few other situations carry such an emotionally powerful charge.

All Cancerians and other members of the Water signs can benefit from greater emotional balance and understanding. Festering emotions can only create poisons in the body, and repressing feelings leads to energy blockages that can cause ill health. For Cancer, one avenue to explore is the drawing through of the latent Air element, so that conscious reason and mental control can help to balance the power of love and sensitivity that they can find difficult to deal with at times.

Cancer parents will find a more natural affinity with children born under Scorpio and Pisces, and the Earth signs of Taurus, Virgo and Capricorn can benefit from the sheer love and stability which are offered. The Fire children of Aries, Leo, and Sagittarius will easily feed off the emotional energies, but may be a little too active for those times when Cancer wants to withdraw into its shell for some peace and quiet. The Air signs of Gemini, Libra and Aquarius may be less dependent on the supportive love of Cancer, and become more independent as they learn how to question and mentally explore the world, and a sense of wonderment and curiosity will dominate their needs.

THE LEO PARENT

There can be a tendency in Leo parents to see their children as extensions of themselves, especially in the context of future achievement, and they really want their children to succeed. Part of this derives from a strong sense of pride in their offspring, and part from a sense of reflected success if the children eventually attain a satisfactory level of achievement. To further this ambition, Leo will attempt to give the child every possible advantage and support.

Leo is capable of a deep loving understanding of their children, and has an emotional need to feel wanted, loved and admired by others. A mutual dependency develops, and Leo is very generous to those with whom they are in emotional harmony. Leo likes to be the centre of attention, and hates being ignored, and can often resort to flamboyant actions designed to attract people's attention. Even though there can be some born under Leo who are 'withdrawn', they are only biding their time until they feel ready enough to leap out and announce, 'Here I am!' and to claim the spotlight. Leo can be fond of socializing, and a child growing up in such a household will have contact with a variety of adults over time, which can serve to enrich their increasing awareness of the world.

Children can enjoy that expansive quality of a Leo parent, that flair for the dramatic and theatrical, or spontaneous activity that offers an exciting and interesting visit. At times, it is reminiscent of an over-the-top 'ham actor', but children appreciate such gestures and indulgences. It can also help to stimulate the emergence of the child's personality, as it offers an opportunity for the child to exaggerate personal characteristics in a fun and entertaining manner, through safely dramatizing certain tendencies of behaviour in a supportive environment. Most parents have to act dramatically at times in their relationships with children – especially when persuading them to behave – but it is probably Leo who enjoys this the most!

Underlying the sometimes frivolous and childlike enthusiasms of the Leo parent is a responsible, serious side. Leo enjoys offering advice to others, and with children will attempt to include a worthwhile 'message' within the playing. Opportunities will be taken to communicate a responsible attitude to the complexities of modern life, educating the child into an awareness of how to become successful in society.

Because Leo expects the child to do well and to attain projected ambitions, this can create problems within the relationship. It is fine if the child is an achiever, fulfilling Leo's private dreams, but can disappoint if the child is not capable of being a success in the way that the parent has imagined. The often unspoken expectations of parents for their children are common; all parents wonder about their children's future, perhaps dream about what they would like their son or daughter to become, and often these dreams are related to unfulfilled parental desires. One such cliché is the mother who wants her pretty daughter to become an actress, because she has often dreamt of being a film star; or perhaps a ballet dancer, a writer, musician or artist. Glamorous careers such as these may appeal to a Leo mother, where dramatic image can be overlaid on her children; special tuition may be given to guide the child along that path, to exploit and direct embryo talent towards a future career. In some cases this can be extremely worthwhile and valuable to the child; in other cases, the child has no exceptional talent and is being pushed by an expectant parent in a direction that will never produce success. It requires considerable parental clarity and realism to determine the real potential of a child, and not just to take the child on a journey that the parent wishes that they were personally travelling.

The death of a dream can be painful, both for the parent and the child. The disappointment of failed expectations can change the relationship and decrease the confidence of the child, who then has an image of being a failure which can affect their adult life. This theme of expectations can come to a head during adolescence, when the Leo parent may finally realize that their child is not going to fulfil those earlier hopes. Reality enters the situation, and the parent is required to adjust to the teenager who is actually standing here, with all those personal 'assets and debits'; poised on the brink of entering the adult world. The problem for all parents is in facing the fact that often our children do not turn out how we imagine. Children develop to express their own unique nature; the problem lies in the parent's desires for them.

In astrological terms, children born under certain natal signs could be unsuitable for certain types of parental career encouragement. This does not mean that they would be incapable, but that some careers would not deeply satisfy particular temperaments. Anyone who is forced to become a 'square peg in a round hole' soon finds the situation to be uncomfortable and impossible to maintain. In the modern competitive employment market, it can be difficult to find that 'perfect career'; most people have to struggle with unsuitable employment, which inhibits their potential and drains away creative energies.

Whilst both the Leo father and mother offer great loving concern and attention to their children, the Leo male tends to act like the traditional 'king of the jungle'. Home is his kingdom, where he expects respect and attention from everyone in the family; his desires are paramount and his commands have to be obeyed. There is often a sense of confident superiority in the Leo male, and that dominating presence can affect certain types of children, especially if he becomes excessively demanding and requires total obedience. Friction can develop with Earth types (Taurus, Virgo and Capricorn), especially if they become stubborn in passive resistance, and slow in doing anything; they can be as fixed and single minded in an opinionated way as Leo can. Water types (Cancer, Scorpio and Pisces) will respond to the loving affection and generous spirit, yet can also have their sensitivity trampled on at times by an overly dictatorial Leo type. Fire types (Aries, Leo and Sagittarius) are in basic affinity, and will be stimulated by the vitality of the parent, especially in that urge for novelty and new interests that Leo often expresses. Air types (Gemini, Libra and Aquarius) can find plenty to attract their minds in the household, but can find Leo a little too imposing, and may tend to withdraw more into their studies to find answers to their questions.

THE VIRGO PARENT

One of the major tendencies of the Virgo parent is to display a more traditional conservative attitude; they will attempt to raise their children in a way which will conform and adapt to the prevailing social lifestyle. This evokes the ideal image of the well-behaved child, trained to perform and behave appropriately in every conceivable type of social situation. Despite parental objectives, failure is almost inevitable, unless the child becomes almost robotic, dangerously inhibiting many of their spontaneous actions and behaviour.

As Virgo wants order, control and disciplined behaviour, the parent will certainly attempt to impose such characteristics on the child. Much will depend upon the other aspects of the parental chart, such as the Ascendant, as to how much this personal tendency is applied to child-raising. Yet in many ways, such a structured parental attitude can be extremely beneficial to a child, and Virgo is a very devoted and solicitous parent.

The Virgo household is organized and controlled; house chores, maintenance, and financial budgets are efficiently and carefully dealt with. The household operates according to a regular pattern, you often find that certain days are allocated to certain chores, and meals and regular patterns of family life are regulated by the clock. Great deviation or irregularity are rarely evident in a Virgo-dominated home. Children are expected to fit smoothly into this lifestyle and, as most children generally express a more anarchic and unconscious attitude which will clash with the Virgo need for order, so Virgo attempts to train them to fit in as a contributing member of the family.

The ability to function is the foundation of human life, and Virgo will ensure that the children are taught how to do things efficiently and correctly, so that as soon as possible the young child learns how to do all those repetitive daily tasks, such as dressing, washing, and eating properly. As children tend to scatter toys around with abandon, Virgo will soon encourage them to have an awareness of the value of order and tidiness, and will expect the child to keep things reasonably tidy and to clear them up after playing. Keeping clean will be another Virgo demand; whilst the parent may be willing to see their child dirty during play, they are only waiting for the time to clean them up again! Cleanliness and hygiene play a powerful role in the Virgo home.

Virgo will soon involve the child in the operational running of the home, and each child will be given certain tasks which will have to be done, perhaps only keeping their own room tidy and the bed made, but the lesson will be firmly applied, and, as the child grows older and more capable, more demanding tasks will be expected of them.

Good manners and behaviour are expected by Virgo, and the child will have to conform to the standards that will be clearly defined by Virgo, or face the penalizing consequences of misbehaviour. Morals will become part of the growing child's home education; the parent will express those socially acceptable attitudes in the hope the child will adopt them as their own personal guidelines. Virgo hopes that the child will develop into an independent, socially responsible person, fully capable of making a good life for themselves.

Money sense will be drilled into Virgo's children, especially over what is thought as 'wasting money' irresponsibly, although most children tend to want to buy things that adults privately consider to be a waste of money. Virgo is aware that – for most people – money does not grow on trees, and so it should be carefully used, buying only those things that are essential and value for money. There is a parental tendency for financial caution, and a preference for building a savings 'nest egg' in case of emergencies, and so Virgo will encourage a careful responsible attitude towards handling money in their children, which is likely to benefit them during their later life. Money will be spent on priorities in the home. Ensuring that there is adequate and wholesome food available, and that the home is comfortable and the children well-dressed are the fundamental areas of allowable spending.

Virgo will consider that a good education is necessary for the child's future well-being, and is often able and willing to help supplement school teaching by giving additional tuition to the child at home. This is especially useful for the younger child, as Virgo has a methodical straightforward approach towards explaining things with a more practical bias, and should be able to help the child to gain a satisfactory understanding of a subject. The quality of patience and a genuine desire for the child to succeed also means that Virgo will persevere with attempting to build a good foundation for the child's future.

The area where Virgo may possibly be weakest is a lack of real understanding and empathy with the emotional nature and sensitivity of children. In the adult Virgo, emotions are often an uneasy aspect of their nature, and the emphasis is placed on material practicality and the necessity for efficient social functioning. It is likely that the Virgo parent will disregard some of the child's emotional needs, seeing them as unimportant and secondary to practical achievements. Virgo can be emotionally sensitive, but prefers to keep it 'under control', and has a reluctance to openly display genuine emotions through physical contact. This can create a situation where the child fails to receive sufficient physical love and body contact, which is often the only way that a young child feels parental love and concern. This lack can lead to the development of child–parent splits in later life, partly as a result of a 'misunderstanding' between them.

Another facet of the Virgo temperament which can give rise to friction, especially around the time of the child's adolescence amd puberty, is that of being critical, possibly over-critical. As Virgo needs order, predictability, stability and a sense of security, changes are seen as unsettling. As the child reaches the first stages of maturation and teenage years, Virgo feels the relationship beginning to change and, as most teenagers are moody and unsettled themselves, conflicts become inevitable. Virgo responds by becoming more critical of the child, over attitudes, dress, interests, etc., and can feel that the work invested to help the child become socially successful is slipping away, especially as that stage of teenage angst and rebelliousness is active. Virgo can nag the resistant child, and be reluctant to extend those personal freedoms that the teenage child feels that they should have, 'because everyone else is allowed to stay up till two in the morning'. Virgo reacts by trying to reimpose order and discipline into the situation. Often these are common parental responses to uneasy teenage relationships, and ultimately each parent determines the appropriate style of relationship with their children as seems fit. But it is of value to note how the Sun sign characteristics of the parent condition certain aspects of the relationship with their children.

As Virgo is an Earth sign, the children that will be more naturally compatible with such a parent will be born under Taurus or Capricorn, as the basic essential temperaments are similar, although even there conflict can occur as fixed wills oppose each other. The more spontaneously active and imaginative Fire signs of Aries, Leo and Sagittarius can be disruptive in terms of wanting to be free of a lifestyle that is fixed into an ordered, repetitive pattern, where behaviour has to be predictable, and where decisions have to be seriously considered before an informed choice can be made, because Fire likes to be free to do whatever it wants whenever it chooses. Water signs of Cancer, Scorpio and Pisces may experience the lack of a deep feeling relationship with their Virgo parent, and probably some insensitivity to their emotional needs. To some degree, the Water sign child will withdraw from a full relationship into their own private world. With the Air signs of Gemini, Libra and Aquarius, Virgo can help by providing a physical base and concept of application for their stream of ideas, helping them to ground them more effectively. If the child developed toward more abstract intellectualization in later years, then Virgo would respect and admire their achievements, but would also tend to ask, 'What is the use of such ideas, how can they be applied in real life?'

THE LIBRA PARENT

A household which has a Libran parent is often one which is quite suitable for children's development; although much will depend upon the Libra parent's ability to maintain a steady and stable balanced personality and attitudes. Despite Libra's symbol being the Scales of Equilibrium, it does not automatically follow that anyone born under that sign is a balanced character. Quite often, a Libra is very unbalanced, swinging wildly in moods and changes of attitude like a mobile pendulum, searching for that centre point of stability and equanimity.

To complete the image of the perfect family, Libra feels that children are essential. Image is one of the directing motivations for a Libra, and visual appearance has a high priority; style, clothes and their own looks are important in creating the right impression on others. Children will be taught how to become self-expressive in this way, especially when they become old enough to have more personal choice in their appearance.

Libra genuinely likes children, and has the ability to naturally understand and sympathize with the childhood perspective, and to communicate fairly easily and successfully with them throughout their childhood. There is a spark and vitality with children that Libra enjoys, and which helps to revive Libra's outgrown child self that still exists within the adult; games and playing with the children are welcomed, and there

251

develops a more open house for children's playmates and increasing freedom for Libra's own children.

The Ascendant of the Libra parent will have a strong influence upon the style of raising children. This is because Libra can be swayed by the Ascendant sign tendencies, and a natural Libran temperament can display apparently contradicting characteristics because of this mingling of influences. Some Librans can become very dominating and determined to follow their own path in life, possibly to the detriment of their children who will not have sufficient time, attention and care devoted to them. They become secondary to the demands of a lifestyle and social life. Others with less powerful Ascendants, for example Cancer, would become more home and family orientated. This will also influence the degree of freedom and parental control over their children; if the parent has a full adult life or career, then the children will be expected to become more independent and mature quickly, so that their demands on the parent are lessened. Yet a Libra and Cancer influence is likely to hold them more firmly under a loving and protective parental arm. Each approach has positive and negative results; again, much will depend on the nature of the child's Sun sign as to the suitability of the parental approach.

Libra tends to treat children well, and does not usually demonstrate a patronizing and superior attitude towards them, even though the child will be clear who is in charge in the home. Children are viewed as young adults, and are given sufficient respect and dignity to enable the child to respond in a positive manner. Conversations with them are more as friends and equals rather then the unbridgeable gap of adult and child. There is often an intuitive grasp of what will be right for the child, and the theme of mutual cooperation will be stressed, so that, over time, the child will grow to be a contributing member of the family, sharing in the necesary daily work.

Unless the child is being especially awkward, Libra's style of dealing with children is to use sensitivity and patience, trying to encourage good behaviour from them with persuasion and reason; being a dictator and using force is not a favourite Libran tactic, although like most parents, it is a technique that sometimes has to be resorted to . . . .

Libra has a high regard for freedom of choice and the concepts of fairness in life, like the symbol of the scales of blind justice. These will be influential attitudes, and Libra will attempt to encourage their children to become capable of making free and wise choices for themselves, so that the process of decision-making is understood even in childhood, because it will be of great importance as an adult. The nature of choices determine lives, and lives can be made or ruined by the personal choices taken. Reason and thinking for themselves will also be emphasized by Libra so that the child does not remain dependent and repeating the attitudes and beliefs of others in a blind and mechanical way. The child of a Libran is expected to become a truly independent person, capable of expressing his or her own uniqueness.

Libra believes in the value of culture and art, beauty and harmony. The family home will ideally become an attractive and organized place for self-development and relaxation, where the unique personal Libran vision of beauty and meaning will determine the type of home decor and environment. Most Librans would like their home to reflect their own artistic sensitivities, filled with items that embody a sense of personal value and meaning to them, an objective display of their own ideal inner life. Through such visual stimulation, it is hoped that their children will begin to develop an artistic and cultural appreciation. Libra will help the child to unfold any natural talents in arts, music, painting and writing, because this is valuable for self-expression, can become a career, and offers a route to eventually meeting interesting, artistic people. Libra has a contradictory attitude towards people and society. Some Librans become traditional, conservative in essence, preferring to see themselves as part of established social life and status, whilst others move towards the more unconventional artistic and anarchistic anti-establishment people. This depends upon the Libran analysis of what 'higher development' is; whether it is towards money and materialistic success and social status, or towards personal growth, art, culture and a freer lifestyle. Certainly, whilst allowing choice and freedom to their children, if the Libran parent is firmly following either of these two social approaches, then the child will be highly conditioned by the nature of the lifestyle chosen, and be expected to conform!

As Libra is an Air sign, and associated with mind and intellect, there is probably a natural talent there for explaining and instructing their children, so that the teaching becomes interesting. Children born under the other Air elements of Gemini and Aquarius will easily respond to the mind emphasis of the Libran parent. Fire children of Aries, Leo and Sagittarius will find plenty to relate with in the Libran home, as personal freedom, independence and spontaneity will be acknowledged and accepted, and their more intuitive and artistic temperaments will be encouraged to develop. Although a Libran preference for logic and reason may sometimes create friction, particularly during the Fire child's adolescence, it can also serve to build an anchor for Fire's flights of fancy and imagination. With Water signs of Cancer, Scorpio and Pisces, Libra may not be so suitable, because whilst there is a mental affinity and understanding of children, the more complex emotional and feeling depths are often not recognized, as Libra is 'head' not 'heart' focused. Also, Water may require more tangible signs of parental affection and love than Libra may demonstrate and, with that tendency to encourage children to become independent and free, can be interpreted by an insecure child as a 'pushing away' action. The Earth signs of Taurus, Virgo and Capricorn are a little too down to earth for Libra. Libra has intellectual, elitist aspirations, trying to 'fly in the skies of life', and a naturally materialistic and practical temperament can be too inhibiting and restrictive for Libra to feel a deep affinity. Libra likes to be practical and organized, but only as much as necessary to ensure freedom to explore those more interesting mental horizons. There can be friction with the sometimes slow, stolid and more passive earthy natures, which appear to Libra to lack a spontaneous vitality.

THE SCORPIO PARENT

Being a child of a Scorpio parent is not always easy, especially when a male Scorpio is in charge. The home becomes a well-organized, tightly controlled regime, where deviations are not welcomed and decisions are clearly made by the dominating Scorpio. This aspect of control only becomes obvious when certain demarcation lines have been crossed, and then the underlying Scorpio rulership becomes evident.

The appearance of placidity that can emanate from a Scorpio is just a mask, formed by their ability to strictly control their real attitudes and emotions. Control and willpower are innate traits which disguise the inner vitality, intensity and rawness that swirls inside a Scorpio, a state of deep and wild emotion that only a fellow Scorpio can ever know. Crossing a Scorpio is never wise, because the proverbial sting will certainly follow at some point, even if the scorpion gets damaged too.

As a parent, there will be great love for their children and considerable effort put into their upbringing, ensuring that they are well looked after with food, clothes and a decent home, and that their natural development proceeds correctly. Scorpio is a solicitous parent, wanting only the best for the child so that any innate potential is released and carefully used to enhance the later adult life. Yet Scorpio does not have a natural affinity and understanding of the child's world and perception. Scorpio has a very responsible temperament, one which has moved beyond most childish tendencies, and which finds it difficult to revive that childlike spirit. Life is seen as basically serious, and tendencies of avoidance and evasion are considered to be immature. Unlike Libra, who tends to relate to children more as young adults, in the Scorpio household children are children until they begin to consistently prove otherwise.

Independence and maturation are encouraged in the children, because Scorpio prefers them to actually grow up, but until that point is reached (and probably not until the child leaves home), Scorpio is still the clear Master or Mistress in the house. Like a leader or traditional ruler, Scorpio commands in a direct manner; there is no scope for argument. As all children argue, either directly or through failing to do as they have been told, this creates friction and the likely imposition of penalties for lack of obedience and misbehaviour. Discipline is a strong factor in the Scorpio home, and is related to order and control; the child is expected to conform to whatever rules have been determined. But these rules – whatever they are – will be clearly stated to the child; if the child chooses to ignore or transgress them, then they have the freedom to do so, but in that case they must also be willing to face the consequence of their actions.

The underlying issue is power and choice. As children become older and more part of the type of society into which they have been born, they find that freedom is restricted by those who 'wield power', and who state those types of socially acceptable behaviour, such as teachers, parents, priests, employers and the state. Choice becomes limited if one chooses to conform to the established social lifestyle, or if personal choices lead towards socially dissident directions, then one will be penalized as a consequence. Scorpio tends to confront their children with this conflict; that free will and choice can lead to social penalty whenever conformity is disregarded. It is a clash of wills; Scorpio will not bend and intends to win on points of contention, yet does not really want to damage the child's will or freedom of choice. It is a small-scale reflection of social frictions, and one that Scorpio knows will be faced by their children.

The obvious danger in this is that it blocks childhood spontaneity, possibly forcing that child to adopt a course of action in order not to be penalized, and thus conforming to the will of the person with the power. The choice is to obey or suffer. Most adults will recognize this 'option' both in their own adult lives, especially through employment, and also in how they raise their children; it is a fundamental pattern of social behaviour. As a parent, Scorpio tends to embody this in a clearer form than most others, although other signs, such as Capricorn, also display this tendency.

The Scorpio male may need to moderate this tendency within himself, to become more aware of the patterns working through him, and to begin to insist less on being obeyed, especially on more trivial issues. Perhaps he should pause before responding to those inner dictatorial traits, to allow more space for the individuality of the child to be expressed freely. This tendency is probably less pronounced in Scorpio mothers, who are usually good home-makers and parents, when they settle down. Certainly an atmosphere of order, security and stability are present in the Scorpio household, which can help the embryonic child personality to be built on a firm family foundation.

The Scorpio home is often relatively traditional in style and attitude to life, but that tendency towards individual assertion can lead to an unconventional lifestyle which creates a peculiarly modern home for the children, with less socially acceptable attitudes but with the virtues of a more autonomous individuality. There can be a tendency to limit children's freedom through simple parental concern and awareness of the 'real world out there'.

Like every sign, a Scorpio parent offers a 'mixed bag' of positive and negative characteristics for the child to experience and absorb. If Scorpio moderates those sometimes excessive and extreme tendencies related to control and imposition of will over the children, then the most potentially negative tendencies will be dissipated.

The children that are suited to a Scorpio parent are those that need a strong fixed structure to develop within, such as the Earth signs: Taurus, Virgo and Capricorn, who will benefit from a stable secure home which tends to operate in an organized and regular way – yet there can also be clashes of willpower between Water and Earth. With fellow Water signs of Cancer and Pisces, one would assume a more natural affinity, yet Scorpio would consider children who reflected the characteristics of these signs to be too emotionally vulnerable and unable to control their feelings. A Scorpio could be too rough and harsh for a Cancer or Pisces child, unless that moderation of control and more emotional empathy had been developed. With Air signs of Gemini, Libra and Aquarius, mind stimulation by Scorpio would be of benefit, although Scorpio may tend to see the child's mind focus as being superficial and lacking in depth; yet if the child grew to be intellectually successful then Scorpio would have a respect for that. With the Fire signs of Aries, Leo and Sagittarius, Scorpio would react against that tendency of spontaneity and selfish choice that can characterize those signs at times; order and discipline would clash with freedom there, especially as the child reached the assertive stage of adolescence. Yet certain aspects, like the more extroverted self-assurance and intuitive or creative dimensions would intrigue and attract Scorpio, and an uneasy mutual respect and tolerance would probably develop.

THE SAGITTARIUS PARENT

Although Sagittarius is a Fire sign, the main influence that these parents will have on their children is on the development and stimulation of mind and intellect. It is the young, unfolding mind that especially interests Sagittarius, and much of the parent–child relationship and communication will reflect this emphasis.

Sagittarius likes to have broad horizons, freedom to explore humankind's storehouse of knowledge and wisdom and freedom to travel and discover new places. They need fresh stimulation to revitalize their own energy and appreciative enjoyment of life. Domesticity is often not sufficient for the Sagittarian's needs and, unless circumstances are totally prohibitive, will ensure that there is much more to the adult life than being bound to home and children. Restrictions will inhibit and depress the Sagittarius spirit.

Children will not be ignored though. As Sagittarius is an idealist, and is influenced by current theories or modern attitudes about child-raising, considerable effort will be made in aiding the child's development. Parental aspiration concerning their child's future is likely to be quite high, and will generally be associated with the benefits of receiving advanced levels of education.

The Sagittarius mother usually has a deeper influence on the children than a Sagittarius father. The male is a great lover of freedom, and has a preference for the outdoor life, perhaps enjoying other male company through sports or socializing and, given the opportunity, will not become overly involved in the demands of domesticity. A natural tendency is for him to be more extrovert and, if he has intellectual aspirations, then he'll also look for those social situations (like public houses!) where he can express his thoughts and views on life with congenial company. He likes children, but prefers them in limited doses. Impatience with them can be common, and often his attempts at looking after them are not particularly effective (although that could be a tactic designed to minimize his periods of child supervision).

The female Sagittarius is quite suited to motherhood, and performs her role and duties diligently and conscientiously. There is less of a need to roam in the mother and, once she has settled into a stable environment and parenthood, finds a sense of satisfaction with her children. Yet as with most parents, she will find that there can be a lack of mental stimulation when spending all day in the company of children, and Sagittarius will feel this lack quite strongly. Other interests and changes of scene become more important to her, and she should ensure that she manages to spend time cultivating her own interests and widening her life experience beyond the children and domestic life. This is a need that should be recognized by her partner, and anyone married to a Sagittarius woman should encourage and support her efforts to make her life more varied and interesting, especially if she has young children which occupy most of her time. She will benefit by ensuring that she mixes with people more, perhaps through playschool schemes, young mothers groups, or by more interesting company at evenings and, if time and circumstances allow, perhaps some educational courses at local centres.

Sagittarius tends to raise children in a basically balanced way. The emphasis may be placed on mind and physical activity, but their emotions and practical abilities are certainly not ignored. The child can receive a rich home education, where an informed and broad awareness of life and world affairs is often part of the Sagittarian's culture. The mother applies common sense and an intuitive wisdom to her relationship with children, is patient and considerate, and will help the child to develop a firm personality foundation and ability to deal with the world. Sometimes an emotional insensitivity can be displayed, perhaps through those tendencies to be too directly outspoken and blunt, although the value of honesty in relationships is not to be denied. Tact and diplomacy can be useful virtues in avoiding family friction.

Freedom is an important theme in the Sagittarian's household, both personal and universal concepts of freedom. Justice, ideals, philosophy, religious and moral behaviour will often be topics of conversation and interest. Freedom of thought, independence and personal self-expression and assertion will be given a high priority, and their children will be encouraged to absorb that set of attitudes. Tolerance and respect for other points of view, other religions and ways of living, different nations and races, will be emphasized, as it is part of the higher philosophic Sagittarian idealism that people should be capable of living together in peace and harmony irrespective of superficial differences such as race, colour and lifestyle. These home 'teachings' can particularly enrich the child as they grow older, offering a framework of attitudes that the child can grow to consider and think out for themselves.

Common sense and moral behaviour or ways of successfully living with people will be discussed, so that the child is clear as to the sort of behaviour that the parents expect, although there is likely to be sufficient space for personal freedom and assertion to occur. Sagittarius dislikes dogmatic attitudes, and tries not to impose them on their children. They can be good guides for the adolescent child, if the child turns to them and confides their problems. Usually it is the mother who is more aware of what is occurring in the child's life than the father. Yet the Sagittarius father is quite capable of giving helpful advice, especially in practical affairs or in discussing ideas about life and the world. He is more uneasy regarding any emotional and intimate revelations however, preferring to transfer these into the domain of the mother. Within himself, there is often a repression of emotional depths, and so he tends to run away from expressions of emotional problems in his children.

Sagittarius is a Fire sign, and will tend to have a basic affinity with both Aries and Leo, although their own particular type of Fire is less idealistic and philosophic in style. With the Air signs of Gemini, Libra and Aquarius, there will be much intellectual compatibility and stimulation, and Air children will find a Sagittarian's home a suitable environment to emphasize their own natural tendency to question and explore. With the Earth elements of Taurus, Virgo and Capricorn, the Sagittarius focus on freedom and mental development may make them feel a little unstable, as the fixed structures of a home life may be less clearly defined, and their own need for practical teaching and application may be ignored in favour of a more abstract intellectual presentation of ideas and concepts. With Water, Cancer, Scorpio and Pisces, the Sagittarian directness and mental focus can inadvertently clash with the child's complex emotional sensitivities, and there may be a perceived lack of that emotional empathy the Water child needs in order to feel secure.

THE CAPRICORN PARENT

A home that has a Capricorn parent will usually reflect the dominating tendencies of that sign, as such personality types are forceful and determined to have their own way. Capricorn tends to create a fixed pattern of household life, preferably undeviating and where all members are expected to conform to that domestic lifestyle.

Conformity is a key to the Capricorn personality, because it is believed that through conformity, security and stability are created, and that this is essential in both the individual and society. Most Capricorns have a high regard and respect for the fundamental attitudes and beliefs of their community and society, and feeling a part of that is personally important to them. Their natural attitude is to support the 'establishment view', and this can be associated with their attempts to be socially acceptable, and to gain positions of social authority and responsibility.

Any child born to a Capricorn will inevitably be influenced by this prevailing attitude, similarly as children born to the other signs are partly conditioned by their parent's attitudes and perceptions of life. In an attempt to organize and structure the household, Capricorn has a tendency to impose order on everyone; firm rules and ways of behaviour will be established as soon as the children are old enough to understand and be expected to comply with them. As far as Capricorn is concerned, society is only maintained when people conform to commonly accepted rules of law and order and those traditional ways of social life, so any child of Capricorn will be taught to develop in a way that will ensure that they become socially integrated and acceptable.

Whilst this attitude is pragmatic, and solicitious of their children's future well-being, if it becomes too firmly applied then it can have the effect of inhibiting much of that child's natural spontaneous behaviour, as increasingly they are expected to perform in whichever way the Capricorn parent has deemed to be acceptable. When concepts of acceptable behaviour are formed the opposite of unacceptable behaviour is created, which is then 'penalized' or builds often unnecessary 'guilt trips' in children or adults. One of the by-products of attitudes which favour conformism is that unique individuality is not allowed to flourish, because, if it did, then the conformity of the status quo and established acceptable ways would collapse. This issue often forms the underlying theme of Capricorn's relationships with children.

The Capricorn male is often most liable to express this more unyielding tendency, emphasizing the themes of responsibility, order, duty and discipline as the necessary roots of social living and personal choice. His own attitudes are essentially serious in nature, cautious, responsible, conventional and starkly 'black and white', tending to dismiss other beliefs, attitudes or degrees of tolerance. Life is seen in a rational, practical way, with the emphasis placed on a successful performance of 'role and function'. As an Earth sign, Capricorn prefers fixed opinions and attitudes, but if this is not carefully moderated, then it can become a form of narrow-mindedness, where there is considered to be no valid alternative to the Capricorn perception. As children have a much more fluid and changing way of living and exploring life, or as they pass through the adolescent changes, there is considerable scope for friction as those opposing approaches to life can clash. Capricorn hates any opposition to its assumed position of authority.

Family life is important to the Capricorn parent, and is often seen as the heart of a marriage; certainly most Capricorns would submit themselves to undergoing personal sacrifice and suffering for the sake of their young children, if the adult marriage relationship was not working or satisfying them, and they would tend to wait until the children were grown up before perhaps terminating the marriage. Children are deeply loved, but Capricorn has a tendency to be less emotionally demonstrative, and so the children may not feel the depth of their parent's love for them. Emotions can be a weak spot for the parent, because that intrinsic emphasis on order and self-discipline can rarely coexist with free-flowing emotions. Capricorn tends to be emotionally self-repressive, rarely showing raw emotions or passion (except at times when they burst through the dam walls and sweep away the barriers), and this can make them lack an awareness and sensitivity to the children's emotional needs and problems. In their own mind, Capricorn justifies their behaviour and style of child-raising in terms of their children's future welfare, but some powerful Capricorns only succeed in having their children conform mainly out of fear, and not out of respect and love for their parent. In such cases, the child is just waiting until they are old enough to rebel and live an independent life, free to act in the way they want to . . . .

In several ways, the adult Capricorn attitude may have been formed by their own childhood experiences and perceptions of their parents. They may have been children of parents whose marital relationships were perhaps 'not all they should be', and in reaction Capricorn tries to create a very fixed stable lifestyle for their children to grow up within, genuinely attempting to protect their own children from any unnecessary emotional suffering that a lack of adult awareness may inflict on a child. Yet what can occur is that, unconsciously, Capricorn creates different conditions that duplicate unsympathetic conditions, possibly through that emphasis on order and discipline which does not suit a particular child's nature.

Finding a balanced approach can be difficult for a Capricorn. The female Capricorn is able to modify her traits more successfully, as the need to be maternal and loving is drawn out through her, and her own emotions can find channels of expression towards the children more easily. She is often very ambitious for her children, encouraging them to do well at school, possibly transmitting ideas of 'social climbing' and perhaps putting them under pressure to achieve. Well-presented and well-behaved children will emerge from the Capricorn home, especially after the time and effort that has been put into the children to be like that! The virtues of careful financial skills will be taught, and it is likely that the child will be expected to perform certain household chores in exchange for receiving spending money; responsible work will be rewarded, but Capricorn will not encourage any belief that the child will get whatever it wants without some form of work being completed.

Capricorn will probably suit children with either Taurus and Virgo Sun signs, the other two who have the Earth element. The firm structuring and stability of the home will suit their needs, and the basic life philosophy will be close to what will naturally emerge through the Earth element. There may be clashes over will, especially with the stubborn Taurus, who can resent the imposed order; whilst Virgo will respect and value the mental organization and attitudes of the Capricorn parent, friction can occur when personal ideas are not similar. Trying to fit the Water signs of Cancer, Scorpio and Pisces into the Capricorn regime can pose problems. Their emotional sensitivity and changeability can be seen as personal weakness by the parent, as fluid emotions cannot be fixed and controlled in the way that Capricorn would like. It is likely that Capricorn will attempt to impose order on the Water children, and that, whilst superficial acquiescence may be made, a later rebellion becomes likely, especially with a Scorpio backlash. Authoritarian parent behaviour can create a passive reaction from both Cancer and Pisces, inhibiting their need to be more self-assertive, and so can have a negative consequence in later years. The Fire signs of Aries, Leo and Sagittarius will have their spontaneity curbed and their innocent enthusiasms squashed if Capricorn becomes too conformist. Their extroverted curiosity and idealistic impulsiveness will be an approach that naturally contradicts the Capricornian caution and pragmatism, and whilst there can be a side to Capricorn that would love to be like that, such disparate life attitudes will lead to friction, especially at sensitive times such as adolescence and early adulthood. With Air, Gemini, Libra and Aquarius, their intellectual interests will be modified by Capricorn's emphasis on mundane life and practical application; this can benefit them by encouraging the child to realize that abstract ideas and concepts need to be anchored in daily life.

THE AQUARIUS PARENT

The Aquarius approach to children is quite different to the Capricorn way, although its effectiveness with children can be varied, and dependent upon its suitability for the specific temperament of the child. Aquarius displays a liberal and *laissez faire* style, determined to allow their children to develop in a manner that emerges naturally from their own personality, and which is not forced to fit parental conditioning. The highest emphasis and priority is placed on the right of the child to unfold their own unique nature, and to learn how to use their minds to question existing adult and social traditions, in order to eventually arrive at their own personal opinions, beliefs and attitudes. Blindly absorbing the standard social way of thinking is considered to be a foolish approach by Aquarius, as they consider it inimical to the development of the child and their latent potential.

Much of the home education revolves around teaching their children what Aquarius considers to be the best ways to live in harmony with others. Whilst Aquarians are very individualistic, they also have a strong sense of social responsibility, and realize that the well-being of the world depends on the right human relationships, and that this humanitarian and altruistic attitude can be shared with children at an early age, so that they grow to become understanding and tolerant human beings. As Aquarius is the sign of brotherhood and cooperation, they believe that the more people can live together harmoniously, the better and safer the world will be.

Aquarius is idealistic, yet does try to live out those ideals in the real world. Like all idealistic approaches, there are often failures, but success comes step by step, through the attempt, and progress is slowly made, providing that the ideals can actually be applied in life. Relationships with their children are founded on this attitude, where the underlying purpose is to help their child become an intelligent, sensitive human being capable of living with others, without aggression and violence. The Aquarian's vision is often more progressive than most, and reflects an unconventional life philosophy, where the expression of the individual and their potential is seen as the 'highest good'; the development of egocentric and competitive attitudes, plus the focus on materialistic success can be perceived as one of the main negative causes of social friction, creating a society of haves and have-nots. Cooperation and consideration for others are valued more, as is personal honesty and integrity; being true to oneself is a virtuous path, and a way of personal empowerment.

Aquarius does have firm attitudes and beliefs, sometimes

viewed as eccentric by others, but whilst they form the core of their approach to children, are not otherwise imposed upon them; resistance to the Aquarian's attitudes can be secretly welcomed as the child grows older and becomes capable of speaking his or her own mind, as it is a sign of independence and personal assertion. Yet even there, if the child is proposing opposite ideas to the Aquarian parent, then the temptation will rarely be resisted to attempt to persuade the child to see the value of the Aquarius attitude!

The mind of the child will be given the main priority, and is the part of the child's nature that Aquarius is interested in; there can be a weak spot in the emotional dimension of the mutual relationship between parent and child. Being more intellectually biased, Aquarius is less comfortable with the emotional subtleties and requirements of children, and so whilst a real loving affection will be there for the child, there is likely to be an emotional gap present. The value on family communicative skills tends to relate only to the mental level, and certain types of children can lack that sense of demonstrative parental love.

The child will receive the encouragement of personal freedom and independence; it can help them to mature earlier, although some children may perceive this as being cast away from the protective arms of the parents a little too soon. Any signs of personal talent will be supported by the Aquarian parent, and importance will be placed upon their successful development; self-expressive, creative talents will be assisted to reach levels of proficiency, and the direction that the child wishes to travel towards will be aided as much as possible.

Discipline can be a problem in the Aquarius home; there is a natural distaste for repression and corporal punishment, and Aquarius often hopes to resolve contentious issues through reason, logic and persuasion. Restricting the freedom of children, or penalizing them for self-expression and assertion, is not an approach that they wish to take. There can be a tendency to leave this aspect of child-raising to a partner, who temperamentally may be more capable of disciplining their children; although this is a way that evades facing the consequences of their own ideals. Generally, Aquarius tends to be permissive, and those unorthodox ways can be criticized by others as being too free and easy. How well this works in practice depends on the other parent and the particular type of child being reared in that atmosphere.

The Aquarius father can sometimes prefer to retreat from total involvement in family life, especially those more onerous duties and responsibilities, in favour of pursuing his own special private interests. His role is often as an idealistic overseer, setting the underlying parental attitudes, but keeping a distance from situations that can create a conflict between his ideals and the reality of the daily work of child-raising. The Aquarius mother is more balanced; her idealism has been tempered by reality, and she will attempt to teach her children to responsibly handle freedom, knowing that, in many cases, giving freedom to children means that they abuse that situation. There are appropriate times for self-assertion, but this must also be done with awareness of others. Fairness will be one of her personal rules, and she will attempt to educate her children in that as a social attitude.

As Aquarian parents are often involved with social reform and politics in some way, the child will also learn that personal beliefs can influence the lives of others, and that great care must be taken in their application. Culture will also play an important role in the Aquarius household, and artistic appreciation will be valued.

The child will always be encouraged to live from the heart of his own true nature and failure to do so will be perceived as a denial of his unique personality. This can be very beneficial and strengthening to many children, who may not realize its value until later in life.

With children of the other Air signs of Gemini and Libra, an Aquarius parent can offer considerable mental stimulus, and a satisfying relationship on that level; although possibly the intellectual appreciation and perception of life could be over-emphasized to the detriment of both emotions and the practical applicability of ideas. With Fire, Aries, Leo and Sagittarius, there can be an impulsive take-up of ideas before due consideration has been made; some friction can develop with these more extroverted self-centred temperaments, as they may not develop that social awareness that Aquarius invests so much meaning within. Ideals take a secondary place to the enthusiastic spontaneity of personal choice and desire of the Fire signs. With the Earth signs of Taurus, Virgo and Capricorn, Aquarius will offer too much freedom and personal responsibility too soon. This will erode their need for security and stable foundations, and their basic outlook on life is much more materialistic than the Aquarian's stance. Children of these signs will tend to look for more order emanating from the parent, and can feel disturbed when that support does not occur. They need that firm protective parental embrace, with clearly defined ways of acceptable behaviour stated. With Water, the signs of Cancer, Scorpio and Pisces, there can be an emotional gap, where Aquarius fails to fully comprehend the world of intense, passionate feelings that children of this element exist within. Head and heart are two opposite ways of relating to life and, whilst they are complementary in the whole human being, are often pulling in two different directions. The Aquarius parent will fail in the relationship with the Water signs if they maintain a level of communication which is only mind to mind. These children need the heart values and empathic sense of relationship to be present, and idealistic concepts are meaningless to them unless it evokes a heartfelt response. The value of love has to be felt and experienced in the relationship; talking about love and brotherhood is not sufficient.

THE PISCES PARENT

Pisces is the culminating sign in traditional astrological movement through the signs which was initiated with Aries. There is a reflective, dreamy and other-worldly dimension to the Piscean character, which, like its grouping as one of the Water signs, tends to have a fluid, adaptable and variable nature. Cancer has moods, Scorpio broods and Pisces dreams.

The Pisces parent will be very soft and loving towards their children, greatly enjoying that state of emotional empathy with them. What is most important to Pisces is their feeling and emotional experience of life and the state of harmony in their immediate environment. There is a degree of psychic sensitivity with Pisceans, and life is often interpreted through the 'impressions' they receive from people and events. Whilst Pisces can have an intellectual ability, most decisions and choices are determined by their emotional response, even if they appear to be wrapped up in logical reasoning. Like water, Pisces tends to fit into most situations successfully, as the water conforms to the shape of the enclosing container. They often have a diplomatic quality, attempting to smooth away conflicts and friction between people and so restoring harmony and cooperation. How Pisces is self-assertive depends upon the Ascendant; if it is a more extroverted sign, then the inner Piscean personality is easily masked, and that vulnerability and other-world focus is not so easily perceived. If it is one of the more introverted signs, then the Piscean traits are more emphasized and the inner focus will be towards a withdrawal from the demands of the material world.

There is considerable sympathy and understanding of children from the Pisces parent, who greatly enjoys hearing the chatter of the young child and is willing to spend time playing with them. As the child grows older, Pisces hopes to develop the relationship further towards previously unexplored areas

271

of life, but the focus of the relationship will always remain on that emotional bonding.

Family love and support will be there for the child, but one area where Pisces may be weak is in the need to train and discipline children. Part of this is because Pisces tends to shy away from areas of confrontation, and the 'harder face' of parenthood – dealing with an awkward and recalcitrant child – is one where Pisces feels uncomfortable. This is often handed over to the other partner, who may be more capable of resolving such inevitable problems. If neither of the parents are able to stand firm with child behavioural difficulties, then it is likely that the child will reinforce patterns of anti-social behaviour which will create more serious problems in later life.

The whole area of demands which having children places on parents can seem daunting to Pisces. The idea and dream of children can appear highly attractive and emotionally fulfilling, but the actual reality is liable to shatter several of those more illusionary dreams. Whilst Pisces is probably perfectly capable of coping with the physical demands of child-raising, there can be a corresponding inner evasion, which can make them retreat into an internal fantasy life of dreams and ideal situations. This depends upon the emotional well-being of the Pisces parent, and the relative harmony and stability of the family home. Pisces can become temperamentally erratic and changeable when pressures begin to mount, and emotional outbursts occur under provocation. The male Pisces has more difficulty with this, because traditionally males are encouraged to repress the sensitive and emotional sides of their nature, and so they are less adept at dealing with emotional flux, and are more likely to overreact under pressure. The female Pisces often has a more effective balance and ability to raise children, although under stress her emotions will become extremely touchy and volatile.

Children tend to be spoilt by the Pisces parent; it is an expression of love (although in excess is unwise), and happens because Pisces so wants to be loved by their children.

Indulgence and permissive behaviour is often allowed, and considerable effort is made to ensure that the children have and do what they want. Children's demands can become unceasing, and the danger may lie in satisfying most of them so that when they are adults their demands are unreasonable and unrealistic. This can have a negative influence on future adult relationships and obviously their own future happiness. Learning to say 'No' and meaning it is a lesson that some Pisces parents have to learn, even though it may cause them emotional anguish.

Unlike Aquarius, Pisces is not an especially unconventional type, and children will generally be raised in a more traditional, socially acceptable manner. This translates into training which emphasizes correct social behaviour, such as speech, manners, and attitudes. As Pisces would hate to feel alone and isolated in the world (it would shake that emotional sensitivity too much), it is important that their children grow to be socially integrated and not excessively individualistic. Sometimes, by being aware of their own difficulties in adjusting to the world, Pisces wants to ensure that their children are better suited. Pisces can suffer from a sense of personal insecurity, which is founded on that experience of emotional tides, and can try to evade a full acceptance of that important dimension of their being by attempting to be extremely practical and socially responsible, and trying to transfer attention into those forms of preoccupation.

The home life will have an artistic or cultural dimension, and the children will be encouraged to develop that type of appreciation, as well as being expected to perform well at school. What may be lacking for children is a clear sense of Piscean stability and life direction. The Piscean tendency to waver under pressure, and the changeability of attitudes, can leave the child puzzled. One of the main tests occurs during the teenage years, when those stubborn, wilful and assertive adolescents openly clash with adults, and emotional friction is common in most households. How will Pisces react then? It is rarely an easy and quiet time for anyone involved; certainly

Pisces will feel it in their hearts, especially as the teenage child begins to naturally reject the parental protection and support in their attempt to become more independent and to express their own nature.

With the other Water signs of Cancer and Scorpio, Pisces will have a genuine, deep emotional affinity. However, the relationships between parent and child will be strongly affected by emotional moods, and certainly there will be times when fierce clashes will occur as moods conflict. The period of the child's adolescence is likely to be the most volatile, and the relationship could be ruptured if direct confrontation occurs. Yet essentially, a deep understanding of each other can be present with the Water children, with a long-lasting, loving relationship being built. Emotional swings and high emotional reactions are likely. With the Earth signs of Taurus, Virgo and Capricorn, the children will probably sense a lack of solidity and predictability in the parent. They prefer a more earthy approach which is related to the physical materiality of life; Pisces may seem too wishy-washy for them and fail to provide the firm discipline and organized structure that they need. With the Air signs of Gemini, Libra and Aquarius, the children may become too individual for Pisces as they reach the teenage years, too questioning of the established ways which Pisces tends to support in a passive manner. Yet a good relationship can develop as the parent tries to encourage that intellectual spirit of those Air children, although mutual emotional rapport may not fully satisfy Pisces. The Fire signs of Aries, Leo and Sagittarius may be a little too boisterous, assertive and selfish for the Piscean taste. Their natural physical energy, enthusiasm and impulsiveness to explore life and experience it as fully as possible is a foil to the Pisces tendency of private withdrawal. A natural affinity and understanding could be lacking and, as they grow older, the Fire children could attempt to be more dominating in the home; certainly Pisces may find it difficult to stand up to their overwhelming powerful energy.

PART THREE

The Astrological Elements

Astrology considers that the basic building blocks of all organic and material structures are composed of four elements, Fire, Earth, Air and Water. Within each individual, each element represents a basic type of energy and consciousness which is expressed through the human personality and body. The four elements are present in everyone, although each person tends to be more naturally in affinity with certain elements than others.

Historically, this concept of elements has played a profound role in the development of several philosophies, myths and religious beliefs. From the East comes the Chinese philosophy of the Tao, where Yin is associated with Water and Earth, and Yang with Fire and Air; and the corresponding health techniques such as acupuncture, with its concept of five elements of Wood, Fire, Earth, Water and Metal. In India, Ayurvedic medicine is based upon elemental concepts, and in Hatha Yoga, the energy centres of the body (*chakras*) are associated with particular elements. In the West, four elements have usually been the foundation of this idea, as the fifth one is considered to be the primary Life energy which has been stepped down as though through a transformer, resulting in the creation of the four elements. This essential energy has been termed *prana*, *orgone*, *Qi*, or the spirit in different cultures. In the Greek world, the elements were known as moral (fire), soul (water), intellectual (air) and physical (earth), which passed through the states of light (fire), fluidity (water), airiness (air) and solidity (earth). In Medieval and Renaissance times, they were termed the 'humours', which included sanguine and melancholy, choler and phlegm.

The elements also symbolize the needs of advanced life on earth, where air, water, earth/food and fire/warmth are all essential to well-being. The natal chart or horoscope of an individual reveals their basic energy pattern and affinity to each of these elements, and the element of the relevant signs shows the specific type of personality tendencies that are foundations to that person's character. For instance, a Gemini/ Air Sun sign is naturally attuned to the mind, and is often

quick-witted and intellectually orientated, whereas Taurus/
Earth favours physical and material reality, relying more on
physical sensations and the material world's pleasures and
comforts.

Each element offers a focus for the individual; Air is
expressed through thought, mental interests, and questions, relying on reason, intellect and logic; Fire sets sparks
flying, offering warmth, radiating energy, enthusiasm, spontaneous love, goodwill and self-assertion; Water can be cool or
passionate, healing and soothing through emotional empathy
and understanding; and Earth is the grounding in the physical
world, capable of effectively using and enjoying material
objects through a pragmatic, practical attitude and ability.

In a full natal chart, each planet in its appropriate sign, plus
the angles, are evaluated in terms of elemental affinity, so that
the relative strengths are considered in terms of 'superior or
inferior functions'. The great psychologist Carl Gustav Jung
used astrology and the elemental concepts in his treatment of
patients, Fire being intuition, Earth, sensation, Water, feeling
and Air, thinking.

The essential lessons to be learnt and expressed by each
element are: Fire=love, Water=peace, Air=brotherhood, and
Earth=service. If these were succesfully expressed by everyone then we would be living in an earthly paradise. Gaining
insight and understanding into these four perceptions of life
can aid in getting relationships right, greater tolerance of other
points of view and more cooperation. Quite often in relationships people are drawn towards others who embody one of
their 'inferior functions', so that over time they can perhaps
learn and absorb some of that other element into their own
personality. Or if someone is doing a job that is 'out of his
element', then there will be a lack of enjoyment and personal
difficulty in continual performance.

There is considerable depth in this elemental concept that
unfortunately cannot be entered into here. Yet, in considering
the basic elemental structure of children and parent, much can
be revealed as to their natural affinity and disaffinity.

The Sun sign element is probably the single most dominant element in the personality. It indicates the root of personal consciousness, where that person is naturally attuned to, creating the experience of life that is most real and important, and is the underlying vitality source, power and motivating impulse. The Ascendant element indicates how that self is actively expressed in the world, and what the natural way is for that person to confront and experience life. These can be in disparate elements, such as Fire and Water. In some cases, the influence of a Watery Ascendant can douse the fire or inhibit its vitalizing spirit; or a Fire Ascendant can make the Water Sun more vital, passionate and extroverted.

By studying the elemental relationship between Sun and Ascendant, inner conflicts or harmony can be indicated, and offer a key to greater personal understanding. Parents can establish their own and their children's basic elements by reference to the Sun-sign dates and the Ascendant tables; and then study the relevant sections to consider both their own and their child's personality structures, so that they can attempt to see life through the child's elemental perspective too, especially if it is a different elemental type. In fact, the section on the elements has been written within an adult context, because parents can find it illuminating to evaluate their own and their partner's nature through such a focus, and it tends to highlight the probable focus of the child in later adult life.

THE ELEMENT OF FIRE (ARIES, LEO, SAGITTARIUS)

The Fire element offers a high degree of physical and mental vitality, which tends to create an optimistic, confident personality, who trusts in the essential well-being of the universe and who intends to express an enthusiastic, direct and dynamic approach toward experiencing it to the full. You will be a basically warm, extroverted character, perhaps a little too self-centred at times, and sometimes volatile and unpredictable.

Fire imagines himself to be a performer on a stage, dramatically playing those romantic and mythologically significant roles, and often you'll see yourself in that position instead of facing the real-life situation. Fire does not like mundane reality, with those responsibilities of family, employment and everyday duties that need to be done. There's a resistance towards being preoccupied with the material world, and a distaste for having to cope with it. The restraints on freedom are often frustrating to Fire, sometimes to the degree where an attempt to burn those imprisoning ties are made, such as impulsively walking out of a job or a marriage, in order to breathe freely again.

What stimulates Fire is a personal fantasy world, one where colour and glamour can be overlaid on the 'boring world' that Fire seems to encounter. Dreams are crucial to the well-being of a Fire type, to keep that inner spark alight. Variety and changes of scene also appeal, and you may prefer to become a world traveller to satisfy that need for adventure and fresh stimulation. Future possibilities will fascinate you, and you need to remain a believer in the infinite sea of possibilities that are available to you in life, as the dreams of new horizons motivates your forward movement. If you begin believing that those possible options have disappeared and are no longer available, then that inner spark splutters and fades away as the weight of the world descends upon your imprisoned spirit.

Freedom is essential to you; you need to spontaneously display that free spirit and follow those invigorating impulse decisions. Relationships can pose problems if this deep need of yours is not recognized and understood by both you and your partner. One way that you may tend to assert this freedom is by insisting that your point of view is right. Obviously, nobody can be right all the time, and expressing that tendency in a forceful, dogmatic manner can lead to negative reactions from others. With charm and persuasion it can work effectively, but you may need to learn to be adult about 'this need to be right', and to invest it with less importance, so that relationship friction becomes less common.

You are likely to have a fairly direct and straightforward style of expression; diplomacy and subtle tact is rarely one of Fire's gifts. This can offend certain people, who take exception to honesty and direct personal opinion; others can find such simplicity refreshing and appealing, cutting away the confusions and smokescreens of interpersonal communication. Sometimes you will wonder what you said or did that has upset somebody. There's an unsophisticated air of naivety and innocence about you at times – or a lack of awareness!

Fire needs a deliberate self-imposed discipline in order to channel a probable overflowing of vital energy towards productive areas. You should have the ability to consciously direct your willpower – although perhaps not consistently – but maintaining your interest and perseverance long enough could pose a problem. You could become highly self-motivated, being creative in establishing new enterprises and projects that require a considerable initial momentum to lift them off the ground.

Often you tend to create problems due to that self-centred and wilful overconfidence, plus that impulse to rush into situations without careful prior consideration. For one who loves the thought of a future filled with possible enjoyable paths, you rarely spend time checking the most appropriate routes to take; just setting off without even a compass! Whether you realize it or not, you create most of your problems yourself, and even most of those prisons through your own choices and actions. More reflective thought and planning would help you to create a suitably promising future.

There may be a tendency to live too 'fully' without thought for tomorrow. Fire can consume itself easily, and some with this tendency can be attracted to an intense lifestyle, perhaps with drink and drugs as an escape from the limitations of the ordinary reality and that sense of imprisonment. Social activity, and a need to be 'where the action is', can lead to a restless spirit, striving to exaggerate all types of life experience, and sometimes crossing boundaries which it may have been wiser to stay within. There can be a private dislike of being bound within a body, and this can lead to a compulsive behaviour pattern to liberate that fiery spirit as soon as possible. Once it has been released, fire is basically an untameable energy, only water and earth can inhibit it, as air fans the flames. Fire can be prone to indulge in sudden, impulsive, violently passionate love affairs, and may not be the most reliable of partners, especially if that self-centredness is still dominant. You may need to remind yourself that there are other equally important people around you with whom you can share experiences of value and meaning, and that they are not just there for you to take advantage for your own personal needs whenever you choose.

Fire tends to be impatient with people who are more introverted, gentle and sensitive, like the Water signs. Earth signs embody that dimension of life that Fire attempts to avoid, and is almost the direct opposite to its own natural tendencies. Yet potentially, a Fire–Earth partnership could work very well for mutual benefits, if the early barriers of essential differences were crossed successfully and a state of complementary harmony was established. Fire is attracted to the potential for action inherent in Air's overflowing ideas, words and schemes, and tends to be highly stimulated by contact with Air types.

THE WATER ELEMENT
(CANCER, SCORPIO, PISCES)

For those for whom the Water element is strong in their astrological temperament, the realm of life which is explored and focused upon is that of the emotions and feelings. These will be experienced as more real and immediate, acting as a 'guide' in your life. You will tend to have considerable faith in the validity of your feeling responses. For you, motivation emerges from feelings, and that whatever is felt is real, as distinct from Earth's reliance on the physical senses. It is a very intimate and subjective inner sense that guides you, as you live in a private world which is instinctual, irrational, weird and mysterious, an ever-shifting, magical world of psychic impressions and sensations.

One problem may be that you do not really understand the nature of your motivations, and that you direct your life as a result of emotional reactions; these may not always be suitable, especially as many emotions are connected with fear and self-protection. Potentially, your sensitivity is considerable, with a tendency towards entering the realms of intuition and psychic attunement. This should give you the ability and capability to act empathically in relationships; this can also make you more susceptible to registering suffering. You would benefit by greater self-understanding, as this will make you less liable to experience those compulsive desires, irrational fears and an oversensitivity to people which can torment those who are at the mercy of their emotional sensitivity due to a lack of personal awareness.

Relationships are a life breath to Water. They are essential, and also serve to provide a focus in directing your energies and purpose. You need others to provide a 'form' for the 'formless' water energies, so that a 'container' helps to focus it into a distinct, definable shape. Earth energies are especially useful in providing form and solidity, so you are advised to draw these energies from yourself, and perhaps cooperate with people who embody that energy. There can be a fear of isolation and being alone in life, as Water needs that constant contact with people and free-flowing energies in relationships.

The Water signs are usually imaginative, perceptive, sensitive and have considerable depth, like the inner ocean that they can struggle to swim in at times. They are moody and changeable, an inner inconsistency is usually evident, except perhaps in the more inscrutable Scorpio mask. Life is sensed through feelings and gut reactions; intuitive antennae track across the world, picking up all sorts of impressions. As

Water is so preoccupied with monitoring its inner seas and emotional responses, there can be a dislike of external change occurring, as it distracts from that inner observation. Strong personal likes and dislikes are often evident with Water; irrational perhaps, unexplainable probably, but they do condition choices and decisions. An Air sign struggling to get a rational explanation from Water over a 'gut reaction' would probably throw his hands up in frustration!

Water can feel more uncomfortable with those who are exuberant attention seekers – such as Fire – or those with a high Air quality, as Water tends to think that they are too superfical and lacking in depth. Unless ideas have an emotionally resonant content, Water is not so interested in speculative abstract thinking. The preference is for those who are quieter, more self-contained and independent, with whom it is possible to communicate in a deeper and more satisfying personal manner.

There can be a tendency to repress feelings at times, but this should not be encouraged as they should be released, or else you may find that the 'dams burst' and create crises out of emotional storms, and such a volatile release of inner pressure (like an erupting volcano), can be damaging within relationships. You may have to be wary not to stimulate too much emotional instability, through an excessive emotional reaction to the vulnerability of your feelings; you have to accept that you will be easily hurt by others, even when it is not realized by them and that in most cases it is best to absorb the pain and release it through a sense of forgiveness. Do not store the pain within yourself, as like water it will grow fetid when contained for a long period. There can be a tendency to respond to such pain by forms of emotional blackmail, or guilt trips laid onto others who have deliberately or inadvertently transgressed your sensitive feelings. Such a reaction to them is pointless, and only serve to perpetuate a circle of increasing emotional suffering for everyone concerned.

Being overly possessive is another tendency in relationships, partly because of that degree of dependence and also because of the genuine depth of love involved. Each person has to be free to be themselves, otherwise friction intensifies, and conflict occurs.

Water will have to refrain from being so impressionable, and being too influenced or thrown off course by any of life's challenges. A purpose and self-discipline to avoid this hazard needs to be developed. You may need to free yourself of emotionally based toxins that can build up in you, due to that emotional way of responding to life. If this is not achieved, then your emotions can grow more confused and contradictory, much like a slowly poisoned and polluted sea becoming dangerous to life. The key to this is through understanding your emotional depths, those needs and insecurities, and either fulfilling them through relationships in a conscious manner, or by adjusting them so that your attitudes are balanced. At an extreme, you can become overwhelmed by your emotions, and this can become devitalizing, resulting in feeling unable to cope with life. Try not to be overly self-preoccupied; a more active involved interest and concern for others can prove to be a viable way to rid yourself of unwanted blocked energy, and that empathic sensitivity can be used to support and aid others. A sense of personal ideals and values can aid you in developing an emotional self-sufficiency and a greater sense of balance. Rightly understood and applied, Water energies can enrich a life, especially when in some form their healing and cleansing energies can be directed outwards for the benefits of others, and eventually for your own well-being too.

THE ELEMENT OF AIR
(GEMINI, LIBRA, AQUARIUS)

An emphasis on the element of Air indicates that you will have an intrinsic preference for intellectual interests, concepts, and theories. This preoccupation will be with words, processes of thought and ideas, and will involve you in attempts to communicate to others through such socializing interests. In several ways, the element of Air is a civilizing factor in our progression, adding qualities of reason and tolerance to human relations, permitting a flexibility of mental response to allow for differences of opinion and viewpoints on life. There is a sense that there is a huge external world out there, with a multiplicity of people and wonders, and that life can be an ongoing series of explorations and appreciations of both the natural world and humankind's cultural achievements. To Air, a personal philosophy needs to be developed which can take account of life's ups and downs, and generally Air is capable of taking such experiences in their stride.

Society is one of Air's preoccupations, where a liberal awareness is often dominant, with a high ideal associated with an image of the progression of humanity. The ideal world of Air is formed from an idealistic vision, based on integrity, ethics and morality as the foundations of a civilized lifestyle; this perspective is future-orientated, and can be especially strong in Aquarius and the concept of social brotherhood.

You value logic and reason highly, believing in an objective approach to problems, social or individual, tending to distrust any more subjective reactions as unreliable. Usually, you will carefully evaluate and assess situations and choices before making a decision, and your mental style is to be contemplative and reflective rather than relying on a watery gut reaction, a spontaneous impulse, or established patterns of familiar response. Your approach to understanding life is through the mind, curiosity and questioning elicits answers which you strive to understand by incorporating them into a coherent pattern or system of thought, similar to philosophy or scientific techniques. Your mind needs to organize through association, and you can become uneasy when experiences or ideas fail to fit comfortably into your own personal 'reference system' and world view. You prefer to categorize and label things, which you believe gives you a sense of understanding the mysteries of life. To you, an explanation that sounds reasonable and logical is better than none at all, hence the appeal of intellectuals towards reincarnation theories.

Air tends to attempt a distancing from the more immediate demands of daily life, so that you can gain a new perspective and rational approach to whatever you are doing, and display a form of considered thought and a contemplative attitude. Sometimes you tend to resist a full involvement in daily life, preferring to remain in the clouds. You tend to enjoy socializing with others, and listening to them, as whilst you may not agree with what is being said, you find the activity and process of mental functioning fascinating, and can at least enjoy contact in that way alone. That ability of detachment can be used effectively when dealing with people, as you feel little need to become involved with their emotional concerns or personal lives, except in the way in which they are expressed or by the information which they reveal which you can use for future consideration. You can appear 'cold', unconcerned with the dramas of human existence in a personal sense, unless you can conceptualize these into some form of theory or idea.

You may have to be careful not to let your mind become too absorbed with those theories and abstract ideas, because this can lead to a degree of mental imbalance, leading you into inhabiting an inner world which is far removed from everyday reality, and whose concepts colour your perception of the world. This can create distortion, and an eccentric or fanatical temperament. As you tend to overvalue the intellect, and are stimulated by pure ideas, you can become defensive if any of these pet theories are seriously questioned or challenged. Your shadow self hides in those repressed emotional levels of your nature, as you lack an immediately accessible emotional depth, and possibly a relaxed attitude to your physical body too. You can try to evade and resist emotional and feeling aspects, as they are not suitable for a fixed categorization and are a fluctuating energy, being impossible to fit into your defined theories. You 'think about feelings' usually, instead of allowing yourself to really feel those feelings and emotions. Because emotions have a wilder and more basic nature, they can clash with that image of the intellectual adult human being that you have developed. Others can sometimes find you difficult to understand in relationships.

You will probably need the Water element to draw you back into humanity as it really is, and to enhance your ability to relate more easily with others on a personal level, rather than just through communicating words and ideas. Sometimes you can resent or try to ignore those who embody Water or Earth energies, because they will tend to point out that often your beloved ideas are not really practical and are lacking in depth and vitality. As their impact on you is to pull you down to earth, you tend to prefer company which is similar to yourself, for mutual interest and protection. With Fire, you find a degree of stimulation towards a liberation of your ideas, plus more enthusiasm and even more ideas to play with. With Earth you feel the confines of a heavy element weighing you down, whilst the sensitivity and dominance of feeling expressed by Water frightens you by the direct immediacy of its impact.

You may have to avoid becoming an intellectual dilettante, turned on by ideas but possessing no depth or ability to relate them into any meaningful context. You will tend to be cautious, owing to that need to think about your proposed actions and decisions first. Unless this is excessive and stops you making any decisions, it can be a useful trait. You will have to be careful not to use your mind too much, as your nervous system is highly strung, and a lot of mental activity can strain it, thus depleting your overall energy too easily. A period of quiet rest, perhaps coupled with regular meditation or relaxation, listening to soothing gentle music, can be beneficial in a variety of ways, enabling you to gain a deeper perspective on the nature of your own mind, and to create a distance between your self and its restless activity.

THE ELEMENT OF EARTH
(TAURUS, VIRGO, CAPRICORN)

Having a strong Earth element in your natal chart indicates that you will be preoccupied with the material level of life, relying on your own experience of your five senses and the physical reality and obligations of daily living. Your approach to living will always have a practical dimension, where your choices and decisions are determined by a materialistic realism, and which can achieve the objects of your desires. You will not appreciate speculation and theories; what interests you is what actually works, so that a tangible achievement is made.

The focus of all your efforts is the attempt to build a secure, stable and safe environment to live in, and your home life will be of vital personal importance and meaning. Order is essential for you, and you will try to create a structured organized lifestyle, because this makes you feel more secure. There is a fear of chaos and disorder in life, and you try to establish barricades to prevent it encroaching into your private world. The Earth elements provide the tendency in us to put down roots, to create an ordered and law-abiding society where tradition and acceptable common lifestyles develop.

To establish this sense of order, personality patterns emerge which reflect discipline, application, hard work, diligence, reliability and fixed routines. You accept responsibility and, once your decision has been made, you will be committed to a marriage, career or job. You will be practical, efficient and apply common-sense approaches and values to problems of daily living. Your home and material possessions will be of great importance, and most of your efforts will be devoted toward improving your standard of living. Your personality expression will be intended to be socially acceptable, and generally you will have a conformist and conservative attitude towards life and people. There can be a tendency to become more narrow-minded and dogmatic, refusing to allow different ideas and thoughts of alternate lifestyles to enter in, preferring to remain with that sometimes simplistic and black and white world view. This is revealed in that fear of the unknown, and a reluctance to venture out into unfamiliar realms of life; security is felt to be residing only in the known and familiar, and experimentation and searching for new ideas is not Earth's style.

You can lack a broader vision, rejecting any tendency to allow yourself to dream about changing your life, or about exploring a much wilder and richer world that exists around you. To do so, you would need to venture out of that secure, stable and repetitive world that has taken you so long to establish, and such a step would not come easily to you. But you may have to ensure that you do not restrict your outlook on life too much, becoming too absorbed in the obligations of duty, family, or routine. It may be wiser to take deliberate action in order to open yourself to new dimensions of this infinitely rich world, and this would greatly benefit you. Also, perhaps a broader set of ideals would serve as an enriching and guiding factor in your life, as you may begin to experience a lack of a deeper meaning to existence. As work and practical concerns tends to preoccupy you, if this was ever taken away (such as unemployment or retirement), much of your sense of identity and reason for existence would go with it; so it is advisable that you widen your interests even as a self-protective act against this occurring.

You have a strong identification with your physical body, and this will be of a sensual nature. There is a natural affinity with the underlying rhythms of life and its cycles of creation and dissolution, and this can offer a patience and discipline to your attitudes and actions. You have an innate ability to be productive and to ensure an adequate standard of living, and perseverance is one of your important abilities in your efforts to achieve those aims. You may prefer not to be openly assertive, although the assertion of your solid, reliable presence will not go unnoticed by others. However, if you feel threatened or some aspect of your security is at danger, then you will fight to preserve those 'possessions'.

Being naturally cautious, you may lack a sense of adventure and imagination. You may be wary of the intellects of Air signs, often questioning the value of that in real life, and may feel uncomfortable if confronted by those who are very verbal and quick-witted; even so, there is likely to be a curiosity and fascination regarding Air, even though you will see them as impractical dreamers. There may be more distrust and unease with the Fire signs, as you see them impulsively and spontaneously attacking life with vigour, being too forceful and self-centred to be absolutely trustworthy in your eyes. You doubt their ability to persist when the going gets hard, and see them creating so many imaginative directions for them to travel towards that they can find it difficult to settle on any. They seem to lack a dependability and that is important to you. You feel more of an affinity with Water, as both elements prefer to exist within a stable environment, and are self-protective in an attempt to preserve what has been worked for. Water tends to enrich the Earth, making it productive, whilst Earth, acting as a 'container' and defining the direction for Water energies, would also be compatible.

Epilogue

INHERITING THE FUTURE

Across the world, parents in every country devote considerable love, time, effort and caring in trying to safely raise their
children to maturity and independence. It is a common
parental responsibility that goes beyond artificial barriers of
nation, culture, race, colour and ideological or religious
dogma. It is a shared worldwide task to perpetuate the future
of the human race, and one to which most adults contribute.
As parents, we have so much in common with other parents in
other countries; for women, the pain of childbirth and the love
for the child is a common language and, for men, the sense of
pride in becoming a father. Worldwide, parents can stand
shoulder to shoulder united in a common experience of the
tears of joy and of heartache that children can bring in their
wake. Having children is a profound experience, possibly the
most creative action that many achieve during their lives; the
act of creating new life.

In caring for our children, perhaps we should also turn our
eyes towards what we may be creating for our children and
grandchildren; a view of the future world, our inheritance for
them.

Demanding as it may be, parental responsibility should not
be limited to just raising our own children, but ideally should
also encompass the world into which they will emerge, both at
birth and at maturity. It is the inheritance of previous generations that the child will face, the results of others' social and
political decisions that have created the current state of our
world and nation. The question is, what will our generation
bequeath to our children?

Humanity is a social species; we live together in large or
small cities or communities, which, spread across a nation,

create 'society'; a collective expression of individual needs, desires, beliefs and ideas which ideally reflects a consensus as to how people choose to live. Through such choices, we create our own future experience.

There's a saying that 'Without a vision the people perish'. What is our vision of the future? What do we want our children to experience as a consequence of the choices and decisions that we are making now?

In the West and in modern technologically advanced nations, the standard of life is quite high. Each of us has those four fundamental elements required for advanced life forms. There is air to breathe, because without air we would quickly die; there is clean water to drink; there is food provided by the earth; and there is warmth provided by our energy supplies. Our social life is rich, cultured, knowledgeable; education and medicines are available; we have housing, forms of transport, employment. Generally, life is reasonably enjoyable for the majority of people, and we often fail to appreciate our good fortune, which is the positive consequence of our forefather's efforts and vision.

Equally, there are as many people in the world who do not enjoy our social advantages – people in the 'Third World' countries, or those where industrial and technological advances have not yet been achieved. Many live in nations where the four elements for life are not all easily available; famines, droughts and floods are common events in their lives. These countries are full of parents and Starchildren too, who have their own dreams and potentials which are rarely realized, because of man-made civil wars or ecological disasters. Their tragedy touches us too, as we see the distraught faces of grieving mothers whose children have just died because of unnecessary starvation.

Yet in the technological West, we are not any less vulnerable to making life more difficult for ourselves. Our choices can determine a much less rosy future for our children. Through greed and an unthinking or uncaring attitude, we can bequeath to them a future of an ecologically poisoned land, through radioactive or chemically dangerous waste dumps, polluting our rivers, seas, and oceans. We can destroy the protective ozone layer in the atmosphere, allowing gaps for harmful rays to enter. We can create the 'greenhouse effect', where the temperature of the planet rises and melts the ice caps, leading to widespread devastation through oceans flooding low-lying land masses. We continually threaten ourselves by the ultimate disaster of global nuclear war, brandishing nuclear warheads against other people who may hold different ideological beliefs to ourselves. We allow ourselves to maintain racialist attitudes in multi-racial societies, thus creating future disharmony. We persist in nationalistic economic policies when it is becoming obvious that economically the world is now interdependent on the financial well-being of all nations. We keep religious bigotry alive, insisting that our faith is the only true one, instead of being tolerant and accepting that there are many roads to real religious and spiritual experience. Is this really the future that we want our beloved children to inherit?

As demanding as it may be, caring for our own particular children is only a part of the whole parental role and function. Our love and concern should ideally expand to make the world a fit place to raise a child, and for our grandchildren and future generations. This doesn't necessarily imply that we all shall become social activists, although that path may suit some. It is that we should all think seriously about what sort of future world our choices and decisions are helping to create for the generations to come.

Let us allow ourselves to dream those Utopian dreams of peaceful and contented societies, mutually living in world harmony, a planetary family of humanity. We can aim to imagine an ecologically healthy world, where we all recognize our dependence upon Gaia, Mother Earth, and that we all live together on One World, and that we should take great care in looking after our planet and home. Let us aim to imagine the family of man, a naturally multi-coloured species with multi-faceted cultures and ways of living, enriching each other by our differences, rather than by dividing us; we can recognize the One Humanity, our commonality of parents and children. We can begin to support compassionate change in the world, by helping those less fortunate then ourselves. And through supporting those social visionaries in every country who are dreaming the Great Dream of the future. Each of us can help by adding our voices and support to those who are more active, and who desire only the greatest good for the greatest number, and to begin to divert support, energy and money away from those dangerous threats to world peace and security. Isn't this something that we should do for the sake of all children? They are not capable yet of initiating the necessary changes. We are, and we hold that responsibility.

A new life education is needed for our future world. A teaching of realizing human potential, life-affirming positive attitudes, right human relationships and values that encompass the highest aspirations of humanity. Utopian ideal? Perhaps . . . but we can take the first steps towards attempting to achieve such a vision. We can start now. At the very least, we can help to build a better world for more children.

This path is embodied in the innate gifts that each of the zodiac signs offers us. Each sign has a fragment, a talent or direction that it points towards. Each child has a task of unfolding this gift to humanity, for the enrichment and good of all. We need to encourage the release of each child's potential; and pay attention to the lessons that they seek to teach us. In their innate latent potentials lie the hopes of a future world.

Aries offers the gifts of enthusiasm and initiative, planting those seeds, ideas and actions that can bring new experience and development into the world.

Taurus is the nourisher of the seeds planted by Aries, the completer of what has been started, the builder of stability, security and foundations, and the appreciator of physical life and the senses.

Gemini offers the questioning mind, the ceaseless searcher for answers and knowledge, the seed of mind that is perpetually unfolding and helps us to understand the universal life process.

Cancer teaches us to value family life, the joys of intimate emotions, domesticity and children. The root of society.

Leo takes us on a search for personal expression, the need to discover our higher humanity, vitalizing life and showing the value of loyalty.

Virgo demonstrates the aim for perfection, through examination, analysis, criticism, a detailed scrutiny and observation of humanity and the world, and the cooperative values of service and helpfulness to others.

Libra offers a view of the potential of right human relationships and cooperation, social obligations, the ability to reflect the other point of view, the potential of balance and harmony.

Scorpio offers the potential of releasing light and understanding through exploring the darkness and pain of humanity, and rising triumphant in resurrection and rebirth; it is the power of conscious change and redemption.

Sagittarius looks towards a far-sighted social vision, aspires towards the highest ideals created by humanity, right relationships with all kingdoms in nature; ecological and social dreams.

Capricorn shows that the way to achievement is through discipline and persistent work, of personal and social responsibility, and an impersonal attitude to achieve the next step forward.

Aquarius displays the vision of the ideal future, freedom and rights for each unique individual as part of a world-wide family of humanity.

Pisces offers the heart of compassion, an empathatic sensitivity and understanding of the suffering in the world, and a determination to alleviate this as much as possible.

These are the lessons and paths that our StarChildren bring

with them into the world. If they can all be released into life all across the world, then the future will be transformed.

Help your StarChild to share his or her gift. And do not forget the gift that you too have brought into the world. You too are a StarChild . . .

Appendix

USING THE ASCENDANT TABLES

It is difficult to provide a fully accurate set of Ascendant data tables, because the Ascendant changes sign so often during each day, and because in a general book like this necessary details like time, date and place of birth of each parent and child cannot be taken into account. Also, differences in longitude and latitude, variations in global time changes, or even British Summer Time do make vital differences. However, the following simplifed tables should be accurate in establishing the sign of the Ascendant in over 60 per cent of examples; the others are usually either the sign before or after the tabled sign. Where there are two signs together during an hour, use the first one for the first half hour, i.e. on January 1, between 1 a.m. and 2 a.m. the Ascendant changes from Libra to Scorpio, remaining in Scorpio until approximately 5 a.m. when it has moved into Sagittarius.

Look down the vertical column to establish your date of birth, (i.e., January 1 to 3 indicates that the respective times and Ascendant positions remain like that through that three-day period, changing by the start of January 4 to 6,) and note the astrological symbol and refer to the symbols below to determine the Ascendant sign. For instance, a birth at 6 p.m. on January 13 would give a Leo Ascendant; a birth at 2.20 p.m. on November 10 gives Pisces; a birth at 8.30 a.m. January 24 gives either Taurus or Gemini.

Ideally, a full natal chart should be erected for the personally correct data to be used. But you may wish to consider the Ascendant sign for your child to be another dimension to his or her personality, one which either complements or contradicts their fundamental Sun sign nature; so reading the sign that is your child's Ascendant can help to illuminate his or her character even more. If it is a 'double sign' on the tabled

Ascendant sign, then you may find it advisable to read both signs to see which seems to fit your child's character the best. Similarly, the parent's birth can be evaluated in terms of a personality composed of the signs of the Sun and Ascendant, or elemental affinities can even be taken into account.

Aries   Taurus   Gemini   Cancer   Leo
Virgo   Libra   Scorpio   Sagittarius   Capricorn
        Aquarius   Pisces

JANUARY

	1st to 3rd	4th to 6th	7th to 9th	10th to 12th	13th to 15th	16th to 18th	19th to 21st	22nd to 24th	25th to 27th	28th to 30th	31st
MIDNIGHT TO 1 A.M.	♎	♎	♎	♎	♎	♎	♎	♎	♎/♏	♎/♏	♎/♏
1 A.M. 2 A.M.	♎/♏	♏/♐	♎/♏	♏♐	♏♐	♏♐	♏♐	♏♐	♏♐	♏♐	♏♐
2 A.M. 3 A.M.	♏♐	♏♐	♏♐								
3 A.M. 4 A.M.						♐	♐	♐	♐	♐	♐
4 A.M. 5 A.M.		♐			♐	♐					
5 A.M. 6 A.M.	♐		♐					♑	♑	♑	♑
6 A.M. 7 A.M.		♐/♑	♑	♑	♑	♑	♑				
7 A.M. 8 A.M.	♑	♑					♑/♒	♒	♒	♒	♒
8 A.M. 9 A.M.		♑/♒	♒	♒	♒	♒	♒	♒/♓	♒/♓	♒/♓	♓
9 A.M. 10 A.M.	♒	♒	♒/♓	♓	♓	♓	♓	♓		♓/♈	♓/♈
10 A.M. 11 A.M.	♓	♓	♓	♓/♈	♈	♈	♈	♈	♈	♈/♉	♈/♉
11 A.M. NOON	♈	♈	♈	♈	♈	♈/♉	♉	♉	♉	♉	♉
NOON 1 P.M.	♈/♉	♉	♉	♉	♈/♉			♉/♊	♉/♊	♉/♊	♊
1 P.M. 2 P.M.	♉		♉/♊	♊	♊	♊	♊	♊	♊	♊	
2 P.M. 3 P.M.	♊	♊	♊					♊/♋			♋
3 P.M. 4 P.M.				♋	♋	♋	♋	♋	♋	♋	
4 P.M. 5 P.M.	♋	♋									
5 P.M. 6 P.M.						♌	♌	♌	♌	♌	♌
6 P.M. 7 P.M.		♌	♌	♌	♌						
7 P.M. 8 P.M.	♌								♍	♍	♍
8 P.M. 9 P.M.			♍	♍	♍	♍	♍	♍			
9 P.M. 10 P.M.	♍	♍									♎
10 P.M. 11 P.M.					♍/♎		♎	♎	♎	♎	
11 P.M. MIDNIGHT	♎	♎	♎	♎	♎	♎					

FEBRUARY

	1st to 2nd	3rd to 5th	6th to 8th	9th to 11th	12th to 14th	15th to 17th	18th to 20th	21st to 23rd	24th to 26th	27th to 28th
MIDNIGHT TO 1 A.M.	♎/♏	♏	♏	♏	♏	♏	♏	♏	♏	♏
1 A.M. 2 A.M.	♏				♏/♐	♏/♐	♐	♐	♐	♐
2 A.M. 3 A.M.		♐	♐	♐	♐	♐				
3 A.M. 4 A.M.	♐						♐/♑	♐/♑	♑	♑
4 A.M. 5 A.M.		♐/♑	♑	♑	♑	♑	♑	♑		
5 A.M. 6 A.M.	♑	♑					♑/♒	♑/♒	♒	♒
6 A.M. 7 A.M.		♑/♒	♒	♒	♒	♒	♒	♒/♓	♒/♓	♒/♓
7 A.M. 8 A.M.	♒	♒	♒/♓	♒/♓	♒/♓	♓	♓	♓/♈	♓/♈	♓/♈
8 A.M. 9 A.M.	♓	♒	♓	♓/♈	♓/♈	♓/♈	♈	♈	♈/♉	♈/♉
9 A.M. 10 A.M.	♓/♈	♈	♈	♈	♈/♉	♈/♉	♈/♉	♉	♉	♉
10 A.M. 11 A.M.	♈/♉	♈/♉	♉	♉	♉	♉	♉/♊	♉/♊	♊	♊
11 A.M. NOON	♉	♉/♊	♉/♊	♉/♊	♊	♊	♊	♊		
NOON 1 P.M.	♊	♊	♊	♊			♊/♋	♊/♋	♋	♋
1 P.M. 2 P.M.		♊/♋	♊/♋	♋	♋	♋	♋	♋		
2 P.M. 3 P.M.	♋	♋								♋/♌
3 P.M. 4 P.M.					♋/♌	♌	♌	♌	♌	♌
4 P.M. 5 P.M.		♌	♌	♌	♌					
5 P.M. 6 P.M.	♌						♌/♍	♌/♍	♍	♍
6 P.M. 7 P.M.		♌/♍	♌/♍	♍	♍	♍	♍	♍		
7 P.M. 8 P.M.	♍	♍	♍	♍					♍/♎	
8 P.M. 9 P.M.					♍/♎	♎	♎	♎	♎	♎
9 P.M. 10 P.M.	♎	♎	♎	♎	♎					
10 P.M. 11 P.M.							♎/♏	♎/♏	♏	♏
11 P.M. MIDNIGHT		♎/♏	♎/♏	♏	♏	♏	♏	♏		

MARCH

	1st	2nd to 4th	5th to 7th	8th to 10th	11th to 13th	14th to 16th	17th to 19th	20th to 22nd	23rd to 25th	26th to 28th	29th to 31st
MIDNIGHT TO 1 A.M.	♏/♐	♏/♐	♏/♐	♐	♐	♐	♐	♐	♐	♐	♐
1 A.M. 2 A.M.	♐	♐	♐					♐/♑	♐/♑	♑	♑
2 A.M. 3 A.M.			♐/♑	♐/♑	♑	♑	♑	♑	♑		
3 A.M. 4 A.M.	♑	♑	♑	♑				♑/♒	♑/♒	♒	♒
4 A.M. 5 A.M.			♑/♒	♑/♒	♒	♒	♒	♒/♓	♒/♓	♒/♓	
5 A.M. 6 A.M.	♒	♒	♒	♒/♓	♒/♓	♒/♓	♓	♓	♓/♈	♓/♈	♓/♈
6 A.M. 7 A.M.	♒/♓	♓	♓	♓	♓/♈	♓/♈	♓/♈	♈	♈	♈	♈/♉
7 A.M. 8 A.M.	♓/♈	♓/♈	♈	♈	♈	♈	♈/♉	♈/♉	♉	♉	♉
8 A.M. 9 A.M.	♈/♉	♈/♉	♈/♉	♉	♉	♉	♉	♉/♊	♉/♊	♊	
9 A.M. 10 A.M.	♉	♉	♉	♉/♊	♉/♊	♊	♊	♊	♊		
10 A.M. 11 A.M.	♊	♊	♊	♊	♊			♊/♋	♊/♋	♋	
11 A.M. NOON			♊/♋	♊/♋	♋	♋	♋	♋	♋	♋	
NOON 1 P.M.	♋	♋	♋	♋							♋/♌
1 P.M. 2 P.M.					♋/♌	♋/♌	♌	♌	♌	♌	♌
2 P.M. 3 P.M.	♋/♌	♌	♌	♌	♌	♌					
3 P.M. 4 P.M.	♌							♌/♍	♌/♍	♍	♍
4 P.M. 5 P.M.			♌/♍	♌/♍	♍	♍	♍	♍	♍		
5 P.M. 6 P.M.	♍	♍	♍	♍							♍/♎
6 P.M. 7 P.M.						♍/♎	♍/♎	♎	♎	♎	♎
7 P.M. 8 P.M.	♍/♎	♎	♎	♎	♎	♎	♎				
8 P.M. 9 P.M.	♎							♎/♏	♎/♏	♏/♐	♏/♐
9 P.M. 10 P.M.			♎/♏	♎/♏	♏/♐	♏/♐	♏/♐	♏/♐	♏/♐		
10 P.M. 11 P.M.	♏/♐	♏/♐	♏/♐	♏/♐							♏/♐
11 P.M. MIDNIGHT					♏/♐	♏/♐	♐	♐	♐	♐	♐

APRIL

	1st to 3rd	4th to 6th	7th to 9th	10th to 12th	13th to 15th	16th to 18th	19th to 21st	22nd to 24th	25th to 27th	28th to 30th	
MIDNIGHT TO 1 A.M.	♐	♐	♐/♑	♐/♑	♐/♑	♑	♑	♑	♑	♑	
1 A.M. 2 A.M.	♑	♑	♑	♑	♑		♑/♒	♑/♒	♑/♒	♒	
2 A.M. 3 A.M.		♑/♒	♑/♒	♒	♒	♒	♒	♒	♓	♒/♓	
3 A.M. 4 A.M.	♒	♒	♒/♓	♒/♓	♒/♓	♓	♓	♓		♓/♈	
4 A.M. 5 A.M.	♓	♓	♓	♓	♓/♈	♓/♈	♈	♈	♈	♈	
5 A.M. 6 A.M.	♓/♈	♈	♈	♈	♈/♉	♈/♉	♈/♉	♉	♉	♉	
6 A.M. 7 A.M.	♈/♉	♉	♉	♉	♉	♉	♉	♉/♊	♉/♊	♊	
7 A.M. 8 A.M.	♉	♉	♉/♊	♉/♊	♊	♊	♊	♊	♊		
8 A.M. 9 A.M.	♊	♊	♊	♊			♊/♋	♊/♋	♋	♋	
9 A.M. 10 A.M.			♊/♋	♋	♋	♋	♋	♋			
10 A.M. 11 A.M.	♋	♋	♋							♋/♌	
11 A.M. NOON				♋/♌	♌	♌	♌	♌	♌		
NOON 1 P.M.	♌	♌	♌	♌	♌						
1 P.M. 2 P.M.							♌/♍	♌/♍	♍	♍	
2 P.M. 3 P.M.			♌/♍	♌/♍	♍	♍		♍			
3 P.M. 4 P.M.	♍	♍							♍/♎		
4 P.M. 5 P.M.					♍/♎	♍/♎	♎	♎	♎	♎	
5 P.M. 6 P.M.	♍/♎	♎	♎	♎	♎	♎					
6 P.M. 7 P.M.	♎						♎/♏	♎/♏	♏/♐	♏/♐	
7 P.M. 8 P.M.			♎/♏	♏/♐	♏/♐	♏/♐	♏/♐				
8 P.M. 9 P.M.	♏/♐	♏/♐	♏/♐							♏/♐	
9 P.M. 10 P.M.				♏/♐	♏/♐	♐	♐	♐			
10 P.M. 11 P.M.	♏/♐	♐	♐	♐	♐						
11 P.M. MIDNIGHT	♐						♐/♑	♐/♑	♑	♑	

MAY

	1st to 3rd	4th to 6th	7th to 9th	10th to 12th	13th to 15th	16th to 18th	19th to 21st	22nd to 24th	25th to 27th	28th to 30th	31st
MIDNIGHT TO 1 A.M.	♒	♑	♒	♒	♒	♒	♒	♒/♓	♒/♓	♒/♓	♒/♓
1 A.M. 2 A.M.		♒	♒/♓	♒/♓	♒/♓	♒/♓	♓	♓	♓	♓/♈	♓/♈
2 A.M. 3 A.M.	♓	♓	♓	♓	♓/♈	♓/♈	♈	♈	♈	♈	♈/♉
3 A.M. 4 A.M.	♓/♈	♈	♈	♈	♈	♈/♉	♈/♉	♉	♉	♉	♉
4 A.M. 5 A.M.	♈/♉	♈/♉	♉	♉	♉	♉	♉	♉/♊	♉/♊	♊	♊
5 A.M. 6 A.M.	♉	♉	♉/♊	♉/♊	♉/♊	♊	♊	♊	♊		
6 A.M. 7 A.M.	♊	♊	♊	♊	♊			♊/♋	♊/♋	♋	♋
7 A.M. 8 A.M.			♊/♋	♊/♋	♋	♋	♋	♋	♋		
8 A.M. 9 A.M.	♋	♋	♋	♋					♋/♌	♋/♌	♌
9 A.M. 10 A.M.						♋/♌	♋/♌	♌	♌	♌	
10 A.M. 11 A.M.	♌	♌	♌	♌	♌	♌	♌				
11 A.M. NOON								♌/♍	♍	♍	♍
NOON 1 P.M.			♌/♍	♍	♍	♍	♍				
1 P.M. 2 P.M.	♍	♍	♍					♎		♍/♎	♍/♎
2 P.M. 3 P.M.					♍/♎	♍/♎	♎		♎	♎	♎
3 P.M. 4 P.M.	♍/♎	♎	♎	♎	♎	♎					
4 P.M. 5 P.M.	♎							♎/♏	♎/♏	♏	♏
5 P.M. 6 P.M.			♎/♏	♏	♏	♏	♏	♏	♏		
6 P.M. 7 P.M.	♏	♏	♏								♏/♐
7 P.M. 8 P.M.					♏/♐	♏/♐	♏/♐	♐	♐	♐	♐
8 P.M. 9 P.M.	♏/♐	♏/♐	♐	♐	♐						
9 P.M. 10 P.M.	♐	♐					♐/♑	♐/♑	♑	♑	♑
10 P.M. 11 P.M.		♐/♑	♐/♑	♐/♑	♑	♑	♑	♑			
11 P.M. MIDNIGHT	♑	♑	♑	♑		♑/♒	♑/♒	♑/♒	♒	♒	♒

JUNE

Time	1st to 2nd	3rd to 5th	6th to 8th	9th to 11th	12th to 14th	15th to 17th	18th to 20th	21st to 23rd	24th to 26th	27th to 29th	30th
MIDNIGHT TO 1 A.M.	♒/♓	♓	♓	♓	♓/♈	♈	♈	♈	♈	♉	♉
1 A.M. 2 A.M.	♓/♈	♓/♈	♈	♈	♈	♈/♉	♈/♉	♈/♉	♉	♉	♉
2 A.M. 3 A.M.	♈/♉	♈/♉	♈/♉	♉	♉	♉	♉	♉/♊	♉/♊	♉/♊	♊
3 A.M. 4 A.M.	♉	♉	♉/♊	♉/♊	♉/♊	♊	♊	♊	♊	♊	
4 A.M. 5 A.M.	♊	♊	♊	♊	♊		♊/♋	♊/♋	♋	♋	
5 A.M. 6 A.M.			♊/♋	♊/♋	♋	♋	♋	♋	♋		
6 A.M. 7 A.M.	♋	♋	♋	♋						♋/♌	♋/♌
7 A.M. 8 A.M.			♋/♌	♋/♌	♋/♌	♌	♌	♌	♌	♌	
8 A.M. 9 A.M.	♌	♌	♌	♌	♌						
9 A.M. 10 A.M.							♌/♍	♌/♍	♌/♍	♍	♍
10 A.M. 11 A.M.			♌/♍	♍	♍	♍	♍	♍	♍		
11 A.M. NOON	♍	♍	♍							♍/♎	♍/♎
NOON 1 P.M.				♍/♎	♍/♎	♍/♎	♎	♎	♎	♎	♎
1 P.M. 2 P.M.	♍/♎	♎	♎	♎	♎						
2 P.M. 3 P.M.	♎								♎/♏	♏	♏
3 P.M. 4 P.M.			♎/♏	♎/♏	♏	♏	♏	♏	♏		
4 P.M. 5 P.M.	♏	♏	♏	♏						♏/♐	♏/♐
5 P.M. 6 P.M.					♏/♐	♏/♐	♏/♐	♐	♐	♐	♐
6 P.M. 7 P.M.	♏/♐	♏/♐	♐	♐	♐	♐	♐				
7 P.M. 8 P.M.	♐	♐					♐/♑	♐/♑	♐/♑	♑	♑
8 P.M. 9 P.M.			♐/♑	♐/♑	♑	♑	♑	♑	♑		
9 P.M. 10 P.M.	♑	♑	♑	♑			♑/♒	♑/♒	♒	♒	♒
10 P.M. 11 P.M.		♑/♒	♑/♒	♒	♒	♒	♒	♒	♒/♓	♒/♓	♒/♓
11 P.M. MIDNIGHT	♒	♒	♒/♓	♒/♓	♒/♓	♓	♓	♓/♈	♓/♈	♓/♈	♓/♈

JULY

	1st to 2nd	3rd to 5th	6th to 8th	9th to 11th	12th to 14th	15th to 17th	18th to 20th	21st to 23rd	24th to 26th	27th to 29th	30th to 31st
MIDNIGHT TO 1 A.M.	♈/♉	♉	♉	♉	♉	♉	♉	♉/♊	♉/♊	♉/♊	♊
1 A.M. 2 A.M.	♉			♉/♊	♉/♊	♊	♊	♊	♊	♊	
2 A.M. 3 A.M.	♊	♊	♊	♊	♊			♊/♋	♊/♋	♊/♋	♋
3 A.M. 4 A.M.			♊/♋	♊/♋	♋	♋	♋	♋	♋	♋	
4 A.M. 5 A.M.	♋	♋	♋	♋						♋/♌	♋/♌
5 A.M. 6 A.M.					♋/♌	♋/♌	♌	♌	♌	♌	♌
6 A.M. 7 A.M.	♋/♌	♌	♌	♌	♌	♌					
7 A.M. 8 A.M.	♌							♌/♍	♌/♍	♍	♍
8 A.M. 9 A.M.			♌/♍	♌/♍	♍	♍	♍	♍	♍		
9 A.M. 10 A.M.	♍	♍	♍	♍						♍/♎	♍/♎
10 A.M. 11 A.M.					♍/♎	♍/♎	♎	♎	♎	♎	♎
11 A.M. NOON	♍/♎	♎	♎	♎	♎	♎					
NOON 1 P.M.	♎							♎/♏	♎/♏	♏	♏
1 P.M. 2 P.M.			♎/♏	♎/♏	♏	♏	♏	♏	♏		
2 P.M. 3 P.M.	♏	♏	♏	♏							♏/♐
3 P.M. 4 P.M.						♏/♐	♏/♐	♐	♐	♐	♐
4 P.M. 5 P.M.	♏/♐	♏/♐	♐	♐	♐	♐	♐				
5 P.M. 6 P.M.	♐	♐					♐/♑	♐/♑	♐/♑	♑	♑
6 P.M. 7 P.M.		♐/♑	♐/♑	♐/♑	♑	♑	♑	♑	♑		
7 P.M. 8 P.M.	♑	♑	♑	♑				♑/♒	♑/♒	♒	♒
8 P.M. 9 P.M.		♑/♒	♑/♒	♒	♒	♒	♒	♒	♒/♓	♒/♓	♒/♓
9 P.M. 10 P.M.	♒	♒	♒/♓	♒/♓	♒/♓	♓	♓	♓	♓/♈	♓/♈	♓/♈
10 P.M. 11 P.M.	♒/♓	♓	♓	♓	♓/♈	♓/♈	♓/♈	♈	♈	♈	♈/♉
11 P.M. MIDNIGHT	♓/♈	♈	♈	♈	♈	♈/♉	♈/♉	♈/♉	♉	♉	♉

AUGUST

	1st	2nd to 4th	5th to 7th	8th to 10th	11th to 13th	14th to 16th	17th to 19th	20th to 22nd	23rd to 25th	26th to 28th	29th to 31st
MIDNIGHT TO 1 A.M.	♊	♊	♊	♊	♊	♊	♊	♊/♋	♊/♋	♊/♋	♋
1 A.M. 2 A.M.					♊/♋	♋	♋	♋	♋	♋	
2 A.M. 3 A.M.	♋	♋	♊/♋	♊/♋	♋					♋/♌	♋/♌
3 A.M. 4 A.M.			♋	♋	♋/♌	♋/♌	♌	♌	♌	♌	♌
4 A.M. 5 A.M.	♋/♌	♌	♌	♌	♌	♌					
5 A.M. 6 A.M.	♌						♌/♍	♍	♌/♍	♍	♍
6 A.M. 7 A.M.			♌/♍	♌/♍	♍	♍	♍	♍	♍		
7 A.M. 8 A.M.	♍	♍	♍	♍							♍/♎
8 A.M. 9 A.M.					♍/♎	♍/♎	♍/♎	♎	♎	♎	♎
9 A.M. 10 A.M.	♍/♎	♍/♎	♎	♎	♎	♎	♎				
10 A.M. 11 A.M.	♎	♎						♎/♏	♎/♏	♏	♏
11 A.M. NOON			♎/♏	♎/♏	♏	♏	♏	♏	♏		
NOON 1 P.M.	♏	♏	♏	♏							♏/♐
1 P.M. 2 P.M.					♏/♐	♏/♐	♐	♐	♐	♐	
2 P.M. 3 P.M.	♏/♐	♏/♐	♐	♐	♐	♐					
3 P.M. 4 P.M.	♐	♐					♐/♑	♐/♑	♐/♑	♑	♑
4 P.M. 5 P.M.			♐/♑	♐/♑	♐/♑	♑	♑	♑	♑		
5 P.M. 6 P.M.	♑	♑	♑	♑			♑/♒	♑/♒	♑/♒	♒	♒
6 P.M. 7 P.M.			♑/♒	♑/♒	♒	♒	♒	♒	♒/♓	♒/♓	♒/♓
7 P.M. 8 P.M.	♒	♒	♒	♒/♓	♒/♓	♒/♓	♓	♓	♓	♓/♈	♓/♈
8 P.M. 9 P.M.	♒/♓	♓	♓	♓	♓/♈	♓/♈	♓/♈	♈	♈	♈	♈/♉
9 P.M. 10 P.M.	♓/♈	♓/♈	♈	♈	♈	♈/♉	♈/♉	♈/♉	♉	♉	♉
10 P.M. 11 P.M.	♈/♉	♈/♉	♈/♉	♉	♉	♉	♉	♉/♊	♉/♊	♉/♊	♊
11 P.M. MIDNIGHT	♉	♉	♉/♊	♉/♊	♊	♊	♊	♊	♊	♊	

SEPTEMBER

	1st to 3rd	4th to 6th	7th to 9th	10th to 12th	13th to 15th	16th to 18th	19th to 21st	22nd to 24th	25th to 27th	28th to 30th	
MIDNIGHT TO 1 A.M.	♋	♋	♋	♋	♋	♋	♋	♋	♋/♌	♋/♌	
1 A.M. 2 A.M.				♋/♌	♋/♌	♌	♌	♌	♌	♌	
2 A.M. 3 A.M.	♌	♌	♌	♌	♌						
3 A.M. 4 A.M.							♌/♍	♌/♍	♍	♍	
4 A.M. 5 A.M.		♌/♍	♌/♍	♍	♍	♍	♍	♍			
5 A.M. 6 A.M.	♍	♍	♍							♍/♎	
6 A.M. 7 A.M.				♍/♎	♍/♎	♍/♎	♎	♎	♎	♎	
7 A.M. 8 A.M.	♍/♎	♎	♎	♎	♎						
8 A.M. 9 A.M.	♎						♎/♏	♎/♏	♎/♏	♏	
9 A.M. 10 A.M.		♎/♏	♎/♏	♏	♏	♏	♏	♏	♏		
10 A.M. 11 A.M.	♏	♏	♏							♏/♐	
11 A.M. NOON				♏/♐	♏/♐	♐	♐	♐	♐	♐	
NOON 1 P.M.	♏/♐	♐	♐	♐	♐	♐					
1 P.M. 2 P.M.	♐						♐/♑	♐/♑	♑	♑	
2 P.M. 3 P.M.	♐/♑	♐/♑	♐/♑	♑	♑	♑	♑	♑			
3 P.M. 4 P.M.	♑	♑	♑			♑/♒	♑/♒	♑/♒	♒	♒	
4 P.M. 5 P.M.	♑/♒	♑/♒	♑/♒	♒	♒	♒	♒	♒/♓	♒/♓	♒/♓	
5 P.M. 6 P.M.	♒	♒	♒/♓	♒/♓	♒/♓	♓	♓	♓	♓/♈	♓/♈	
6 P.M. 7 P.M.	♓	♓	♓	♓/♈	♓/♈	♓/♈	♈	♈	♈	♈/♉	
7 P.M. 8 P.M.	♓/♈	♈	♈	♈	♈/♉	♈/♉	♈/♉	♉	♉	♉	
8 P.M. 9 P.M.	♈/♉	♈/♉	♉	♉	♉	♉	♉/♊	♉/♊	♉/♊	♊	
9 P.M. 10 P.M.	♉	♉/♊	♉/♊	♉/♊	♊	♊	♊	♊	♊		
10 P.M. 11 P.M.	♊	♊	♊	♊			♊/♋	♊/♋	♋	♋	
11 P.M. MIDNIGHT		♊/♋	♊/♋	♋	♋	♋	♋	♋			

OCTOBER

	1st to 3rd	4th to 6th	7th to 9th	10th to 12th	13th to 15th	16th to 18th	19th to 21st	22nd to 24th	25th to 27th	28th to 30th	31st
MIDNIGHT TO 1 A.M.	♌	♌	♌	♌	♌	♌	♌	♌	♌	♌	♌
1 A.M. 2 A.M.							♌/♍	♌/♍	♍	♍	♍
2 A.M. 3 A.M.	♍	♌/♍	♌/♍	♍	♍	♍	♍	♍			
3 A.M. 4 A.M.		♍	♍						♍/♎	♍/♎	
4 A.M. 5 A.M.					♍/♎	♍/♎	♎	♎	♎	♎	♎
5 A.M. 6 A.M.	♍/♎	♎	♎	♎	♎	♎					
6 A.M. 7 A.M.	♎						♎/♏	♎	♏	♏	
7 A.M. 8 A.M.		♎/♏	♎/♏	♎/♏	♏	♏	♏	♏	♏		
8 A.M. 9 A.M.	♏	♏	♏	♏						♏/♐	♏/♐
9 A.M. 10 A.M.					♏/♐	♏/♐	♏/♐	♐	♐	♐	♐
10 A.M. 11 A.M.	♏/♐	♐	♐	♐	♐	♐	♐				
11 A.M. NOON	♐						♐/♑	♐/♑	♑	♑	♑
NOON 1 P.M.		♐/♑	♐/♑	♑	♑	♑	♑	♑			
1 P.M. 2 P.M.	♑	♑	♑				♑/♒	♑/♒	♒	♒	♒
2 P.M. 3 P.M.		♑/♒	♑/♒	♒	♒	♒	♒	♒/♓	♒/♓	♒/♓	♒/♓
3 P.M. 4 P.M.	♒	♒	♒	♒/♓	♒/♓	♒/♓	♓	♓	♓/♈	♓/♈	♓/♈
4 P.M. 5 P.M.	♓	♓	♓	♓/♈	♓/♈	♓/♈	♈	♈	♈/♉	♈/♉	♈/♉
5 P.M. 6 P.M.	♓/♈	♈	♈	♈	♈/♉	♈/♉	♈/♉	♉	♉	♉	♉
6 P.M. 7 P.M.	♈/♉	♈/♉	♉	♉	♉	♉	♉/♊	♉/♊	♉/♊	♉/♊	♊
7 P.M. 8 P.M.	♉	♉/♊	♉/♊	♉/♊	♊	♊	♊	♊	♊	♊	
8 P.M. 9 P.M.	♊	♊	♊	♊			♊/♋	♊/♋	♊/♋	♋	♋
9 P.M. 10 P.M.		♊/♋	♊/♋		♋	♋	♋	♋	♋		
10 P.M. 11 P.M.	♋	♋	♋	♋						♋/♌	♋/♌
11 P.M. MIDNIGHT				♋/♌	♌	♌	♌	♌	♌	♌	♌

NOVEMBER

	1st to 2nd	3rd to 5th	6th to 8th	9th to 11th	12th to 14th	15th to 17th	18th to 20th	21st to 23rd	24th to 26th	27th to 29th	30th
MIDNIGHT TO 1 A.M.	♌/♍	♌/♍	♌/♍	♍	♍	♍	♍	♍	♍	♍	♍
1 A.M. 2 A.M.	♍	♍	♍							♍/♎	♍/♎
2 A.M. 3 A.M.				♍/♎	♍/♎	♎	♎	♎	♎	♎	♎
3 A.M. 4 A.M.	♍/♎	♎	♎	♎	♎	♎					
4 A.M. 5 A.M.	♎						♎/♏	♏	♏	♏	♏
5 A.M. 6 A.M.		♎/♏	♎/♏	♏	♏	♏	♏	♏			
6 A.M. 7 A.M.	♏	♏	♏								♏/♐
7 A.M. 8 A.M.					♏/♐	♏/♐	♏/♐	♐	♐	♐	♐
8 A.M. 9 A.M.	♏/♐	♐	♐	♐	♐	♐	♐				
9 A.M. 10 A.M.	♐						♐/♑	♐/♑	♑	♑	♑
10 A.M. 11 A.M.		♐/♑	♐/♑	♑	♑	♑	♑	♑			
11 A.M. NOON	♑	♑	♑				♑/♒	♑/♒	♒	♒	♒
NOON 1 P.M.		♑/♒	♑/♒	♒	♒	♒	♒	♒/♓	♒/♓	♓	♓
1 P.M. 2 P.M.	♒	♒	♒	♒/♓	♒/♓	♓	♓	♓	♓/♈	♓/♈	♓/♈
2 P.M. 3 P.M.	♒/♓	♓	♓	♓	♓/♈	♓/♈	♈	♈	♈	♈/♉	♈/♉
3 P.M. 4 P.M.	♓/♈	♈	♈	♈	♈	♈/♉	♈/♉	♉	♉	♉	♉
4 P.M. 5 P.M.	♈/♉	♈/♉	♉	♉	♉	♉	♉	♉/♊	♉/♊	♊	♊
5 P.M. 6 P.M.	♉	♉	♉/♊		♊	♊	♊	♊	♊		
6 P.M. 7 P.M.	♊	♊	♊	♊			♊/♋	♊/♋	♋	♋	♋
7 P.M. 8 P.M.		♊/♋	♊/♋	♊/♋	♋	♋	♋	♋			
8 P.M. 9 P.M.	♋	♋	♋	♋					♌	♋/♌	♋/♌
9 P.M. 10 P.M.				♋/♌	♋/♌	♌	♌	♌		♌	♌
10 P.M. 11 P.M.	♋/♌	♌	♌	♌	♌						
11 P.M. MIDNIGHT	♌						♌/♍	♌/♍	♍	♍	♍

DECEMBER

	1st to 2nd	3rd to 5th	6th to 8th	9th to 11th	12th to 14th	15th to 17th	18th to 20th	21st to 23rd	24th to 26th	27th to 29th	30th to 31st
MIDNIGHT TO 1 A.M.	♍	♍	♍	♍	♍/♎	♍/♎	♍/♎	♎	♎	♎	♎
1 A.M. 2 A.M.	♍/♎	♎	♎	♎	♎	♎	♎				
2 A.M. 3 A.M.	♎							♎/♏	♎/♏	♏	♏
3 A.M. 4 A.M.			♎/♏	♎/♏	♏	♏	♏	♏	♏		
4 A.M. 5 A.M.	♏	♏	♏	♏						♏/♐	♏/♐
5 A.M. 6 A.M.					♏/♐	♏/♐	♐	♐	♐	♐	♐
6 A.M. 7 A.M.	♏/♐	♏/♐	♐	♐	♐	♏/♐	♐				
7 A.M. 8 A.M.	♐	♐					♐/♑	♐/♑	♐/♑	♑	♑
8 A.M. 9 A.M.		♐/♑	♐/♑	♐/♑	♑	♑	♑	♑	♑		
9 A.M. 10 A.M.	♑	♑	♑	♑			♑/♒	♑/♒	♑/♒	♒	♒
10 A.M. 11 A.M.		♑/♒	♑/♒	♒	♒	♒	♒	♒/♓	♒/♓	♒/♓	
11 A.M. TO NOON	♒	♒	♒/♓	♒/♓	♒/♓	♓	♓	♓/♈	♓/♈	♓/♈	♈
NOON 1 P.M.	♓	♓	♓	♓	♓/♈	♓/♈	♓/♈	♈	♈	♈/♉	♈/♉
1 P.M. 2 P.M.	♓/♈	♓/♈	♈	♈	♈/♉	♈/♉	♈/♉	♈/♉	♉	♉	♉
2 P.M. 3 P.M.	♈/♉	♈/♉	♉	♉	♉	♉	♉	♉/♊	♉/♊	♉/♊	♊
3 P.M. 4 P.M.	♉	♉	♉/♊	♉/♊	♊	♊	♊	♊	♊	♊	
4 P.M. 5 P.M.	♊	♊	♊	♊				♊/♋	♊/♋	♋	♋
5 P.M. 6 P.M.			♊/♋	♊/♋	♋	♋	♋	♋	♋		
6 P.M. 7 P.M.	♋	♋	♋	♋					♋/♌	♋/♌	♋/♌
7 P.M. 8 P.M.				♋/♌	♋/♌	♋/♌	♌	♌	♌	♌	♌
8 P.M. 9 P.M.	♋/♌	♌	♌	♌	♌	♌					
9 P.M. 10 P.M.	♌							♌/♍	♍	♍	♍
10 P.M. 11 P.M.		♌/♍	♌/♍	♍	♍	♍	♍	♍			
11 P.M. MIDNIGHT	♍	♍	♍						♍/♎	♍/♎	♍/♎

STARLORE ASTROLOGY

Every individual is unique and important, and the world is enriched in some way by every one. Each person has certain talents, qualities and abilities that can be used for their own betterment and for the benefit of others. Through the focus of an astrological analysis, it is possible to indicate the innate potential which you are capable of expressing during life; the ways for you to discover more meaning, purpose, self-understanding, life direction and ultimately a sense of fulfilment. Challenges and lessons that are likely to confront you in life are considered, and suggestions made to help you recognize these, and also the ways for you to resolve recurring problems which are often caused by a lack of self-knowledge. StarLore seeks to indicate positive life directions and purpose for each person, and the interpretations can reveal a new dimension to your life, a new way of perceiving yourself in a creative and positive light. The basic attitude of StarLore is that a greater self-understanding is the key to fulfilment, and a wiser way to live in a good relationship with others.

If you are interested in personal analysis, for yourself, children or friends, then please send an s.a.e. for additional details to: StarLore, c/o 9 Brechin Close, Hinckley, Leicester, LE10 0UX, England.